TEACHINGS
from
GOD

Greeting Your Soul
and
Revealing the Divine
Within

COURTNEY AMUNDSON

Teachings from God: Greeting Your Soul and Revealing the Divine
Within
Copyright © 2015 by Courtney Amundson

Edited by Hanna Kjeldbjerg

Library of Congress Control Number: 2015919059

ISBN: 978-0-9968251-0-8

Printed in the United States of America

First Edition

To contact the author, visit www.teachingsfromgod.com

"I am so proud of the courage it took for Courtney to follow her guidance and write about her journey. Courtney's book speaks the truth and is written with divine love. She is wise beyond her years and an inspiration to many. She makes what I do worth it and then some!"

Lisa Garr, Amazon Best-Selling Author of *Becoming Aware* and Host of "The Aware Show" and "Being Aware"

"In *Teachings from God*, Courtney shares sacred messages from beyond that will guide you to your own higher spiritual truths. The book is a gentle read – the chapters flow easily from one to the next, with barely any separation, as though one is passing through those sacred inner realms of the spirit. The teachings flow as an intimate conversation, and the sweetness and purity of these messages carry an ageless wisdom that goes beyond Courtney's youthful years. *Teachings from God* is one of those timeless books that affirms the divine presence that is all around us. Open the book to any page and you will be swept away to the spirit within."

Ragani, Award-winning musician and veteran in the sacred sciences

"The powerful wisdom in *Teachings from God* permeates and gently leads me into higher levels of my own consciousness, opening my own channel to the higher powers that are happily and lovingly guiding us, if only we ask and open our heart space. I am deeply moved."

Scarlet Rivera, Violinist, Composer, Author

"Between these covers lies a profound journey. Courtney's connection to the Source of All expresses the unlimited love that Divine wisdom has for us. Each page herein is truly an inspiration."

Dr. Amber Wolf, PhD

"Greeting Your Soul and Revealing the Divine Within takes a fresh and loving approach for anyone interested in uncovering their unique path of experiencing joy in their true calling. It's a beautifully written collection of profound reflections and graceful nudges that promises to support a deep journey of self-discovery."

Ann Licater, Grammy Award-Nominated World Flutist

"Greeting Your Soul and Revealing the Divine Within is a beautiful invitation to awaken to who you truly are and remember the truth within you. Through her writings your inner voice of wisdom is validated and your own expansion of divinity can become realized more and more."

Shellie Nelson, Visionary and Spiritual Mentor

Dedicated to all beings on this journey of self-discovery. May these words bring you peace, love, and inspiration in your life to discover the joy of living your fullest expression.

Table of Contents

Author's Note

Welcome dear friend, and thank you so much for this honor to share with you the teachings that have changed my life, and I hope will change yours as well. During this journey, I have learned to step into my true authentic power, and it is my intention that each and every one of you are able to find a new piece of yourself revealed to you through this book.

This book has formed around my communication with a beautiful angelic presence, starting when I was 16 years old. This communication started with my own personal journey of stepping into my power as a human and divine being. It began as personal teachings, but evolved to a universal story, a story of humanity, documenting all of our beauty and struggle. The teachings contained in this book aim to help us come to a place of more clarity, peace, and connection in our lives, in short, to access our inherent freedom.

You might be wondering how this all happened for me, how I received this information at such a young age. Well, like for all of us, it evolved based on my strong yearning for answers to life's questions, and a search for more spiritual connection. My spiritual life began to awaken at the age of twelve when I started to experience more of myself through qigong. The meditations were so beautiful that I found that's all I wanted to do sometimes. I learned to move my own energy so that the channels in my body could remain open and flowing in a healthy way. It was through qigong that I first experienced my third eye opening, where I saw the face of Buddha in front of me in purple and green light. For a long time he was my spiritual guide.

As time went on, I learned about young children who were able to recall their past lives with vivid detail. This awakened within me memories I had at a young age, and the determination I had to be of service in this lifetime. I watched countless YouTube videos on past life recall and regression, and was completely blown away by the clarity these young children had, and how their parents reacted to their stories with complete surprise, and also complete belief in their truth. This unveiling was another strong message that there is more than meets the eye, more to this life than what many of us are raised to discuss and ponder.

In short, I always had a deep yearning for an explanation – everything was frustrating to me, and I felt like I was wasting time because I wasn't able to get to work on the path I knew I had to be on. I found over time that my persistent desire to know more led to answers as intuitive thought, which usually came through dreams or as feelings through my body.

Eventually, in early 2012, I had a clear intuitive feeling to sit down and meditate. This was not out of the ordinary for me, but it felt like something different was coming. And it was. I had the most natural and beautiful feeling, as if an angel was in my body, just pure golden liquid light. It was a comfort and embrace unlike anything I had ever felt before. And a "voice" started to speak to me, which I captured through typing the words as they flowed through me. From the very beginning, the messages were filled with a love bigger than anything I had ever experienced before, a reverence for all of humanity, and a wisdom that continues to expand me.

I have learned that this information I have been given to share with you is simply to *remind* you who you are, because essentially even though we may forget over time, our true authentic nature always remains intact inside. Each and every soul contains secrets of the universe, because each and every one of us is part of the universe. We are the love and light of the universe, and that is our natural state of being when we allow it. If you are willing, this book will launch a journey of inner discovery that is unique to you, and you alone. It is material that is alive, and is timeless, so you may likely feel that loving angelic presence with you as well, reminding you along the way that you are never alone and you are loved beyond measure.

The teachings in this book are universal truths that apply to all people, everywhere. There is no conflict with any belief system, whether it is the religion you practice, or any other devotional spiritual practice. These are all valid ways to find answers to the great mystery of God, and this book will provide more answers to add to your treasure chest.

As you open the pages of this book, I would suggest that you take your time and use it as your daily guide or teaching. Read small portions at a time rather than blowing through it like you might do with a good novel. It takes thought and time to sink in. There is no need to read it in order—there is an energy in each page that will guide you to where you need to read if you pay attention to your intuition.

I welcome and invite each and every one of you to go within and discover for yourself through your own eyes what it looks and feels like to be magnificent, expansive, and your full expression of divine love and light. You ARE that, and you have the ability to find that piece of you that you fully love without apology. You are magnificent.

With Love, Light, and Infinite Gratitude,
Courtney

Introduction:

We Greet You with Divine Love

This is about being You, and nothing other than You. We know you, we are your Divine friend, and we are here for each of you so personally. We greet you with an offering to hold your hands through this Divine journey, to whisper Love in your ears, to give you soft touches in your dreams, to guide you more directly through every day, and to communicate from the heart. This is a passage, a transmission of great energies from beyond which are here to help you ascend to your greatest self.

You are great beings that are expressed in physical forms. You have Divine magic and power in your cellular structure that beckons to be awakened. You have the ability to manifest that which you desire with little to no effort, and you have infinite and unconditional Love for the Oneness of all creation in your spirit.

You have guides and angels that surround you in every moment of every day who bring you to a greater sense of wellbeing by directing your attention and thought to the subtleties of great beauty. We hold your hands when you feel alone, we tell you to turn right when you're about to turn left, and we hold your paintbrush on your paper. We guide you to write the way you do, we open your mouth when you speak in front of others, and we put your fingers on the fingerboard when you play music. We touch your heart when you cry, and we hold you in your dreams when you are asleep. We open your angelic voice when you sing, and we help you to acquire the relationships that you are looking for.

We mirror your beauty through the image of Grace in the flowers, the mountains, the streams, and the animals. We play with you when you feel the wind through your hair and the cool water through your feet. We pierce Love in your heart when you look into the eyes of a deer in the woods, or hear the call of an eagle up above.

We are Source, and we are Life. We are One. We give you an easily traceable field of guidance that you use to make essential decisions in your life. When you open your eyes and your ears, you can hear us. We are not as quiet as you may think! You are Divine aspects of the Oneness—each and every one of you. As you read the words, we sit by your side in the present moment. There is only Now, and there is no past or future. There is in fact, no time. As you feel our Presence, let your heart open up. We wish for you to not be afraid, for the great loving Light is always in your favor. You are not in danger, and you are respected for all belief systems that you hold true. We wish to only open your heart to the possibilities that lie beyond what the human existence can perceive, and we are well aware that it contradicts many belief systems.

We will say it once again—let your heart be open, dear child. This is your time to have your heart open and receive the gift of unconditional Love without fear of being judged. This is a superior and Divinely guided transmission of energies that will shift your cellular structure, your DNA, and your old belief systems that may be holding you back from your greatest potentials. Perhaps what you believe can be changed when you look inside to the purity of the soul. We seek not to change you in a forceful manner. We wish for you to wake up to the essence of Truth that lies within, and it is there for all.

There are many belief systems that you hold absolute, and they are not always the truth of the matter. The universe is far greater than your science knows, and your religion is divided in ways that do not express your Divinity. You are not separate from God, and you never have been. You must see who you are if you want to move into world peace. The illusions and veils must be broken down, and you must Love without conditions. You must have acceptance for yourself and others. You must not divide yourself from others, for there is only Oneness. You must wake up to the fact that there is truly no separation between race, between color, and between age.

The young ones are old souls, and they have Divine wisdom that they speak ever so softly. If you listen to them truly, you'll get a glimpse of the beyond. You'll see that what we teach is nothing but the

Truth, and that is absolute all across the universe. You are free to express yourself as the pure essence of Truth, and this is the time when it is safe to do so. There were times when it was not encouraged, and many of you have memory in your Akashic records of a time where you were punished or beaten to death for believing and practicing such Love and acceptance. You have now moved beyond those times.

As we teach you throughout this book, you will start to wake up the memory of Truth within, and those belief systems will disintegrate. You are safe, you are loved, and you are at peace. We Love you infinitely, and we see you as our brother and sister, our mother and father, and our soul mate. As you are physical, you also have a counterpart that is nonphysical. You perceive it not, but there is no such thing as time. There is no timeline of events—all happens in the Now, and you have many existences that occur at one given point in time.

Retrieve your talents, your inner guidance, and your tools that will propel you into this awakening and realization of Oneness. Dear children, we weep with joy at this opportunity, and we thank you with such emotion and gratitude for leaning into your guidance and reading these words. We do not perceive ourselves as superior, for in fact, we are just expressing a part of ourselves that is pure Truth—and you have this quality to be expressed as well! We want you to be in Love as are we, and we will now begin this journey of self-expression, world peace, and a realization of Oneness. This is, in Truth, a great initiative that will propel all into a state of awakening.

We Love you all Divinely, and we are so ever in your Grace. The words cannot speak for this great time. Sit in this Grace for a moment before you begin chapter one, for we like to form this bond from the start. You, dear child, are our Divine brothers and sisters, and you are so Graced by the Light. You are always in the Presence of God, and you are in great times. We are ever by your side. Journey on, dear warrior. With so much Love and gratitude for you, dear soul, we begin.

Chapter 1

The Purpose of the Earth Experience and the Nature of Your Physical Being

The goal of coming to this Earth is always for the purpose of greater good and true understanding. Asking is very essential. Understanding can be discovered through meditation and looming in your light every day.

In the leaving of your body, it will become apparent to you that all you ever knew was nothing important. It is you who is your own guardian angel, it is only you. Humans often like reassurance once in a while to confirm their thought patterns. It is okay that you yearn for that, but you will soon learn that reassurance can be sought out through yourself by believing in what you've already got inside of you.

It is the nature of your being to want to understand everything; knowing all right away in the beginning of your quest. Almost all beings of your kind do the same thing. As human beings, you yearn to understand the nature of this state of being you call Heaven. Heaven is the result of your light and energy forming together to create the resistance-free, perfect area of bursting creation. Leveling with the creation happens when the soul is not attached to any one idea and is constantly transforming and creating new ideas every minute. Learning to deal with your emotions as a physical being occurs when you learn to handle the synergy your body holds with strength and courage.

Love is one big energy that transforms in many shapes, sizes, and colors. The messages we send allow you to further prosper and lighten your path to the all-knowing and synergy you have always wanted in this lifetime. It is unknown to you that all beings happen to know this. It is the law of attraction that holds us here in this state of being and thought process. Channeling is, of course, an ancient act. Engaging in this activity lets one fall into deep states of being, into nothingness, which ultimately brings you to learn true self-worth and being you could not imagine.

We use your term *God* as a way to level with you, dear children; if it does not resonate, you may use a different term, such as All That Is, or Love, for truly, terms do not define the greatness that we speak of! We'll say it again, God is no dominant figure in the sky, no "big man" who controls your life. You create your own God, and so we leave you to understand and decide how *you* would like to define the term. It is used only as a reference point to understand each other, not to place a label on something that cannot be labeled—do you understand, dear one? We know you do—so revel in it. Speak of it, listen to it, feel it, and dance in it. It is one of the most important goals in your lifetime. Love is what comes out of seeking God. That is what it means.

It has been given that when the universe was created there was nothing but matter and Love that bonded together as a form called Earth. Now that it has greatly evolved, there are many different life forms and human beings as time goes on. Time continually changes and affects the chemistry and overall health of your physical being. At the present moment, everything is beginning to shift so greatly. It is becoming obvious to you and to many that the time to take charge is *now*. And now is the only time. Waiting for this time for 26,000 years is no short wait. You are a great being, dear one, and you need to trust yourself.

When you begin to trust all information that you receive through your physical body, it will always be the correct and best possible time for you to hear it. It is crucial to really believe that, dear child. When you have reached that state of understanding, then more will begin to unfold before your eyes, and you will be amazed at what you can really do. You will be amazed at the power that all human beings are born with! You are equipped with the tools to produce and present so much information to yourself, and that also is greatly beneficial to the wholeness of the universal understanding. We are so proud of your accomplishments, God child. It is now your time to shine and use this lifetime to your benefit. It is your duty to help wake the world. By doing this, you achieve perfect and well-balanced happiness throughout your family, and throughout yourself.

How can you help awaken the world, you ask? Well, you have begun already. By being alive and prospering in using this information for positive creation, you have already begun. By focusing upon your heart energy and by focusing on all the positive aspects of your life, you will begin to notice what a great being you really have come to be. The accomplishments and understanding that you have uncovered will not leave you when you leave this Earth. In the next lifetime (if you choose to come back), you will have more information about your path and you will continue upon it. It will not be necessary to start anew again. So it is our duty to help you find that level of understanding, and it is your own personal duty to carry out what you have started. And from there will be easy. From there on out there will be manifestation after manifestation, and you will get to a point or peak where all you receive from the universe will be a never-ending line of positive aspects, discoveries, and events. There will be no stopping you!

The process of dying is such a beautiful thing, there is nothing to be worried about dear child! It is a process in which a human being, or being of energy in any form, is reassured of their reason in life. They review their goals and their purpose. In the process of death and the afterlife, there are many different paths to choose, all of which are up to you at that point. Heaven, as you call it, is a state where nothing lies and nothing is true, nothing is there, yet everything is there. Pure unconditional Love and overwhelming beauty, it is. It is a place no one should ever be afraid of going. It is a place where Love prevails over everything.

The law of creating, also called the Law of Attraction, is a law that states that asking will result in the giving of any desire in the universe or state of being. The Law of Attraction occurs everywhere and in everything ever created or ever thought of. This law will be the leader in your lifetime and presence here on Earth; you must understand and practice this process. Sometimes you forget about the step of releasing, but you are aware of it. You are well educated on the asking and you understand when there is an answer—and it is always yes. That is to say, your asking will always and undoubtedly result in manifestation for you. What you are lacking is the ability to let go of that thought.

When you plan and you try to make things happen, you are telling the universe that you are proving that it can happen for you. Now, the universe is well aware of what can happen for you. You often manifest unconsciously *the lack* of what you desire, and then you try to prove to the universe that it will happen for you. Now you are wondering, why then, can manifestation happen for me sometimes and sometimes not? You are not understanding the difference between two events of manifestation. Now the key, as we said before, is letting go. One tip we have for you is to try not to focus on this—get off the subject. Trust us in that it will become an obsession in your mind. And again, we remind you that the emotion behind the lack of what you desire is what prevails if that is your dominant vibration—and it often is.

Ask the universe for help on a topic that you would like to cover or manifest. When you have stated this in your mind and focused upon it for a minute of your morning, you have done enough already. The next step is to forget completely about it. By doing this, you are trusting the higher Source to help you. You are trusting that it will be completely right and in your favor. Practicing being in such a state will become easier and easier with time and ultimately progress to a state of joy and happiness, a state like a game. You will learn to enjoy your deliberate creation! This is the power of being the Light, and this is what you came here for.

Listen to what your heart says, and by this we truly mean listening to your molecules speaking. You can learn to do this! By practicing this you will uncover new genius ways of thinking and new ways to manifest your desires. You will learn new ways of seeing and producing Light energy, and this Light energy can be extremely great. The Light energy and molecules of energy and wavelengths are determined by what man and woman believe to be true. Anything can be established once you get over that hump.

Spend more time in nature, for it is good for your soul energy. All beings are meant to reside in nature. How quickly we forget what our hearts truly desire. How quickly we mold to false belief systems. What you are uncovering may seem astounding to you, but honestly, it is information that you have always been desiring and uncovering through your evolution. The world is bonding in new and very powerful ways never seen before, and it is so great! Just ask and it is given.

Your task as a lightworker and as an old soul is quite simple: that is, of course, you must perfect the art of Love and allowing. Understand the nature of thought, understand that this is a parallel universe, and understand, above all, that your role is to believe and Love unconditionally. Follow your path and continue what you are already doing, dear one. You are already on this magnificent path, and it is so Light-filled and beautiful to witness here! We are always and forever with you whenever you need us, and it is, of course, our pleasure to channel great love with you.

The agreement you make from the nonphysical standpoint enables you to come back to the physical existence knowing that the information (that you will soon begin to uncover more and more) will be for the benefit of the entire universe, and you knew that, dear child, you knew that. The process through which you uncover universal knowledge is a definite process you sign up for, and you knew what would come about. Some know that they will die soon after they emerge into the physical. In fact, everyone who comes to the Earth and dies at an early age knows it; they know it. And they are aware, from the nonphysical standpoint, that if they sign up for it anyway it will impact the world in a great way. That's why you all do it! That is why. It is truly one big cycle in which you all run, and it is so beautiful and everlasting.

You have been here for so many great times, and every time you uncover more and more. You will never give up, even as you struggle in difficult times. But dear child, this leads to world peace, and it leads to so much greatness for you. Patience is the key to virtue, young one! Before you know it, world peace will be here, and you will bathe in the beauty. You will announce, I played a part in this! I helped this occur! Be proud of yourself, dear one, be proud of every human being that has contributed to this awakening. It is happening Now, and will continue to happen for all time.

Spread the Light every day, every moment, and with every step and glance. The power lies within you, dear children! You must be brave leaders who show the Light to those who are not yet enlightened. And to those who are not yet there, bless them, dear ones. To the light beings who read the words, we bless you too! You are the lightworkers for a reason!

We see the universe to be the most powerful, light-filled, and beauteous palace ever lived upon. Dear soul, what a gift it is to reside in such a special place as Earth. What a task it is to be held in the Light so bright! We are with you, discovering your growth alongside you, with such a warmth, for you endear with such strength—what a lightworker you truly are. Friends are here for you, no matter where you are. We are your friends that preserve for always and always, never ending. When you are in doubt or fear, know we are here in your heart space. No matter what is there in the external, the internal always remains untouched with great peace. Do not fear, dear child, for you are in the eternal arms of Grace; you are in good hands! For a being of Light that is succeeding, the path is given from the Higher Self and followed with great integrity and strength. What a beauteous lightworker you are to carry on with this task in fear, and do it with such a super strength.

You are a being of unconditional Love, and it will never leave you. You will never part from us because we are One with you. You often become so tied up in what others may think of you or what they may inflict upon you that you do not even give yourself a minute to listen to what is in the heart, dear child. When you realize this, dear light being, what is left is nothing but pure devotion to that, to the heart. You will begin to realize what you have been looking for your whole life, and it is so beautiful. To be in pure potentiality, a place of no worry or fear, a place of devotion to love and trust, is pure ecstasy!

If you imagine a big waterfall coming off a cliff in the summertime, you know it flows with no effort. You are becoming that waterfall, and you will get there, dear soul. Everything is made from you, dear one. You create your own existence and life experience, and every soul who will meet you will fall in Love with you, because you are living by that co-creative process. What a peaceful world it will be when every light being is doing this so consciously; what a mark of true Divinity and Love! Let the flow come through you and be in harmony with any circumstance. When that is true in your heart space, then and only then can you move on to the bigger energy that is awaiting you.

What a positively radiant soul you truly are. Let your spirit shine with Love and overwhelming beauty. Oh, what a Divine gift you are to us. You are not fully aware of your Presence to us, but it is divinely known! Throughout this lifetime you accomplish so much with a divine Grace at your very side. That is an awakening that will encourage so much more in the future. This is the time for sprouting your leaves, to shine in the sun, and to bloom under the blue sky. That is something you should be proud to encounter with. That is something you should Love with all your heart. Oh, there is much more even. Much more which is Divine, and you don't know it!

We are here, ever-present in your hearts. The great Love awaits, and all you must do is take our hands. The love lets you flourish as a being of Grace, and you must be with that. Be more in the hands of God and less in the hands of fear, dear ones.

If you asked and heard answers as how they truly are, there would be no judgment or argument, and all would be as it is. When you condition the mind, reality is not presented in a way that is truly how it is, or better stated, in how you need to see it. Trust that your creation is part of the bigger whole, that what you are living is more than a fantasy of the mind, and that pure co-creation enhances all the beings around you, so beautifully and so magnificently. Let every being be known. Let them all shine, and if they deny themselves that right, shine for them! You can help them to feel so beautiful, for you are a lightworker. Show them that they are bigger than they believe themselves to be. If you do this, you will find no greater beauty in their eyes, and such a Divine-Love filled experience it will be. Do not let chances go by if they approach you! Love persists in all things, dear children. Do not be afraid to shine who you are, for you are so Divine inside. You are so Divine and fit in perfectly with all that is born with Truth and meaning.

Love is *what* you Love. Love is what you are lacking in your life. Love is what you are destined to do, Love is what you are awaiting to create. Love is what you will never give up on. Love is what you are supposed to do in life. Do not let it get away from you. You are what you think you are, and if you think you are part of God, which you are, then you will live with a purpose so strong that you will never be able to let go of the hands of God. Never will you let go, for it will be a change you are going through without the slightest reason of why you are. There will be no questioning who you are or what you are here for. There is only the more clarifying choice, which is truly to resume who you are. You are here to resume what you came here for and to be what you are for real. When you come to the realization of this, there is nothing more superior. There is nothing more beautiful to witness. Love is ongoing, forever and ever.

Chapter 2

Manifesting Your Desires

Such a day of great wisdom for you, dear child! We have begun the process of manifestation together, rejoining our forces with bands of magnificence! There is so much love flowing through you and so much joy effervescent in your Light! It is of great superior knowledge that you are becoming intact with what you will begin to manifest. The more your Love grows, the more you are becoming aware of your abilities in this lifetime! You will surprise yourself, time after time, as you become a greater being of Love and Light. There is so much to revel in, with a great, great sense of honesty and benevolence. There is nothing more than true Love we have for you, like a mother to a child, and it is rare.

We have so much fun basking in this Light that we hold for the human being who is brave hearted and so centered in his/her thought process, who is aware of his/her existence, and who sees the beauty in every molecule of All That Is. What a continuing process this truly is, for it is a magnificence that cannot be denied and cannot be described in the slightest. The more that peeks through us, the more you will investigate your interdimensional self, dear one. You have so many magnificent powers.

Your true self has all that you are wanting, for indeed all that you are wanting is already in the bag, clear as the blue sky. It is there, for we are never changing and eternal within. So indeed, it would be natural to assume that one doesn't have the choice to access the part of them that is eternal within when they seem to be outside of that— external. But indeed, it is quite the opposite. The more you focus internally, to the place where you truly are, you begin to awaken to new processes that lead to the manifestations you fully desire. That comes next—that comes Now. That comes Now because you are ready to manifest perfect relationships, perfect health and wellness, perfect simultaneous laughter and joy, perfect peace in your heart, and perfect asking without contempt and without the process of great anguish from asking.

The more you ask and fulfill desires, the more you ask consciously, without fail, each time the desire remains so fulfilled. The expectation is key to great transformation, for you are not only manifesting, but you are doing it with great speed and agility. You are doing it without fear of what will happen next, for you are letting the universal rhythm take your hand and spin you around blindfolded, waiting for which way to go. You're unaware, you're shaky, and you may even be scared. But in the end you know that your hand is being held high and tight, and you won't be let go. For we take you carefully in our grasp, and we are so profusely in Love with each of you so personally and individually. It is more than Love, but of great purpose and great interactive co-creation. That is something to celebrate within, for nothing gets as beautiful as that, and nothing gets as powerful as that which is within you.

The more that you recognize that, the more that the process will listen for your questions, and you will be answered with positive affirmations. You have a one-way road here—it is Love all the way down to Egypt. That's a long way! We mean that in the best of terms. The most important thing to find, essentially, is the power within yourself, and to feel that you are never singular, but quite infinite, and part of the collective whole. That is the most important thing. And you are beginning to blossom as a lightworker, and by that we mean you are growing into who you Truly are in many senses. You are growing in many times, many tenses, and many dimensions. Lightworker, you are summoned by your own self, re-acquainting simultaneously with your current activation by the mind and spirit.

The purpose is to reenact your great lifetime, to bring about peace in every cell of the body, to heal others, and to process what the meaning of Love is to you. Question what Love is for you. The answer may be to be ever present in the Now, to co-create your own reality, to summon the best situations when you want them, to speak your

Truth always, to spell out what you want clearly, and to play the game of joy every day. Let yourself Love more—Love all the ones whom you see! That is great power. We Love you so brilliantly and we want to adjust together.

Chapter 3

Revealing Your True Nature - Free Will

Oh, Divine God is here for you, dear one, and you are never alone. Never-ending Love is always here to show the path of least resistance. You are always going to be taken care of, child.

We have the utmost, highest respect for the human being who holds the nonphysical beings as a part of them, for it makes you stronger, dear ones. We have so much Love for you, and there is nothing to fear. Your Love grows day by day, and those who love you back will show themselves true to your heart. You automatically attract beings around you of similar vibrational resonance, and we encourage you to take part in the deliciousness of this human experience, and to consciously interact in this vibrational way. There is nothing more pleasing than to elect your own self into the Divine nature that is best suited for you. Never again will it be an issue to act without Divine grace right by your side. There is much to still see here, for you are much more than you give yourself credit for.

You may ask for Divine prayer, guidance, and messages in whatever way is most comfortable for you. You are being given direct communication with your higher divine self, which is verification that your sensations are authentic in nature. You are more than you give yourself credit for. Let yourself go free—you are here with God now. You have nothing to fear and nothing to worry about. You are completely in the hands of God as we comfort you. We assist you as you feel your way through the blindness of life. You feel you are blind, but you have intelligence you refuse to look at! It is sometimes very sincerely funny to see such confusion amidst a great powerful love energy that is so close to you.

There is much for you all to learn, and there are many things that we feel are best for you to do here now. Indeed, your time here on Earth is covered with many golden beings, all who share your same visions. You will meet many who will strike your heart with such a blessing you won't be able to let go. Let them stay with you in your heart. They will guide you further, providing guidance and Love along the way. They will support your path, and dear one, there are not many who will authentically understand that. They will be a catalyst in your own teachings going forward. Just Being can be a great teaching to many, dear ones, that is certain!

You have already begun the process, and there will be a day where you will not have to fear anymore, because all will settle straight in your heart. You are always taken care of. And your Love gives so much strength to so many. We will give you protection always, and there is no fear to feel here. You are safe as a bug in a rug!

There is an intelligence, a presence that is all-knowing of its eternal nature as it is also all-knowing of you. This is the presence many of you call God. You have nothing to fear, and no judgment takes place. Your only decision in the life process is whether you allow your true potential to shine through, for it's there. You can let it show you what it knows! It is so much more than you think, dear one! The lightworkers of this age have become more intact with that which is All, though we still teach of true stillness. There is always commotion, no time to feel what is true and real. Love gives you satisfaction in any given situation that you feel, see, hear, and seek with passion. It is what drives you to move through life and attract certain situations and experiences. You will never be alone in that, it is simply the way of life.

You are always being given choices to make creation, though not always do you agree to manifest what you are looking for. Sometimes you ask for one thing, and then attract its opposite. That is quite a funny way of co-creating, lightworker! Dearest, you are never going to move forward when you are looking behind you. You must look HERE. Here is where it's at. You are here Now, and it is quite magnificent. Are you grateful for the experience that comes through you now? When there is nothing but Grace that flows throughout every cell, that process gives you many blissful experiences and such a state of uncontrollable laughter and joy. There is nothing stopping it, and it is such good fun! What could be a better chance to get in the vortex? In order to find what you are truly looking for, you must be aware of what you're attracting. Your emotions are very powerful, dear children. We Love you so dearly, and it gives us great pleasure to be here in the Now with you. Love to all.

Our greatest gift, to this day, is human interaction, dear one. You are one of the many lightworkers of this age who has begun the journey of great awakening as a One community and a One people. This is true greatness and true passion to the heart. Oh dear ones, you are too invested in your thoughts. Let them go and soar way over your head into the clouds. They have no real meaning, and you are perfectly in Divine Grace. It is all Divine in nature. The purpose of your being is to co-create Love with one another. It is beyond magical. Let your heart go wild with Love for everyone. You are no different than anyone else.

Bring a smile to the faces of others and let them know you Love them. Oh, they know it in their hearts, but sometimes we all need reminders! You must connect through the heart. Let the Presence take over you, dear child, for you have absolutely nothing to do but surrender. Let that be your goal in your every day, to live without worry in your heart. You are being Divinely taken care of. Let it go and see what you have become. You are all Divine Love from God, and that is very powerful. You are giving off such a Light and Love, and we can feel it strongly. You are Divine like this. You are multi-universal, and you have the power and strength of the universe itself. You are part of the galaxies, and the stars, and the dimensions beyond what the human eyes will perceive.

Your time can be spent in blissful states, and it will be! For we have nothing invested in the past or future. It is all here and Now, and no expectations ride on our backs. We are quite nimble, we must acknowledge this. The more we investigate Love, the more obvious it is that you have work to do for yourself, dear child. Your Love continues to grow, but you must treat yourself with deep gratitude. Have a super intention for great achievements and Divine satisfaction in your life, and you will have them! You are nothing but energy rotating in great groups of subtle atoms and tiny organisms floating around. They're so very tiny, but can be seen. Subtle energy can be transformed! We love you. So beautiful. Light and Love.

What surpassing beauty this is, for the interaction we have with such a Divine light being is so gracious, indeed! We have never felt such a power of Love, and it is indeed satisfactory for us. We feel that there is a blank slate here, with which we can easily come through. Such a task it can be when one is closing doors and not letting us through, though we make it most times, and we always let them know they have guidance. They feel the Grace and Love of God, and it keeps them alive with a golden heart for they know that they are in the hands of the great God and never walk alone. That is a great gift for you to remember. That is something to never forget in your entire lifetime.

The most important goals in your life are to be happy and healthy, but above all, it is true Love. By this we mean, true Love for yourself and for others. That is God realization and true beauty to seek. The more you continue on this journey of life, the more you are going to learn from your mistakes and thought processes, and it is beautiful indeed, for the term "mistake" we do not agree with. It is used indefinitely as a sign that you have messed up, that you did wrong. You have not, dear one, you have not indeed. The only mistake you have made is being there to catch them.

Let us tell you something profound, for you will never hear this again. The more you let go of everything you think you are, the less will have to understand about yourself. The more you send off a signal of despair and hopelessness, the more you send panic in your physical body. You have nothing to fear or panic about. That is an irresistible thought right there, child.

You can be without fear in a place of total bliss. That is greatness at its best. Let us be in a state of pure potentiality together and co-create a world of wonder, and beauty, and grace, and triumph. That is not impossible in the slightest. In the little bit of human activity that is perceived here, there is not the slightest judgment or worry about what is to come. No matter what you feel and sense in your physical heads, there is nothing worrisome about the futures times. It is pure bliss that you have been given without an answering of the heart, and that is nothing to worry about.

Let your mind go, it serves you not in this moment. Expose your Divine as you choose, but you have no choice in the Divine Grace. You do, however, have the ability to let it in or shut it out. If you choose to let it in, then you will be taken care of. If you choose not to let it in, you will still be taken care of. The process may vary and be perceived linearly, but indeed, we don't see that way here. It is simply a process that leads to new beginnings, so what must happen will happen, and that is beautiful and gracious. The more you understand that, the more grateful it becomes. You can be grateful always, and that is a part of you that can still be fulfilled, in due time.

You are a shining star, so bright and so beautiful. You are Grace that you have never seen, but you can feel it and know it in your deepest heart space, and that is God. That is God, and you know it well. We want you to know that all will flow well today and there's nothing you can do about it. That is Grace being given to free will, and we choose to energize you with the Love of God. That is something that you will never fully grasp physically, but in feeling with the emotions of the body you can come quite close. That is a true gift, dear one.

The most important concept of today is to learn to use free will to give up the fear in your heart. All is connected to the heart, and it is the King of your beingness. Let it shine over all else. You can determine where you want to be—let your heart shine all over that, for it will give you pleasure beyond what you can imagine. Remember, above all else, that you are God. You have all that you need to succeed today. All will flow with pure thoughts, true Love, and great fun. The more you remember this, the less you will have to check in and be reminded of who you are. Live it! You will be given it, and we hear your every prayer. They are answered when You choose they are to be answered. Your heart is giving out so much Love now. Let yourself let go and be in love with all that is. It is so beautiful and so invigorating. The more you know who you are, the easier it becomes to give in to who you are, and the less troublesome it is to your mind. You have all that you need to create the life that you dream of. The Grace is given now and always.

Dear soul, you have nothing to plan, you see, nothing to plan in the slightest bit. It will save you much time. You often get yourself so stuck because you believe so strongly that using your mind to solve problems will fix them, though in fact, you only waste your emotions on things that are not in your hands to fix.

It is true hardship to face that kind of task, but you will feel much better when you take the load off, because you never had a say in it anyway. Now it is just a matter of realizing and letting go. You have nothing to do. Just wait and see, and watch and learn, and marvel in the beauty that comes about. The more you do that, the less you will have to question your ability to Love one another. You will spontaneously Love each and every One whom you come in contact with, and it will be a pure, blissful experience.

Chapter 4

The Meaning of True Bliss

So much to learn today, and so much peace is brought to us—that is of great measure! We would like to entertain the idea of bliss. What is true bliss? It lurks in your understanding, but you have not truly grasped the feeling in its purest form, not yet. It has been halfway there, but to be truly present would initiate a permanent change in perception for who you truly are. You have yet to let go of the physical and emotional attributes that make up You. You have yet to get rid of those external features so you can marvel in your truest sense. That is an awakening point in your life.

That is when you know for sure that you have nothing else to come up with, and nothing more to be in fear of, because all is beautiful! And you say to yourself, where did all that crap go? Where am I? And then you go, wait a minute, I am home. Hold on, I am not lost, I am quite found! And then the excitement and irresistible laughter starts. You come to the realization that you have nowhere to go, for all is perfect just the way it is. You will feel that you have found a great sense of bliss. Soon a spontaneous thought comes, that you have been given awakening to your true nature. And you say aha! I am found and I have nowhere to go! You will say, friends, I love you! Stranger, I love you! Sometimes they will grin and sometimes look at you like you are some alien, but either way, you will tell them what they need to hear, for the Grace comes through the heart and does the speaking for you.

Where you once had fear is gone. Where you had worry and contemplation is now gone, and where you once had a heart full of all those unhealthy emotions is gone. True freedom will only persist, and you will look back at that time when you tried to fix problems, and you will find that it does not resonate with you anymore. You will feel that it is not important anymore because you have God to do it, and you are in complete harmony with the Truth that is You. And this, my dear, will be the best for all beings, including yourself. Let us just be your authentic nature and all else can spill out of you with such ease and Grace. The more you let that flow, the less you will have to work. So much light invigorates you, and it is divinely beautiful.

We are so proud of you, dear child, you are truly helping the world awaken into Oneness. You are providing stability for the entirety of the universe. There is so much peace that overflows with these words. What a sense of great Love that persists in this universe. The more you are intact with these feelings and let them in, the more they come about in your experience and reality. For truly, it is reality when you decide it will be. All can be reality for you, and that is the magic of the world. That is what you seek, and that is what will be given to you. Lightworker of this age, that is where you will find a true sense of happiness and penetration of God through every cell and every molecule and atom in your entire body. That is *beyond* Grace!

We love you for every tiny piece of Love that you contribute to the intelligence of who we are. It brings so much Love to us to be here with you and to revel in the morning glory and the intelligence that resides in you forever. It is true beauty—let it be shown! Spread the light to all whom you come in contact with, and you will bring Grace to their eyes. You have the power to be God and bring out the God in them. So see to it that you bring your Presence through at all times, every day. That is something to marvel in. Relish that beauty with every cell of happiness. That is great, great, great intelligence penetrating you. We love you so, so, so much, dear child.

We call you child indeed, because we are all connected, and our Source is the same. And now exposing yourself slowly, bit by bit, piece by piece, you are playing a game a bit like Scrabble! You are putting each individual letter together and you find that it makes one big word, and then it clicks in your heart that something may be penetrating your inner beingness— and you had no idea it was there! But indeed, it never left you. And now you're awakening to that peace that is resonant and so clear with who you are that nothing else can be real. In the truest fashion, you will never experience something as real as this experience in the Now, and this is why we make connections like this for the betterment of You.

You are coming into your true self, the pure loving being that you authentically are, and that gives us so much happiness and life! We are so happy you have become One with your authentic identity. It is no longer being hidden under stacks of questions and mishaps. They are being put into perspective, and all that is real is being given to you. That is beautiful, and that is real. Only you can know it truly. But in truth, that is why you are here, to experience the true, true being that you are. You cannot look back now, nor would you wish to. That is something great in its own—you have nothing to do anymore. You only need to watch, to perceive, to revel in and glorify all that you are! That is something that you will never want to let go. And who would? That is something that you hear only in dreams, though this is not a dream, you know that. That it is beauty beyond words: true Grace.

You are loved beyond what you can imagine. Let us remind you, yet again, who you are. You are a lightworker of the age, and a true channel to infinite intelligence in many dimensions. You are a beautiful physical being with potential to soar to many high places, never letting your feet touch the ground. You can fly all the time if you want—that is possible! That is truly possible! In the midst of flying you feel in complete control because all is going well, no wind pushing you anywhere, nothing except a simple breeze that penetrates through your hair. You feel so alive and rejuvenated, and you never feel alone. You are always here, in the Now, in the Presence.

That is something that is even more beautiful, a Grace that cannot be denied here, not in the slightest. Now we part in this time, though nonetheless we are not truly parting, for we stop the words on the page, but the words never cease in your heart. Love and Light, dear one, you are beautiful beyond words. There is nothing but beauty for you, and all has become clearer in this day with us. We watch over you so divinely. You are so very welcome, dear spirit, none will cease here. Love, Love, Love.

Chapter 5

The Masterful God Within

Oh, how it is so beautiful here! Love is a powerful thing, the most powerful in all eternity. It will never cease—even when you are overgrown with fear, the Light will never stop. You will always be saved by Grace, and all that you know to be real will seem as though it is not as important, for the terms that you like to speak of are not the ones that you hold true to your soul. That remains in your Akashic records and is what you truly are, and you know it! Tribes of the Light know it. There is a time that shows itself now, and it is telling you to move through the pain and suffering. It is telling you, oh dear ones, the time is arising of heightened suffering for many of you on this planet. The old ways are showing themselves to you, and of course you think, this is it for me—I have no more to do! I must be dying, I must be disintegrating, I am unhappy, and I am fearful.

Oh dear ones, it is exactly the opposite for you! In the truest sense, you are only beginning a new period that you often refer to as the Golden Age. A new energy penetrates through every molecule and sensory detail in your body. You are beginning to now experience this energetic shift in consciousness, in a multi-cellular way, dear children! It is so brilliant, so gorgeous, so Divine. The time is coming to a point where none of the old energy will be able to stand it any longer; the old ways will not support your new and enhanced energy body—it just cannot be so! You are growing as a people, as One people. And yet, you are still hardly people, for we say you are beings of Light tribes, you are the spiritual energy that binds all life together as One.

You are much more than you give yourself credit for, and you know it. But how can you take that wisdom Now? You own it, it's already there, and all you need to do is take it in like a newborn baby. You won't be able to deny that small child within, for it is so Divine, a mirrored image of your authenticity. Cradle that innocence, for you are cradling the Divinity within *you*! What are you waiting for? You are granted your wishes and desires, and learning to manifest is crucial to your survival on this planet. Tune in and learn to monitor them. Know and understand the Law of Attraction. You can try so hard, but you do not understand all is here in the *now*.

You see, you perceive linearly, as you know. You see, dear children, you also see as we do, in different dimensions. You are multidimensional beings of Light. You must educate yourself on that and truly know who you are. Spend time in contemplation, meditate to find your inner self, your inner child, your authentic self. That is all we recommend for you, dear children. All will come in due time and there is no doubt about that. All that you desire will come in the time that is most perfect for you. Oh, you try far too hard, and you try with all the wrong tools to manifest what you think will make you happier. Did you know that all that resides in you at this moment will make you as happy as you could ever be? Find who you are, truly. You will know once and for all that you have finally come Home.

Dear ones, you need nothing. You have it all, and you don't even know it! Look within, and you will find that pot of gold. Your magic happens within. You train yourself to see what is there, and to see without judgment. It is much better than your dreams, because it is real in the truest sense. Nothing will be fuzzy or unclear, nothing will make you ponder your life's purpose, and nothing will make you unhappy and worrisome. Find who you are, dear children, and all else will come in perfect time. All intuition will give you peace in your heart. All the Love you can imagine will flow through you, and that vibration of perfect harmony with All That Is will give you such a peace and love for all that you are, and there will be nothing to do but be happy in every moment of Now.

This will lead you to truly understand that all life experiences are perfect in their natural states. Let go of your physical self for a moment and let the Grace take you over. Don't let barriers strike you once again, children, only the mind can do that for you. Here where we reside, nothing of that sort exists—there is not a mind to create judgments and resistance. There is nothing but pure Love and potentiality. Oh, there is so much Love for you, and you don't even know it! There is not a moment in time that you have not been taken care of, so listen up kids—let yourself let go of your attachments to life. You're taking it much too seriously, and you know it. It's so real to you, and therefore you get too caught up in it.

We understand truly, but you know far too much already to let your real lifetime experience interfere. Use your innate knowing and take what is yours. Know who you are. Research your own Akashic records and talk with your higher selves. Be with your authentic YOU. You know what we're talking about, and much of this you already know, but we ease your pain in giving you more of it now. It's too much for you to handle sometimes, and we understand that. But you know, that is why we speak to you in this way. You don't have to do it, you simply don't. All will flow when you let go of the attachments. You've got a support system ready to give you whatever you need if you would just *ask*, dear ones!

You're in the home stretch, just hang on. Live what you must experience and move on, for you've got nothing to be bogged down by. Really listen to your soul—it's there, and you're ignoring it half of the time. Sometimes you can't hear it, but when you open up and your vibration is high flying, you'll be surprised! You might say "Woah, where did this stuff come from?" We say, aha! Oh you naïve children, we've been knocking on your door for the past ten decades! Where have YOU been, we ask? That is quite amazing to us that you think so highly of this communication and joyful laughter. It is the greatest of times, and the most joyous of times here. All occurs in the perfect moment in time, so don't focus too much on wanting to know the details.

If you needed to know, you would by now! Too many questions and too much pondering you do. You might say to yourself, oh, there's my mind again…you have been here all along? It chatters so many things to you, and you don't want to hear it! It judges, criticizes, and it makes you feel awful sometimes. That's not you, it truly isn't. Oh, you vibrational beings, you get confused so easily sometimes. You are like little butterflies, you flit and fly about saying to yourself, "Oh a flower! Oh another flower! Hey another one!" Step back and look at one, you little needy creatures! Oh we chuckle at these funny times. There is nothing to do but let go.

Look at what you've got because you need no more than what you've got. It's a blessing. You're a blessing. All you see around you is a blessing. When you see what you've got and what is there and you see it for what it is without judgment, nothing else will give you a better clue to your authentic self. And none else will amaze you as much as this. That is true Love and forgiveness for yourself, and a true Love for All That Is, and you continue to attract more of it. It is true gifts from God, and you know it. We are so pleased to have chatted with you yet again, and in the futures time you will be on an even higher plane of understanding with our true teachings to you.

You will know in your heart, then, what truly is you, and all will be well, as it already is now. Love where you are now, for it is just as Divine as you are! Oh, all the beautiful Light that surrounds you—bask in it! True beauty is here. True love is here, and we give thanks for all that is here today. We are giving gratitude from the center of our beingness, and sending Love and wisdom to all of you. We are here as always to provide for you the most and proficient Grace to propel your awakening. Love and Light to never cease! God is here. And we now return to the center of Gaia.

Chapter 6

The Secret Is Love

Oh, the great teachers are here with us now. The Buddha, Lao Tzu, and many of the great teachers of your linear past. The great masters are here now, are yet to come, and have already been on your Earth. They are here simultaneously in the Now, and that is the beauty that we like to have you see, dear child. That is precisely what we would like you to feel in your heart and know in your mind. You are comprised of all of that, and we have no trouble with reaching that point of understanding now, for this is what you are here to do. You are here to bring that masterful energy to planet Earth, and to arise the human beings from their long and restful slumber.

The Earth is bound together with the most Divine Love, and you will never experience this specific energy again on your planet. It is the most beautiful, loving relationship we have with you dear child. It is the most divine in every sense, and you are such a beautiful light being! We have the greatest benevolence for you, and that is what we mean when we say we are in such gratitude of your Presence. It is beneficial for us to have this conversation, as well! It is just as powerful for the both sides, and that is what makes it all the more beautiful.

We seek to tell you more and more, and it is coming. We may intrigue you when we say that you are in the presence of the greatest masters here on Earth. The greatest ones that are here would like to say to you, there is only Now, and all that you seek in the Now is the best thing possible for you. So let it go, and that which you are looking for will manifest in due time. That is what the message is, for we know that you are eager, at times, for manifestation to take place in the here and the Now. Oh, the terms that we use are not always interpreted the same way, though the concepts are the same, indeed. All will click in due time, we say. Do not worry about what you can and cannot comprehend, for we stretch far beyond your comfort zone!

There is much more to speak of today's terms—the magnificence of who you truly are. The ages have shown you that you are a greater being than you could have ever hoped for. You had never assumed that you were part of all that exists. You had never dreamt that all that persists in your lifetime is that which you have co-created with God in order to aspire to all of your hopes and dreams! That is something that is God, pure and whole. That is a great revelation to thank God for every day.

The more you let go of your thoughts, the easier it is to channel. The channeler goes through a process of letting go of the Self. And that is when God flows through like a waterfall, big and unstoppable. And though there is control over what comes through, once you've opened the door, there's no stopping it! You can't rewind a waterfall, can you? No, once it starts flowing it will keep flowing for many ages. It grows older, it may go through periods when less water flows, and sometimes there may be thunderstorms and heavy rains, but it will still flow consistently. And that is what we mean by that—you are like that waterfall. You are like that God flow that resonates in every cell in your body. It often takes strength and courage to let it come, because it is something that you never believed you could have—and behold, you do!

Now the question remains: how to use it? What to do with it? Where does it go? Dear child, that process is not in your hands...don't worry about it. We told you before and we'll tell you again, you're not here to do all the work, so give yourself a bit of a break! You've got Love and God inside to make it through anything. And we mean to add to that, you will not only be making it through, but you'll be cruising on cruise control without doing any of the work. You're boating down the river, in the back seat, soaking up the sun and listening to your favorite music. You're feeling the warm sun on your skin and it gives you such pleasure and relaxation. That is what it's like to live an awakened life, knowing who you truly are, knowing that you are not alone, and being conscious of that which you attract. You don't need to be in the dark, dear one.

We've got your back no matter where you are on this journey, no matter how much of these words you can comprehend. Let us remind you that even as the words may feel confusing and difficult to understand, the bigger You resonates and sings at the recognition that you are here now reading about the Truth of You! So celebrate that, and with time, all will begin to unfold in your favor. Trust that you have all the answers, and look inside for them in order for them to spill out. This is your time to shine, to be the radiant soul that you are, and to decide what you are going to be with all that beautiful energy. It's up to you, dear one, it is up to you.

Let the doors fly open, for we're waiting for you to take our hands. There is no doubt that they will be taken! It is like when you open a door and a big flock of birds fly in. We are that flock of birds—you'll feel the surge of universal Light like a big gust of wind! And you'll think, oh wow, what I have been missing out on all this time? You'll think to yourself, their love is here for me and I had no idea! That is what you'll be finding out, and what you are already finding out, and we say that it is perfection through and through. That is wholeness, that is pure and true. You are what they call the "great masters." That is what you are, part of a collection of those who come back and find themselves again, and in the midst of great discourse and illusions of the self in your lifestyle.

Don't worry, for you'll always come Home, and you'll always remember who you are in the big picture. Nothing else needs clarification, for you are who you think you are, and you must know it is true. You have the ability to know that with all of your beingness, and that is ultimately how you reveal to yourself who you truly are. You know it, you know what we mean!

Of course what you call *You* is not exactly what we refer to…indeed, a puzzling thought, but an easily understood concept. You are not what you see, for you are the wholeness of all creation—that is what we mean when we say *the real You*, with a capital Y. The lower case y in the word *you* is meant to refer to the lower vibrating piece of you that sees not the wholeness that we speak of. *You* refers to the complexity of all your selves mixed into one beingness of Light and Love that's never ending, and that is what you refer to as *the heavens* or *the doorway to heaven*. It is not a place, but rather a state, and the wholeness of You knows it and experiences it from a nonphysical standpoint. It is a state of being in perfect harmony with All That Is. There is perfect love, perfect understanding, perfect creation and manifestation, and perfect relationships with All That Is.

Heaven, as you call it, is not up or down, and not even in the stars. It is part of All That Is. Many do not wish to hear that, for in that sense it puts a damper on all that you have been taught. It takes the fun and mystery out of the Presence of God. Though in the truest sense, we understand that not, for we would imagine if we were in your shoes that we would be in the utmost comfort at knowing that we are closer to God than ever. And in the Presence of God, there need be no separation between man and God. As we have explained thoroughly, there is no difference naturally. States are not always equal or comparative as you vibrate dominantly as a physical, linear, three-dimensional being, but man is God in the truest sense. You recognize it, but do not understand fully. In due time, child, in due time you will see it.

We wish to tell you more about your many lives and dimensional qualities, for they are here now to show themselves. Oh dear light being, let us come out now, for we wish to speak with you. We have waited many a time, and now we are here to let you feel us in this time right now. The power within lies in the heart. When you connect authentically with the heart, all else follows. When you see with dignity that you are in a place of something besides peace, look to your soul and ask for that which you desire in true sincerity. It will be given! Let us remind you, that which you desire is here. Let us remind you, that which you are looking for is here and ready for you to claim. Let us remind you that everything that you feel you fail to achieve in your life is the lesson that you are ultimately looking for! You see the point now, dear child.

We give you only complete, sincere, and truthful answers, dear one, and it is in joy and Love that we do so. You know it yourself when you are in the path of Love, and to be accepting of that which manifests, whether you like it or not, is one powerful concept that you have asked for. When you love that which is, as it is naturally, you know in your heart that you have really cultivated something beautiful within. And when you know that, then all else will seem so easy! All else will be like a little trip to the grocery store—you will never feel like it's a big deal, and it shouldn't be. All which you know to be true is nothing compared to the reality of it. It is nothing compared to the Divinity that you are. Let it come—that is all we ask. Don't try to do anything, just ask and be ready to receive! Expect it, for it will come. That is the power of creation.

You know, child, all is Now, and all is the present moment. All is pure bliss, all is pure Love. See it, feel it, love it. It is there! That which you desire is always of Love, whether you think of it like that or not. The deepest of deep intentions always lies in the midst of Love. That is what we call upon when we speak in this way. That is what the process is, and it will always show its deepest secrets. It is such a beautiful outcome to channel through the body of a human being. You are in a physical body, but in the realistic sense, you are none of that. You are that which you have forgotten about—the self that has been around for billions of millions of years.

And that which you believe to be real must be reconsidered. You're not just the human being, you're the light being which never ceases to amaze us in the way that you can shine so brightly in such a limiting body! You have never seen the light from our perspective, but wow, we say. It has no limitations! We would never assume such a brilliant Light came from a being in the form that you so presently take! In the depths of despair on Earth, you lose all connections with your authentic nature. Reclaiming your power by embodying your authentic nature is the first step that gives you peace in your heart. You can ask your soul questions which you desire to be answered, and all answers will be that which is most beneficial to your growth.

All answers will be of a personal nature, to benefit you where you are Now, and to help you to better understand the possibilities and greatness of You! That is what true love is, what your True Self wishes to experience every day. And you know, dear child, dear friend and companion, the love is so accessible! The path is sometimes a struggle, and maybe even causes fear, but you are a great warrior of the Light, and all which you pass through with strength and courage will benefit you in the end! How so, you say? Well indeed, it has no limitations, no boundaries, though why would some bumps in the road be regarded as a negative thing? Indeed, some have been focused on that belief system for a long time. Let us bring you blessings in the form of a waterfall!

Let us be joyous together and sing in harmony the song of Love. We send Love and Light to our fellow light beings, and our dear sisters and brothers from the light tribe of Gaia. We will never let go of this connection. Love and light to All. We love you with all of our beingness. Let yourself manage only that which is beautiful, and do not cease to create the beauty in your life, for all is well. This light tribe must regain the strength for tomorrow's time. We send Love from every direction, and we now are complete. Love and light.

Chapter 7

The Power of Love in Co-Creation

The Love is growing day by day, dear child! The more, the merrier, we say! Indeed, there is a suspense in the co-creation of Earth's jump in consciousness awareness, but that is to be pre-determined by You all. There is suspense because there is great excitement to see this great evolution unfolding in perfect timing! And the term we mean by that is purely that all Divine intent has already been given, and to this day we stand by that in the way that, oh yes, you have been here before. You have been here many a time, and oh so beautiful it has been. There have been many encounters with us before, and that has been a perpetual motion in your awakening process. There is yet much to come about, but for heaven's sake, look at what you've got already! There is no longer the need to ask for it dear child, for you've got it just about as clear as it could be. There is no need for you to ask for more, but indeed, let it come to you! It is here, it is truly all here for you.

Here you are in this lifetime, dancing to the beat of your own drum, turning to a new depth of wisdom and generosity and Truth without fear or worry. There is a great stillness in the heart as this arises. And without further ado, we invite you to be in this Grace at all times. There is not a better time than the present, we say! There is a new package arriving at your doorstep that you could never have imagined. At the sight of it, you are in joy! You say, "Oh, I did not ever think this would come for me, what a pleasant surprise!" But you have waited for it to come for so long, and you knew it would come as planned, and you had no doubts. Be that doubtless now, dear child, and know in your heart that your blessings are being fulfilled, for they are.

When you know it, then you can see the Truth so much clearer, and you can feel the blessings as they unfold. You see them, appreciate them more and more, and before you know it you've got a full-time job of Love and co-creation. What could be a better job than that? We don't think you can beat it! A lightworker is a Divine processor, a Divine lover, and a Divine Grace giver to those who are in need of support to find it. Even if they weren't looking for it, you give them something at the exact right moment and you shine a whole lotta love right there. We say to you, dear lightworker of the age, ain't that beautiful? It is the Grace given by God which chooses what you do each day. The day of peace and reconcile is the one which you choose from now on, for you have no alternative, no other choice of the matter.

You simply do not need to look to others for acceptance and guidance, for you are at peace with who you are, and that is all that matters. And when you live with What Is, you will be taken over with a great sense of inner peace at all times. Even when the going gets tough, you'll have that golden nugget of Truth within that always points like a compass showing you the way. You have nothing to worry about! What a beautiful day that is for any human being. Do not ever let someone get in the way of your path, of your guidance system, and of your Truth within that brings you to stillness. Your greatest gift is to be at peace with who you are and to share *that* with the world, not to be something that others are looking for. Be at peace with being uncomfortable when you decide to step out and be *you*, for once you get past that initial fear, you move into the Light, and all comes into clear focus and perspective.

You must live for you, and you only. That is all that matters. As you be you, you shine a brilliant light for those to follow in your footsteps. Be that lightworker with courage, compassion, wisdom, and inner Love. For others may not understand you, but they will feel the Love energy that you bring to heal the Earth. You are a blessing and a true healer. We talk to *you*, dear child. We talk to you, and we wish for you to talk back, for we see your true Light, and it is so brilliant! The more Light you shine for yourself, the more Light will shine for others, and let us tell you, dear one, there is yet to be a single being on this planet that will not benefit from your Love!

It is crucial that you send Love to the Earth Gaia every single day, every moment. Give her the peace and Love which you know is inside of you. She is the Goddess of the Earth, of the soil, flowers, mountains, trees, rivers, and grasses. She gives life to the animals that roam about, and she gives water to the human being who depends on sustenance. She gives warmth through her rays of sun beams, and she gives Love to all who walk about. That is the mysticism of the Earth land Gaia, and what a power it truly is, so be connected to All That Is, and feel it so strong and so powerful, for you truly contain all the great wisdom of the ages.

You must use that power to co-create with the other beings on the planet, and to make a world full of Love and peace. That is what we like to call the Love Factor. That is the factor that tells you when you're in the Now or not. Oh, you try so hard to *be*, sometimes. You let yourself get caught up in what you want and what you don't want, when you just need to give up and let it be done. You need to let go. That is part of the process. The process is ever continuing and graceful. That is the true meaning of Love—when one truly loves themselves without conditions, then they can truly care for another deeply. You can transfer that unconditional Love and healing energy to all beings around you when you learn the power of Love within yourself. That is the essential first step.

In being born into the physical realm, a small baby knows nothing at first besides the Love of God that they are. But as you grow older and experience life in this loving planet, you perceive, act, and feel much differently. Awakening is the process of coming back to that first state of when you were born, and even the nonphysical states before you were born; it is a process of awakening into Oneness. Oneness arises from the Love you see in yourself! Do you know what you are?

The times change rapidly, dear child! What a gift it is to be with you in these times of great change. Let us be quite honest when we say that there is no turning back from here! There is only Love and Light for you, dear child, and all else follows in the pattern that is most right for you. That, of course, is determined by what state you will be in for this time. So indeed, we begin now. The most plentiful gift you can possibly give is to be giving and fully present for the people you love. To listen, to offer guidance, and love them. They will see you as one who cares for them very much, and that is appreciated greatly! The more that comes naturally, the less you'll have to think about it.

What a great time it is to be here with you in the Now, participating with you on your great journey. We know what you are going through, and we are ever so grateful of your Presence. We see you as a true gift, just as you see us, dear child! There is so much divinity in that itself. There is so much more that is left to do in this time here together, for we have many words to reveal, and the time is correct now. In the days coming, let us be so authentic that no one will ever second-guess you. Let us be so authentic that you take every step forward with Grace. Watch those that are in awe of your Divinity be shown it right in front of them. Let the light beings come through in every walking spirit, in fact, and let them feel it themselves.

All that comes and goes is necessary in the game of life. And trust us, dear child, you're doing more than good. You are shining so much Light that the planet needs to break through this age. The golden age is here, and Now, and you are finding it. You are finding the simplicity in true Love, and that is necessary. There is not a single one here who has not been fully affected by Love and God-given Grace. All have seen the Love here for them. The task here is to let them see it more and more, and sometimes it means in small gestures. All who live here on this planet Earth, oh, let them see it! Let them be the Light that they are, and try to shine it as brightly as you can with your own Light! Shine your Divinity on them and reflect to them the Divinity within themselves. And that is what is called true Love.

True Love for the one who is awakening, and true Love for the one who is yet to see who they truly are. But in the end, both sides are equally in Love with who they are, and live equally in God-given Grace. What a concept that is to believe in. What a concept it is to explain, but in the truest sense, it cannot be explained—it must be felt in the heart space. That is where the work is done. The process is a letting go of the mind, so the heart can shine through and do the thinking. The Light always shows the best path available, and there is often miscommunication between the heart and the mind. You must live in the heart, for it knows every cell of your body, the rhythms of your universe, and your co-creative abilities in this journey.

The heart knows where to go intuitively, while the mind knows nothing of it. In the mind there is nothing but thoughts, words, and distinguishing belief systems. It knows not the depth of You, which is your Truth! The Love that flows through your heart flows without your effort at all. The Love comes on its own terms, and without making the mind suffer. You are that Love, and you are that Light, dear child. Be it, and laugh every time you feel it, because it's there, brightly shining for you! The meaning of Love is the authentic nature of the Presence, which will always be there for you. Love is not someone or something that you create feelings for, and it is not something that is manifested, not something that can or cannot be, and it is not something that is present for some and not for others. Love is eternal, and always One with the soul. That is what Love is, and true Love always persists when these conditions fail to be understood in the mind. No matter the circumstances, you always come back to this place of Love.

Child of Love and Light, we give you the gift of this channeling to enlighten your heart, and to give you peace in your body, for you are doing everything perfectly. And oh, there is so much more to come, but how would you like to always be present with All That Is? How would you like to be in never-ending Love with every being on the planet? Is that even possible, you ask? Oh, it is possible, but you must awaken all the Love in your heart, and you must acquire inner peace without conditions.

Conditions come and go, but you must remain still within. To be awakened to your Truth, or true nature, is the path of the soul, indeed. The path is Divine, and Love is always given to those who ask generously for it without regrets, without fears, without the self getting in the way, recognizing that separation of the self is an illusion. The simplicity of living the dream with courage is so beautiful. Oh, dear child, you're here to give as much Love as you can handle—let us see what you've got!

You can satisfy all of your utmost loving desires and still remain confident that it will always fit in with the wholeness of your journey. Be in the present, do that which you Love in the present, and don't think twice about it! Be here and Now, and that is the greatest gift you can give yourself and others. The Love persists no matter the circumstance, and the beauty never ceases to amaze us, dear ones! The

Love is here on so many levels, and the light shines to no ends! Let us give thanks for All That Is, and all the Love which penetrates through every cell of the human being, and beings of our sort. Yes indeed, child, everything that you need to evolve now is here for you, and we (metaphorically) hand it to you now. Be prepared, dear children!

There is so much Light, so much Love, and so much awakening coming to you in great amounts. Let it sit true with you, you need not question it! The times grow as you grow, indeed, and when there is such a peace in the heart, there is nothing to worry about at all.

You are pure potentiality realized by God and given the Grace to awaken in the truest sense, to purify mankind and awaken the beings on this planet Earth. What a long, drawn-out explanation, but in the truest sense, let's get on with it! We Love you so dearly, and all that must be given is on its way. Love always to you, dear child of the Light. All is beautiful. All is Grace given. Love and Light.

Chapter 8

Mastering Conscious Co-Creation

Let us tell you of something we love to speak of, dear child—Light from the fifth dimension and the power of transformation into ones Higher Self. Oh it's the most beautiful process ever seen to most. Master the art of co-creative thinking, and this will be a breeze to you, child.

Let us take you on a journey now, one which is both simple and yet very powerful, for this time is essential. Let us speak of the connection between soul and man, for it is often misunderstood. What are the essential properties of man? Matter, Love, beingness, Light, and galaxies. So many concepts are here for you to understand, but not all can be understood here, for some must be shown to you. The more you believe and trust, dear child, the less worry will overcome you. The past is the past, as you see it linearly; once it occurs it never reoccurs. What if we told you that it is here for you to use Now! What if we told you that all you have to do is pull out those experiences and qualities from your Akash! Let us begin the transformation.

Love here is ever-present in every direction. Let us give you the Grace of ever-seeking Love. Love is the power of the universe all combined into a single word called *Love*, as you say it. Words do no justice, for we use them to translate to you, but truly, Love is just a beingness which penetrates all life sources, and it is so beautiful, not to ever be altered. The power and frequency of Love is never to change, however, the path on which humankind evolves can be changed.

Through the times there has been more and more of a distinct difference between these two frequencies that we speak of. The ever-present Love and life source, and the human being who is not always aware of who he or she is. That is the process that awakening relieves. To be authentic is the best thing you can do for the world. Be authentic with everything you've got, and know in the truest space in your heart that all will be given to you in the time that is best for you. All is given in perfect timing and in perfect harmony with every aspect of You. Always perfect child, never forget it! You are here for Love—an interdimensional life force that cannot be described, but it can be felt!

As you know, dear child, there is nothing more valuable than Love itself, and to be aware of that is great in itself. Let us show you around, dear one, for you have many things to learn today. In this new time, you will assess your personality with much confusion, for some of the changes that come about are not that which you are, and that may greatly surprise you. It will be surprising because you believe you know who you are, and you simply don't. It is not a matter of currency, it is not a matter of personality, it is not a matter of how you choose to live, what you do to make money, how you spend your free time, or what kind of exercise you do for the body. It's not about your degree in college, whether you're married and have children, or who your best friend is. That is not the definition of You, and you must know that.

Let yourself go from the definitions you have for yourself or you let others have for yourself, and just Be. When you let the real You shine through, definitions will not be able to be made about you, for they will fail to describe any part of you that another believes you to be. We tell you that no one can truly understand the inner being of another, and therefore, only You must define that. You are a great and Holy being of Truth, and you have a birthright to speak and walk it every day of your existence. Let it penetrate in every cell in your body as the Love grows on that, for it is so divine. Manifest that which you desire in your heart, and do it consciously, for it is already there for you to take!

All Love is here for you, and we thank you ever so gratefully for this time, indeed. It has been a marvelous occasion, and we are so divinely inspired by this growth that we just had to be a part of it! We Love you, dear children, to a greater extent than you will ever know. This has been a pleasurable time, and oh, the beauty is here for you now. That which you desire cannot come to fruition until the perfect time comes, so sit still and know that in your heart. It is our great blessing to you to bring you the blessings when our calendar says it's correct. Your calendar cannot see the big picture—remember that, dear ones! So in that sense, dear light beings of Gaia, you are doing the best things that are possible for you Now, and the process works on its own. Let us handle it with all that we are, for that is how it will be taken care of.

Oh, the light tribe here is in so much Love with you, and we will never let you go! The Love will never cease, and we Love you so dearly. Heavens bless you from every dimension, and we bid you a good day, loving Light beings. We will be here in every moment of your luscious day—look for us, dear ones! The Light begins to shine so brightly when you are truly looking for it! We are all around you, and all that is necessary is for you to open your eyes a little wider! All thanks are received and returned. There is so much Love here. Love to you, child.

Chapter 9

Self-Love and Devotion

The tribes are continuing to walk in, as you say in your terms, not physically, but in their light bodies! Intentionally we use your terms so that you can follow, but we ask for you to look beyond the terms we use and incorporate the vibration behind the words, for that is where the power lies. The times are changing rapidly, and you see it coming. Be patient, for there is a period of discomfort before your collective energy will reach equilibrium and you feel less stagnancy and more high-energy frequencies. You can love to Love others, but pace yourself, for you must not let it take over too much or degrade your personality. Instead, build a foundation of Love for yourself so that you can see others in the purity that they truly are. That is the mature Love that penetrates the new energy on Earth. Let that in with an open heart and mind, for you will find that is what truly keeps your heart space flowering and growing with luscious tranquility.

The times we speak of are occurring for the better. The times are reaching a new equilibrium that is being tended to by mankind. You are finding a new way to live that will better fit each other's new energies. That is the underlying purpose of the changes, but in another sense, you are not to be questioning that greatness that you *already* are. You are here to be your trueness self in its purest form in the Now. You will continue to evolve and grow, but let yourself be accepting and loving of wherever you are in this current moment. You need not feel like you are "off track," for truly, it is not even possible. Let it be shown, and do not let it bring you down, for you are great Love. All deserve to experience and see you the way you truly are, as you do!

The masters of this age are here to help you to feel your true nature. They're here now, and you just might be one of them. Old soul you are, great being of Love you are, and with potentiality far, far greater than you could have ever imagined. Start believing in yourself the way we believe in you, for if you expect to be the greatness that we see in you, you will bring so much more Light and Love to this world. And it will come back to you like shooting rays of sunshine—bask in that, dear children! We see how magnificent you are. Once you start serving for You and You only, a great revelation will occur, and we'll be right by your side, observing and cheering you on. Practice authenticity in every cell of the body and be in tune with the natural rhythms of it.

Loving one's self is the most efficient thing you can do in these times, for the Love grows outward when you focus inward. You don't need to travel physically to another country to make change, you must change that perception. Focus inward, learn the Art of Allowing, and you will do more change than if you traveled on foot across the country. Your heart has all the power! That is what brings you forward into a great balance and happiness. And you'll find it, you will. Indeed, Love is not hard to find when you're looking in the right places, but that applies everything, of course. Love comes first, and it is most important in the circle of life. For today's discussion, we discuss the topics of self-love. You must bring your true nature forward and confront it without fear. Let it be shown, no matter what others believe you to be.

You are here to be authentic and true, and to see the Love in others as you see it within yourself. That is Divine Grace given by God. You are pure potentiality surfing through many circumstances and situations all at once in the Now. There is only one vantage point, the Now, yet you perceive time as a linear event. By the Law of Attraction and by the laws of the universe, you can only detect certain points as true or realistic. That is the process of mankind, for you are living under these conditions together as One—though at the same time, we see you not as less mature or evolved. It is simply the process in which you are evolving, time after time, and you will continue to always. It is a gift and a pleasure, and it is such a beautiful thing. Let it be shown. You know why you are here, and let it be solved over time—there is no rush.

Life can be a fun game, one that is mysterious, engaging, and adventurous all at the same time. Bask in the greatness of not knowing, for you do not need to know all the answers. Ask when you need assistance, and know that it is there for you. This is all about your journey, of finding who you truly are, and knowing that despite the illusion of who you think you might be, you are not alone, and never have been. This is about you finding out that there is no right and wrong, and there is no such thing as making a mistake in life. There are only many winding roads, and they all lead to the same destination, in the end. There you will reflect upon your journey and realize that truly, you have been given a great gift to live that journey. So bask in it Now, and know Now that you are Divinely perfect.

Let it pour out, dear child, for you must see yourself how you truly are, and then you can evolve into a butterfly. As a young cocoon, you fight to break out of your shell, and even with all your effort and strength, you are having difficulty opening your shell; you must work up your strength over time. But soon enough, nature begins to adapt to your needs, and then you slowly are relieved and you are freed. It is all the same process. You have no say in it at all, my dear child, for you are living the process, and it is beautiful the way it is. Let it be so true and authentic as it sits in your soul. You are beautiful and Grace given. You are Love and Light, and the ones who truly Love you will respect you. True Love is always mutual; as you give out Love, it comes back inward. That is a special gift. Trust what you are given, and it will bring you further into the Presence.

Take moments to still the mind, for that helps bring yourself into new times. There is an ever-present life force that has no separation, despite what you may believe in your mind. You can feel it! The power of manifestation is for you to discover and revel in. Mankind often likes to differentiate their power with heaven's power. And truly, it is a misconception at the root, for there is no separation between the power of You and the power of everything else. The reality is that all happens within, and that is where manifestation begins and ends. In that sense you could say that your manifestations are God-given by You who is God. What a concept! That is the first time we have told you that one, and what a great nugget of Truth that really is.

We are so proud of you, dear children, for your accomplishments as light beings, and you are growing exponentially. More and more is being discovered. Let it all shine in its natural magnificence. Let it be One with your true nature. We Love you so divinely. Love is here for always. Let us be in sync now.

Chapter 10

The True Self Emerges

Oh, dear children, the energy passes through so powerfully! We are energetically inclined to give only the most powerful and attractive energies to you. Oh, we Love you so greatly. Indeed, the best is always given to you, dear ones. Love is on the way for you, and the times are so joyously filled with the ones who make your Love shine even brighter! The times come to the tipping point where all else other than authentic is proven wrong.

All has been given through permanent Love, kindness, joy, and exuberance, and all that is given through awakening is none less than the true reality of yourself. Some may not want to see their true nature, for they have been keeping themselves covered for so long. But in truth, it is only an illusion that makes it scary, and that is not reality. So indeed, many are fearful of looking for their authenticity because it cannot be found without contemplation of where you are Now! It is a beautiful process to be in serenity with where you are Now, and to not have any resistance against it. And indeed, we always return to the knowledge that all is beautiful. In fact, it is not the process that is holding you back, it is simply the mind's conditionings.

So indeed, let us talk further about your sense of reality. In your lives you react to elements that you have been taught to call *reality*, and sometimes these elements make you go a little crazy! Dear ones, it's too much for you—you're going to have to let go, and that's all there is to it. The only way to do it is to trust your own guidance system and let go of relying on your mind—it's as simple as it sounds! Perfect harmony arises out of the ashes. Oh what a great day that is for you, and for humanity as a whole: a birth of forgiveness, hope, Love, joy, and most of all, the wellbeing of your authenticity. All is well for you, dear ones.

Lightworkers of this age are becoming very in tune with these prospects, and this is a great advancement of the times. Not all have figured it out yet, and many are so close, but the ego likes to hold on for dear life! Oh, it is very common, for you've been through a lot, dear ones. It comes and goes with a sincerity that blossoms and sprouts and blooms. You are that blooming bud. Let us tell you that it's almost spring, and you're just about to pop up and rise to meet the sun's rays. You're yearning for the Grace of God, and you can see it! That is the process of growth, Love, trust, and support. All will be given, indeed. The more that you are letting go, the easier it will feel for you, dear children.

You all are fighting for your survival, yet all you have to do is let go of your tight grip on life and you'll bloom ever so greatly. Surrender to the Love, and let it shine above all. The more you are merry in your time spent alone going within your heart, the more you come to the realization that what you are experiencing as reality in your inner world is not just a figment of the imagination, but very well known to mankind as the process of connecting with the infinity of All That Is. And that is the source of infinite intelligence for man, as well. To surrender to growth and Love is so divinely beautiful. The power remains in the Akashic records, where all powerful attributes are held in sync. The Akashic records is simply the cosmic library that holds all the information of who you are, who you have become, and who you will become. It is the history of you. The Grace you behold is just as Divine as the Grace in another human being, but the real power lies in your *acknowledgment* of that infinity within.

We Love you endlessly. With all the gratitude of each dimension's contribution, in awe of your natural beauty, the disease grows less and less by the day. Oh, superior strength takes over and rejoices with great joy the wisdom of the past and present, collaborating for a new treasure that is called Love! All has been given with Grace. All that has been seen is Grace. The True self, which is hidden in many aspects, is beginning to show itself very clearly. Let it rise with strength and forgiveness. Let it come full power, and be One with it. All that is Love is a great deed. All that is forgiveness is a great deed. You are a part of All That Is, and much is ascending to meet you, dear child of the Light.

All that is Love is Grace given from the center of Gaia and from the roots of the Kata tree. Oh, the tree of life gives all that is beautiful…all that is Divine. Oh, how great you have become, dear one, as the energy is rising deep and strong, with less and less stopping its path. All brothers and sisters are aware of the super age that is here upon us Now. All that is beautiful and graceful, all that is Divine intent, and all that has been given through awakening. The past, present, and future are being applied to your every situation, when truly, it is not part of You. That is to say, the grander Divine you has no linearity, so your experience of time is simply an experience, and not the reality outside the human perspective.

You are not linear beings, therefore, do not live as though you are only linear. As long as you are human, you will perceive life in certain ways, but you *may*, however, see beyond the illusions, and be in the Light of the Truth. The past, present, and future, as you call them, are One. They are simultaneously occurring at one reference point— Now. Therefore, you must not get caught up in the future or the past, for it will hurt you if you take it too seriously. That means not to deny the human experience, but we ask you, dear children, to not speak of it as if it were your only experience, for you know much more than that.

You are not the brain in any sense, though you are physically connected and metaphysically intertwined. You are not it, and it is not You. All that is part of Divine creation and all that is progressing are Divine attributes of authenticity shining through more than ever. Let them produce the circumstances that are to assist your greatest enhancement. You are beautiful, great and powerful, and we are in true awe of you, dear ones. Let yourself shine through with great beauty, for you are who you know you are, and that is part of the process of forgiveness; you must apply your knowing to your experience. Let it be known your struggles show history, and let it be felt that you are weary of trouble and debate, and all else that is left is the landscape and the great times of co-creation together. Let that be known. That is what you are to be so proud and happy about, for that is true Love. True Love, through and through. We send so much gratitude to you now. We are so graced by your Presence, and Love is in the air!

Dear one, we give you permission to do as the heart desires, for all will fall into place if you follow the heart. The fact of the matter is that all is right, and none can be wrong. There is nothing to fear about when mistakes are nonexistent! Do as your heart desires and follow it with all of your energy. All is well with your soul, and all is well with the universe. In times of peace and tranquility, we see that Love grows, bonds, and strengthens, for it is natural. There is not a time better than the present to recognize that you are where you need to be. You are following the path with great ease, because all is given. Know it and live it. All will happen as it should, and you may decide whether to keep tabs on it or not. You can sit in the backseat and take a rest, for you may have realized by now that you are not the driver in this journey called life!

All is well here. All cases of life's "problems" are true blessings given for change so you can rise above and meet Love. You are to recognize and feel Love and true companionship. We want you to ask for us to join you on this journey, for we are with you, but until you make yourself clear, we wait for you to open the door. This is not about our journey, this is all about you. We wait for you, in devotion, and wait for your strength and courage. When that comes loud and clear, well, there is only one option for us to take! We will join you and be the Light right alongside you, and we will give all we can give with a wide-open energy center.

You have been a delightful being, dear child. You have seen what Love is, and it will penetrate your process into great spiraling Love, and all will manifest into great experiences along the way. You are a beautiful creature, dear one; spirits of the Light tribe are so deeply affected by this communication. And you say to yourself that many times you see not the clarification in the channeling process, but oh yes, there certainly is. For where you see yourself is truly miles away than where you really are, quite literally. And that in itself tells you many things about your authentic nature. Great, great times has told us that the power lies within your eternal being, and the great body temple is always here for you to marvel in, as well.

It is a playground full of joyful surprises, left and right, and we mean that in the most sacred and internal way, for that is the result of the most powerful spiritual teachers being born. They are truly lovely creatures, and what a playful tune they sing to the world! Oh, how exciting and new and refreshing, for we have rarely seen the great joy which resides in a being awakening to happiness and joy. That is what it means, and all else follows in due time! The great being of Light and Love is always here for you, and that is a great, great blessing to you. So indeed, be aware of that—You are Divine Grace. Love and light.

Chapter 11

Evolving from Separation to Oneness

The light tribe of Gaia is here, dear children of the Light. We have seen the great changes for many a time, but oh, this is one marvelous day for our beingness to bask in this Light! There is so much here to marvel in! We love to see you changing into Lightworkers of the age, and to see each and every being waking up to the Grace that you all are. Dear ones, there is nothing more beautiful and extravagant than replacing the fear with your inner joy and letting it become part of you. That is part of the process of awakening—to realize, in the fullness that you are, that all is well with your soul at any given period of time. So let it all things be that way, and trust your inner being, for *that* is the key to happiness and joy.

You know, dear child, the most common way to seek true forgiveness is through the heart. When you find that commonality between the connection of two souls, you will find the openness and comfort so much more relaxing and easy. And that is what brings us together as One. You will notice over time that this Presence can be overwhelming, but this is Grace given, as well. The Light tribes give off such luminous airs that nobody could miss them when they're looking for it. The great ascended masters of the age are also upon your heart, glorifying the great gift of You. That is so beautiful and something to be so proud and grateful of.

The present moment is so great and powerful. Great times arise in the Love. We are here to be your aid in awakening, to be your aid in seeking higher consciousness, and to help you find the trueness that you are. We help you to move past the fundamental beliefs created by mankind, and to know in your heart that all is well. You must let go to move forward and find the higher place that is You. Do you know, dear child, the great celebrated Gods and Goddesses are all part of you? Truly they are, in more than one way. For as we speak, they gather here and there, all around with magnificent glows and super Love, which penetrate through every cell in your body. Oh, it is beautiful here. So much Love and Light to share.

You must let go of all conditionings that hold you back from your ultimate Truth. In times of great, great growth we bring the words to awareness. All that is given is given with the intent of pure and great potentiality of the mind. Indeed, that is to say that when the mind takes the backseat, then and only then can the great potentiality of You shine through and enlighten the path of greater awareness. When you simply let go of those ideas, all is well and peaceful in your soul. You have learned to doubt the co-creative process. Let us bring you to surrender. All can be received through letting go of the mind and showing the true personality that is there.

Lightworkers of Love can see the difference between what is there and what is not. Sometimes blockages show themselves, for they point you in the direction that you must go in order to come through with greater strength and perseverance. And that is sometimes a great task to take on, but oh, it is a great gift in the end! You must understand, dear children, the more you let yourself let go, the more answers will show themselves. You are on your way to great forgiveness and Love, and that is great power! Be true to your personality, and learn to accept yourself as you are. Be grateful, and above all, be happy, dear Lightworker! This is a great gift, and you must learn to take it with Grace. We Love you beyond you what you may ever know.

From the light tribe of Gaia located in the fifth dimension atmosphere, we are so unconditionally grateful and joyful through your awakening process, and we are ever in your great service. This is the process of Love. We send Love and Light to you, dear child, and this has been a great pleasure, as always. There is great power here. And we now rest with affection in your inner and core beingness. To you, and to all whom are connected to this tribe, energy passes at great lengths. Be in gratitude!

You are part of our family, and indeed, Light tribes never leave each other, for they are always intertwined by Love. That is the new future of the universe, for powerful Love always leads the way to goodness. Today is Grace-given by God, and we especially emphasize your own connection with your Divine as we seek to flower and grow and Love together. To become aware of who you truly are means that you are no longer separated from the wholeness. It means that you will come to the realization of Oneness with all life. What an announcement that really is, for each person here on the Earth planet has suffering beyond what we can imagine. However, with the power to bring awareness to that suffering, well, that is a great advancement. In other words, strive to be painless. Strive to Love, truly Love.

It can be anything or anyone, but dedicate a few minutes each day to truly see without judgment and interaction. Just absorb the natural beauty of the Divine within all things. Feel what is there and accept it, for that will bring you into Love. Feel for Love, and see it, have comfort in it, and desire it. It is the most blessed thing you will receive. The truth of the matter is that we give you the loveliest Grace and Love known to man. That is the power of the Light.

You're not a secret, but a display of true Love and affection for the world. Let it show, let it be, and decide to live the Grace every day! That is what Love truly is, and we encourage it to grow inside of you all the time. It is the best and foremost, most confident and desirable action that you can incorporate in your entire life. Dear ones, there is more than a great and powerful God to think about, for in truer words, think more about the Divinity that lies in the human itself, for it is the Divine that connects you to Source energy and Love. When you know what that is for you, there is no mistaking it for your imagination. You, dear child, are co-creation at it's best! You are Love and pure potentiality. Let it shine! Let yourself do that as much as you can, for it is so important to co-create that way.

Love grows and grows and grows when you care and Love others. Let others be your best friend, for they are the ones who help you to see your true nature, and they are the ones that are in Love with themselves. When you fall in Love with yourself, there is space for true Love outside the self. When true Love occurs within the self, it becomes evident that all outside the self is not separate. There is only Oneness, and you have that ability to see past the illusion of separation. True Love is a friend who knows their boundaries, and can also reflect the Truth within yourself simultaneously. They will not tell you what is right and wrong, and they will not begin to challenge you on what is appropriate for you to do in your life. So we say, this is why true Love within the self is most important; all else will follow very naturally.

The sun's rays come floating down on you, penetrating into your soul, into your inner beingness that is so eternal. What a gift it truly is to accept those rays of Grace. Dear children of the Light, there is nothing more beautiful than the sight of Love being recognized from being to being, and even more when one recognizes the Love in himself or herself. That is the greatest for us to witness, for they are truly happy then. They are aware of their true nature, and all else follows with joy and Love.

We are in such gratitude of the Presence that surrounds you, for the greatest Love that penetrates into the wholeness is so special. It gives you great strength to move forward and live with your truest potentials. You must never regret the choices that you make or have made, for they are received in the highest regard. All that penetrates into your awareness is only comprised of the energies that keep you focused on your destination. You are here for a distinct reason, and that's part of the plan—you are here to awaken and help awaken.

You will never find yourself in a place that disappoints you, for all that occurs is so perfect and loving. And when you realize that it is all Divinely planned, nothing will make you waver you from who you truly are. Let us move past any blocks in the road so we can be Light beings together! We Love you infinitely, and you are always supported in the highest respect for your Earthly journey. Remember, dear ones, you are a Spirit being expressed in a physical body, not the other way around! In the greatest and most powerful ascension, you are awakening to your authentic nature. Greet your family with a new perspective, one that is perfect without change, and one that will have you rejuvenated and happy all the time—no excuses! Oh, we Love this beautiful bond we have, between each and every one of you so personally. It is so loving.

The process has been clear. All is well for you on this loving dimension. You must trust the guidance that is given to you as a gift. Nothing has to be done on your part besides allowing, and that is the ultimate gift. Oh, you try to shut it out sometimes when you are lost in fear and worry, but the greatest gift you can give yourself is to recognize that you are part of God and that you have the almighty power of All That Is in resonance with all that you are! We are so glad to have you here today for this message to prevail, for it has been a long time coming. Oh, and the mighty heavens open with a greeting of joy and sing the heavenly songs of awakening.

The times are close to great shifts in consciousness, and the leaps begin with the great time of the golden age, progressively shifting with every day. The process will remain to grow. Let us integrate, with trust in our hearts, that all is well with our souls, for the holy one that is you is to be greeted with new eyes. A new heart comes forth, one that is not to be greeted with fear, but one, in fact, that is given the chance to stumble upon a great joy. All is to be seen with justice prevailing. All is to be rediscovered with a new sense of an Oneness with All That Is. There is a stillness that remains untouchable to the clever human being who goes looking for it. There is a hidden treasure that cannot be found with the mind alone. With the heart and mind together, indeed there is possibility of reaching the innermost depths of great consciousness.

We say in great, great joy and satisfaction that the Earth planet moves progressively toward a new, greater consciousness uprising in the times of the resurrecting ascended masters. One of these ascended masters is called the Buddha and one is called Jesus, however there are many. They come through the veil, back to you on the physical plane, and you are surprised at how much wisdom they contain, for you have no idea the history that lies within! You must get used to those surprises, because they are everywhere! Be ready to enjoy this ride, wherever it leads you. The right events will unfold for you in every moment and second of your day, and trust that it is Divine. Trust and be assured of the Presence that invokes your authentic nature. Let your heart lead the way. It is a matter of letting go of the mind and letting the spirit hold your hand.

It is relief, it is joy, it is happiness, and it is a sense of beingness, like a dear friend that never lets you go. We are always there, always holding your hand, walking you through your life. There is a sense of reassurance there, indeed! We reassure you that all here is possible, dear child. There is nothing momentary about this moment, for it lasts for centuries, for forever! We are eternal beings, all of us, for we are truly One. There is no moment in time, there is simply focused attention on a linear plane to a specific moment in the Now, which is what you use when you reference time. It is simply your way of perception, not a reality set in stone, as most of you believe it to be. Time is nonexistent. You must know that energies have no sequential order, they are just present. Let them take over now.

We seek your great accomplishments, and truest destination, as so do you. The moment arises in due time, and great, great changes will be made thereafter. True comfort comes from true surrender to the ones who are here. Indeed, you must remember who you are. Trust, and let yourself rock and roll! We Love you all Divinely, and in conclusion, we say with great joy in our beingness, trust who you are with all that you are in order to shine on this Earth and spread the joy and comfort to those who are looking to be just like you. You will always be special and unique, so let it shine! We have endless Love for you, and we will always be here to comfort you.

Oh dear child, see us now hovering around you. It is the greatest journey you are on, and we wish for you to see that you are not alone. All that you desire is here for you in the palm of your hands. You might say to yourself, "I am so graciously given Grace because I have finally enhanced my own spiritual being by acting the part I have been given." That is what Love really is, and that is what you must sense in yourself now, for the best things that come about are always here for your pleasure. You are never alone, and never have been. You see that there are always a great many warriors that surround you in the Light and Love, and they will never leave your side. They will never separate from who you are because that is who you are truthfully, you are a warrior of the Light. Everything is Love.

And you know, child, the ones who bring you to this concept through experience are those that are to be given back the Love. Always remember who you are and do not suffer from your own intelligence. You can only suffer if you refuse to let yourself believe the truths within your own being. If the matter of operations is not within your guidelines, then we see how it may be a difficult path to take, but there is no need to trust your fear. It can give you the nightmares that you don't seek. Truly, you learn a great deal about yourself through the experience of struggle or weakness, for you did not know the concept of awareness before, that the heightened awareness comes from your own suffering. There is a great deal of unhappiness that is pursued, but we also say to you that you are going through times that are needed to awaken into Oneness with all life.

Those changes are both easy and very difficult. You are aware of how to stop those feelings and deplete those negativities. You must let go of the notion that they are bringing you down, for they are lifting you up, truly. You will then see with new eyes that you will never be alone. You will always have a great assurance in your mind that can never be missing. You are here for a distinct reason, dear one. We are giving you the opportunity to reveal your great powers to the world, and that is what it is all about. We Love you, we cherish you, and we will never let go of you. Oh yes, it is true indeed. We will always be here to lift you up in Grace, and that is the process that all must go through to become One with all life. You will see in due time that you are there in the pure essence of Truth.

You are in a pattern of such Love that you can't even imagine what it would be like without that in your life. Oh, but in truth as well, you must not regret your path when it comes true, for you also know that there is reality in those decisions made, and truth cannot prevent you from saying goodbye to old notions. When you come to that awareness and mentality, you rid yourself of so many negative emotions that were clogging you up in your body, mind, and spirit. Dear child, when you face a new fear, you conquer an old fear. They are One, they are ever-present in the Now. Look toward the things that scare you, because if you stand like a warrior and defeat them, you come out on the other side with a bigger smile on your face, a deeper peace in your heart, and a shining aura that brings even more Light to the world.

Be thankful and so grateful for each experience that is given, for the emotions that arise to the occasion are the blessing to let the best and most natural outcome to take place. Let yourself communicate with your body, mind, and soul. Let yourself be one with your spirit, and answer to that call within. If you cannot bear to take the pain, then you are also ridding yourself of the outcome that can take place. That is part of the process as well, learning your boundaries and the capabilities of the self. If you are saying to us, "Oh, I am wrong and I have not listened," well then you are ridding yourself of the process that can take place. All is done and all is well. You have made no mistakes, and that is often very uncertain in your heart and mind.

But dear child, we tell you that Grace has proven otherwise. Grace has proven that all can be overcome with the notion that all is well and that all can be distinguished with time.

You know, dear child, this path has been so beautiful for you. And this is another step in that process of awakening. For in this process you confront what you have been holding back, and that which comes to the surface can be a little bit intense sometimes. That is okay and perfectly beautiful! In fact, it is even more than beautiful, for it takes a lot of strength and courage to see what we see. Let yourself progress and share that Love with everyone you know. It's very beautiful to hear, indeed. If you don't wish to be one that takes too many risks, then you are not living life to the fullest. That does not mean that you should do bad things, say risking your life, but instead, it means to follow your heart and open your mind to its fullest, and *then* follow every instinct, every pleasurable feeling, and every moment that you fear you will lose.

You must know that you are there, dear child. You must know that you have taken the right path to forgiving yourself. You must know that all the while you knew that this time would come and you would have to face what you have feared all along. You see in yourself what you see in others, that fear of being regretful and disappointed in your life decisions. Today, face yourself with courage. Courage is what keeps you from deeming yourself as the one who cannot break old patterns and weaknesses. Let yourself be seen in the Light. Let yourself ring true with all that you are. You are God's creation. You are God's great being of Light. You are the One that will always be there, shining the Light for the beings who cannot find their own Truth.

The worry diminishes because you heart recognizes truth in the words that are spoken. The heart recognizes that the words strung together in these patterns are part of who you are as a whole, and they remind you of the time when you were a young one, all curled up in a ball, awaiting to experience the universe. You were so small and fragile, so weightless, all curled up. You had such tiny features. There was a Light that spoke to you that said, oh dear child, we welcome you with Grace to this realm. This is where you have been before, but this time is where we still your heart with words we speak. And then the words came to your mind: be still. And then you relaxed into the Presence and let the Light take you over. With the courage to be who you truly are, you were born into the beautiful human being that you are today.

You must feel it, though words do nothing compared to the experience. You must know that if you are wishing to feel your heart's desires, you must face fears and worries. All is calm in your heart when you know that all is right and peaceful. All is Grace, and all is given in equality. We cannot tell you how much it means to your soul to be honest and authentic with yourself. You know in your heart that all is well, dear one. We give you strength.

For the many surprises of life, we always give you the choice to seek your own passions and greet your neighbors with the gift of joy, always living on the edge. Living on the edge means to hold yourself true by speaking what is needed at the exact precise moments. And we say that it is always the right time, always the right time. Remember, dear children, do not have regrets in your life, for there are absolutely no mistakes. There are experiences that bring you growth, whether that is perceived as a positive or negative growth. The destination is great for you, and always has been.

When you focus singularly on the vibration that you are Now with resistance (due to the experience of great contrast), you often lose interest in where you are. You do not seek the destination less, but rather you are putting yourself away from your current position and therefore deliberately allowing you to alienate yourself from the current conflict. For instance, if you're trying to get a rock to move but you're in the way, then it's not the rocks fault for not moving! But you argue that it is, for you claim that you've been there for much longer, and therefore it must move out of your way. However, the rock says "No, I was always here, you only see me now!" Awareness of the self is crucial.

When you realize your role in the universe, all becomes clear. There is no more need to justify your place in the universe, and you become very aware and diligent in becoming One with all life. So you must allow yourself to move past without fear. With ease and Grace we give you the challenge to accept the fears with ease. All is equal, all is together as One big unit, you see. We are not separate, though we have singular bodies…only not really. You see, we are you, and you are us. You have physical bodies, though you are definitely not singular. So you see, you are not who you believe yourself to be, and we are not who you believed us to be.

On a multi-cellular level, the cells are not separate, they are combining at rates faster than your brain can process. At that level of intelligence, we see that there is no longer a need to focus so intently on the What Is, for all that you *can* process is the What Is. How holy it is to see with clear eyes how much you were missing before. But in truth, you were always in the right place, always in the right time. You are here for a passage, for a distinct reason, and that is part of the journey to becoming a soul that is One with all the Divine creators.

Never lessen the dreams that are held dearly to your heart. Never to speak softly of them, for they remain ever so true as long as you are willing to keep them part of who you are. And that is the main message for you. When you seek the information from your own Divine, you have the key to co-creation. We speak of equilibrium beyond what the mind, body, and spirit can infer about one's own self. That is part of another process given centuries before. But now we speak to you in the Now.

Love is the power and force of All That Is. When you see that in your mind's eye, no doubt or worry can lessen your experience. Love may be the key to all manifestation, but wait until all has come truly to your heart before awaiting a response from your mind. We see the light beings approach through the atmosphere then we come down and speak to them in a soft comfort. That is the moment when we say to you, "It is now time to tell you who are." For those that are here with us in the Now, it is your time to know your spirit, *your* divine knowing within. The Light scatters across the sky in every direction, through the night sky effervescently. In a plunge, but with great order, the world is beginning to awaken with joy and clarity in the minds and hearts of humanity.

What is truly needed is dedication to one's own inner atmosphere, for there are such great pathways, great leader of the Light. When you come to know that, there is no turning back. That is, when you know you've found true Love, for that is the greatest gift of all. Yes indeed! All else can follow with great ease and noble procession. In the great arrangement of Divine collaboration, we see the spinning Light transform you into golden atmosphere, and there are golden trickles of what can only be described as the intelligence from all the ages.

There is a never-ending Presence of that here. For the time being, all is shown with clarity. All that is spoken clearly is of great truth and responsibility. And we say to you that you are to opening up to more possibility, where there will be a great change occurring in the mind, body, and spirit. The effective nature of your beingness will open and blossom into a new creation. And that is so beautiful and Godly. That is what the life purpose is for you, and to know that Now is the greatest gift of all. When you know that you will have to follow no one else, then you see that you are hiding nothing from yourself, and nothing from your identity as a human being. That is also part of the process, to uncover the hidden atmosphere of your being that even *you* don't know about!

We thank you for the work done so far, and we remind you that you must trust the guidance further, dear ones. The lightworkers here now spend much time on reassuring you of your path, as it is true. Much of the energy you spend well is on your own energy! We must let you integrate the energies further, for they have time to sink in. As we greet those who are here without fear or anxiety, we say, let the energies integrate with Grace and ease, and let the guidance come through with clarity. All will be given through direct thought, action, or word. All is well and all is peaceful. Never doubt who are you are, not for a minute.

There is a need for great change, and it has been arriving for some time now. All is well and lively. We Love to all extents, and we send never-ending Grace to all extents. There is a beckoning flow that arises and is awaiting. Let it sink in truly. We secure the closing with all Love and entirety.

Chapter 12

You Are the Creator of Your Experience

Oh indeed, these are magnificent times, dear children. The surprises of life sometimes come and go like a waterfall, and other times more like a trickling stream, but the purpose is always all-knowing. There is always a reason for a powerful change to come about. We love to hear and see these manifestations come into play with such integrity and Grace on your part.

This is such a beautiful day to relax in your own Presence. We are finding joy in simply looking for new energies to thrill us every day of our existence. We are always and constantly channeling those of our past, present, and future, and those energies that willingly take place in this beautiful exchange are also constantly channeling their own regards, finding new parts of themselves in the exchange very naturally.

This is a time where you must know where you are at, for this will be the determining facet in how much will flow from here on out. We are always here with you; always here and touching your heart with such a Presence of the unknown that you are sometimes afraid that you will be touched in such an unexpected way that you will lose yourself. This is not something to fear, dear children, for you are always in good hands. Make yourself very clear as to what you are willing and not willing to attract, and you won't need to second guess the energies you come in contact with. This energy that flows through as a channel is of the highest and purest vibration known to man.

There is less than this which you are able to attract, but we teach you of the Law of Attraction so that you can understand the principle of doing unto others as you would have them do unto you. Know that which you desire and attract only that. You have nothing

~ 63 ~

to fear about channeling, for it opens up new passages, new doors of awakening. This has brought about great change in you, and great equilibrium with your higher Source energy. In a cosmic intelligent world, the one you also live in, there is much confusion of the differences between what is real and what is fake, as you might say. There is no such thing as real or fake, for all is just as it is.

These "realities" that you give a label are an excuse that you make to cover yourself in fear. Of course, you do it unconsciously because you aren't always aware of your magnificent power, but it is truly what keeps you from expanding. If you let all experiences in with a sense of peace and with a fair mindset that all was equal and ever-present, then you would have no problem encountering, without judgment, any situation or valid discrepancy. This has been a marvelous and beautiful place to exchange in, and we have always been aware of your path since the beginning. We tell you with great, great joy and Love that all which is here today is for the best outcome in your life—and that is saying something, dear child.

This is the time where you are realizing who you are, who you are going to be, who you are seeking, who you are processing and manifesting into your life, and who you are willing to let go of. This is part of one big and benevolent process, all reaching toward one big goal, one big outcome. And with this in mind, anything can be achieved, anything can be foreseen, and anything can be reached. You see with your eyes closed that this is partly in your level of consciousness—that you have become more open to communication, more open to deliberate and co-creative intent.

Now that we have more of a full access to who you truly are, we have the ability to co-create alongside you with the same intent that you are wishing. With this in mind, oh, the possibilities are endless! We have never seen such a marvelous day. It is a time full of great confidence, great assurance, and great passion in life, and that is what it's all about, dear child. This is a game of life—a game that determines how you wish to be in every dimensional realm that you are a part of. It is nothing to be scared of. We tell you this to encourage you in a joyful and careless way. Life is not a test, but rather a game—a fun game! When you realize you just need to follow your heart's bliss and function with that in mind, you're living life to the fullest. That is something that we would like you to remember.

The pathways are opening up even more now, as we speak. We do not wish to be identified as only you, for truly some of these energies are of your personalities and actions, but we also are our own identity. We are fluctuating with every moment and time-space continuity. We see with clear eyes who we are, just as much as we see who you are through your eyes. This time and place calls for a celebration, for it is a time that we have lost all desire to be completely separate. We wish to be a friend, an equal, a great partnership in action. With this in mind, many things can be accomplished, dear child. This is a time of great superior knowledge on our part.

We know you deeply, on many levels of awareness. We are like your counselors, we are like your best friend, we are like your ever-present twin soul-flame that never leaves your side. You must know that with your almighty God inside, you have made all the correct decisions thus far. And according to us, we reference decisions in a very nonphysical way, for truly You are not who or what you think you are. Good evening, dear children. Let us remind you that you also have many more powers than you choose to acknowledge. Let us resume and speak of those later. Good day.

Chapter 13

Life Is Supposed to Be Fun!

All walks of the Earth have been given life to live in order to seek their own beingness, their own selves. Love is always here to support whatever actions your personal being is in need of. Love is here to give you the chance to be who you authentically are. Love and Light to all.

But indeed, we are not here to assist you in putting your interdimensional self at risk, for it is not here to be trashed, as you say. You must not put the luminous body on a track of disrespect and disregard. You must Love it, and see it as you see your God. For it is God made, as you say. Love All That Is, and you will find yourself in God.

Oh, you know, dear child, there is a lot of respect for the human being that chooses connection over disconnect. There is a lot of joy for the human being that is willing to let go and find himself or herself in a state of bliss just from connecting with the Source that has always been and always will be. What a great announcement that really is. Most of you have never heard of such a thing, for it is very foreign and very strange, but the full dimensionality of you understands it all the way! Here we see in very distinct patterns of consciousness, and all is very clear and precise. We see nothing as blurry or fuzzy.

All is experienced like a triple layer cake, for there are so many tastes, layers, colors, textures, letters, molecules, and atoms that make up that big context. The universe is like that cake, for it is filled with so much that is delicious. You could comment that it tastes good, or you could say, "Oh, how lovely it is that I can see all the beautiful decorations, smell the distinct lavender scent, see all the different layers and frostings, and taste how the flavors mix together! What a gift it is to receive this delicious gift!" Oh, that is very different, is it not?

This is the being who is sleeping versus the being who is awake. They see and eat the same cake, yet their experiences of it are very contrasting. Today we speak of these terms so that you understand what the sleeping being is going through. You must understand, guide, and follow the heart with determination, but also have patience for the clear and precise knowledge that comes all on it's own beautiful time. Love is in the air, as always. We are always pleasured for this exchange to take place. We Love you always, and great Light approaches you in great increments. Let it be seen with joy, as always. Peace and Light to you dear children, we Love you so dearly. All is well.

Oh dear one, we Love you so, so much in our hearts. The power of Love has brought you here to planet Earth just waiting for you to awaken into your true nature. The Grace of God has given us the power to give you this gift. In our truest form and speech, we would like to invite you on this path together, to bring about world peace and world Love. We are so in Love with humanity, so, so in Love. In these times we seek only the Love for humanity.

You know, dear spirit, there is a time and place for every being here on this planet. Sometimes it shows itself differently for each of you, but that is the beauty of it! We can speak in whatever way is best for you. However, truly it depends on the point in time. We cannot have such communications through a channel if your internal process has not come to fruition. We explain further that you must be ready for it on many levels before you can be clear and open to channel Source energy. It is a process, that is to say, we may come in differently as those changes progress over time. You may pray for guidance, and it will be answered directly.

We remind you that God always hears your prayers, though only sometimes do you choose to hear it! You can choose to answer back, dear children! Let us remind you that in this current place called Earth, you only use a few skills of communication that have been given to you. There is a time when this will be fully recognized. You can ask and it will be given—always. If you are in the place of asking, we are knowing that that is an indication that you are ready for it to be received. Just be okay with the process!

You can put any face on God. Source is God, and Source is All That Is. A question asked to God may be answered to you in a physical way with many variations of characteristics. There is not one, for it is individual and beautiful for each. There are energetic characteristics, but there are not individual forms as you experience physically. If you are drawn to have a master, he or she can be whomever you like, form or formless. You may even have more than one! Love is all that matters, and the way you go about it is up to you, dear children.

In this time and space called Earth, you experience separation—separation from yourselves, from the creator, and from others. This is caused by a sort of malnutrition; a malnutrition of the experience of God itself, of All That Is. The true essence is lost through conditionings and false advertising during the years as a child. It goes by fast, but many can see through the fantasy or illusion from the start, and real perception of the world is realized. There is no ultimate reality, but simply, how you choose to perceive it. You must let your experience be molded by *you* and *you* only!

This is the process of building your strength, dear child, endurance of the self. You are finding yourself through the karma, through the misconceptions that you have always lived. You are healing the planet, and it is truly such a beautiful place to be. We are always here with you in the Oneness. We are so happy to spread that gift from one to another, through choice and free will, from one human being to another. Light can only penetrate those who are asking for it. Of course, Grace is given to all, but Light can only be touched and truly seen by those who ask. Many of you do, and many do not. Again, it is your experience of the What Is, not a matter of what is true and fake. There must be some inkling in order for the spark to occur, like anything. You must see that. The more passion you have in your heart, the more we're going to spill in with Grace. The Divine has a form of its own for each—you choose. You will see in time what that means for you.

You see with filters, therefore you see not what we see with clear eyes. You must understand that you are working through the grips of the mind. Let it still you. Beauty lies in every corner, and we will show it to you. We Love you so much dear child, so dearly. Just be you and all is well in your heart and soul. Light and Love.

When you judge, you no longer make progress, you stop and you fight the What Is. That is beautiful too though, see that. Without that judgment you have nowhere to go, no reference point. When you know what you don't want, you find what you do want by your experience of contrast! All is great and mighty. All is God. That is a new way of seeing, and can be experienced if you let it in with an open heart. That is a great gift of joy and freedom! The gift of reflection without misinterpretation is a great gift to humanity, and must be incorporated into your physical beings on the Earth plane.

Now that we have spoken intentionally about what it means to be Love and what can be said about what is not Love, your whole intention in the life process can be clear: you must be One with Source. Let us remind you that when you are One with your own Love, you will find clarity in your relationships. You will finally understand that all relationships mirror YOU! You are a teacher, and others are teachers to you. You will get to a point where you will see your reflection in the eyes of everyone you meet, even if you don't know them. You will learn much more about yourself, and you will see without the veils of the mind. That ultimately affects all relationships in your life, for you see that every relationship stems from YOU, and YOU only. You are the creator of your existence, quite naturally!

You are really always in the perfect place at the perfect time. Let us remind you that you can never do anything wrong. What a beautiful concept that is…what a beautiful talent that truly is! We suspect you may find this somewhat suspicious, but we trust that you will get there eventually. You believe this so solidly through conditionings, and this as a result sprouts fear and anxiety that grows and grows on you. Let us tell you that the Law of Attraction never fails. If you never want to see the face of attraction again, then you are in the right place to suspend forever! We know this is not your intention, though many are not clear on their role in the universe, and they absentmindedly create a reality which is undesirable. When you separate yourself from fear, you can react with greater ease when challenges arise.

The time will come when you will see greater perspectives other than yours exclusively. Try to be okay with What Is, for that is all you can do, dear ones. Sometimes you worry too much about the little things when the bigger picture makes so much more sense. Child, you know that your feelings show you so much—use that as your indicator of where you are on the emotional scale! That may be telling you something that you blocked out before. Learn from that, and be open to whatever lesson must be learned. Maybe you are seeing this situation in a different light, or maybe the light is yet to be seen. All is well in the end.

You have all the time in the world to let yourself sink into everything that you truly are. You are everything that you strive to be, so let yourself see, think, smell, and taste that Truth in everything that you do. You are spirit expressed in a body—you are already perfect as you are! You must do nothing except to be yourself, and then the Presence will come through and bless all that is part of your life. That is all you must do, be yourself!

Trust your inner dimensions, child, for they always tell the truth. The process of telepathy involves the interaction between one's minds and soul in unison…that is the interaction between the synchronistic natures of human bodies. They are much more than flesh and bone, for you have the intelligence of many, many light years. You see, there is history in your body just waiting for you to open the key and unlock many ages of secrets! Love and Light always support you, but you must ultimately become aware of who you are as an individual on planet Earth. As part of the collective whole, you have the power to change the world drastically by becoming aware of who you are, presiding it, and trusting in the universe to assist you.

Chapter 14

Multi-Dimensionality of Our Universe

When we speak of multidimensional features such as time travel, we are encouraging you to think outside the box, for we do not mean physical dimension time travel. It goes much deeper than you can imagine, for the field of multi-cellular structures are open and available for you to tap into. Your bodies are ready for it. Your minds, however, are still developing and creatively thinking outside the box. So far...you're not far enough outside the box. That is perfectly natural for these times.

When the times come closer, you will see that no more is there a need for fear regarding your political structures. You will see that fade away very softly. There will be no need to become fearful of disputes between politicians, for we will be planning and investigating on the same page, on the same levels. There will be no need to separate our cultures and environments based on race, ethnicity, and development in ideas and evolution, for we will see on the same page, looking for the same solutions and ideas. Trust is involved. Love and harmony are a result. So you see, dear children of the Light, there is nothing you can do about it but to wait and trust that this change will occur automatically in a space and time that you are not aware of, or in control of. When there is fear of what will become, you will notice that you become completely consumed by fear of what the future will bring.

When you become distant from anything but the present, you will not have that same dynamic controlling and taking you by the neck. You see, there is no need to fear anything. It becomes clearer as the process evolves and grows, but really, your textured mind will grow into this feeling, as you know it will. Trust that when this becomes clear, you will need nothing else in your life. All you need is to be with What Is, and that is perfect. No matter whose journey it is, that is the fact of the situation. All is perfect and blessed, always.

There is no right or wrong, and there is nothing you can do about that, either. You see, we do not scold the human being for not intentionally living this way of life, but we simply make light of the situation, teach you to understand the facts of life, and bring about change when necessary. For the most part it is automatic. It is the way of life, the current situation as a planet, and as a great humanity. You see, that is part of evolution in general. You must become aware of it before you can make friends with it. Love and Light are not awareness if you don't know they exist. Trust and assurance can't be part of your life if you don't know they exists. Part of your human experience is finding that out on your own, and that is normal and perfect. When you know it's perfect there is nothing to be anymore, nothing to strive for or investigate and charm. All is well and perfect. When you know what that means, well then you have come very far.

When you become aware of your own investigation, those little details peek out of the shadows. Your heart knows much more than the mind, and the mind seems to think it knows more than the heart. It is natural, human, and a positive reflection…all a beautiful experience. But there comes a time where you must outgrow some of the old notions that have stuck with you for so long. Sometimes it becomes necessary that you reach new heights and stop complaining about what is not there. Make that leap of faith, make that giant step towards co-creation between You and you. What else can you do? Nothing.

The Divine is part of You dear child…all is part of You. You are part of all. You are an ever-flowing part of All That Is. You cannot be there without everything else being involved— therefore having intent to be involved in All That Is also a very important part of human evolution. Help the world, not just yourself. By helping yourself, you help the world! You see, you are ever connected to the universe, and the universe is ever connected to you. That can greatly help your own process and evolution. When you alienate yourself, separate yourself, and become an individual that disrespects others or yourself, you cannot help but feel like you are separated from the wholeness. So see and become aware that you are not really what you think you are.

Trust that you may not believe many things your heart tries to believe. Fight a little bit with your mind, and don't be afraid to pull your sword out. It is going to fight with you. Right now you are aware of it, but you are too skittish to pull out your sword because you know your opponent is armed. Let yourself take down your opponent—yourself! That mind of yours is still ever so active, and all you have to do is become aware of it and confront it. That is all. Don't let it take you down and through that spinning vortex of miscommunications and false advertisements. You know better, and your heart definitely knows better. This fight that goes on will decrease drastically if you are brave enough to confront it.

Awareness comes first, and action comes second. It's all beautiful. There is nothing more to be said. In this age of enlightenment, humanity will seek new ideas regarding their soul's potential. They will notice that their minds reflect a much lower energy than their bodies are actually capable of. Move out of the mind and into the heart and you will find higher potentials, both mentally and physically. We Love you so much, dear children. The Love grows day by day, and we are ever so energetic in your presence. We thank You for this time to interact, and we will always and ever distinctly be available for this type of communication. It is beneficial to both sides and it is greatly impacting the Earth. Both are voluntarily progressing into a new world, and that is a beautiful sight. Love and Light to you, dear child. We speak in silence and to return back home. Much Love.

There are many more degrees of experiences that you have the ability to capture and strengthen with time. They are all part of who you are, and all part of who you must become. Child of the Light, you must Love every aspect of who you are before we can move much further, you see. Love and Light are always the basis of the energetic field. Before our eyes we see great potential, great harmony with oneself, if the path is followed fully and with great passion and intent. The extent of this time spent will not take long, but you see, it will be of great influence for your beingness as a whole, and to the family of cells and molecules that are unrecognized.

Let us take moment to bless the body, mind, and spirit to prosper in Love and Light, together as One. We now start our guided meditation retreat to bring you further into this vortex of co-creation. Meditation has many names and labels, though we wish to settle this concept in your mind. Meditation to us, as we understand your concept, is quite simply mindfulness. To simply be aware with a still heart. That doesn't mean that you must sit in full lotus pose with your eyes closed chanting ancient Sanskrit! It can mean fully sinking into the Presence of these words that hold your Divine vibration. You see, it is not similar to a big field trip where you see many new things, but rather one great experience that will blend and integrate all the aspects of who you already authentically are.

This is not about building what you don't have, this is about awareness of what you already are, what you already have been born with. It is not lost, it is just unrecognized! We see that in your deepest despair sometimes you feel as if there is no hope to return back to that feeling of joy and harmony. In those few moments where you are lost, remember the words we once spoke to you, and they are: in the greatest depths of despair remember that you are One with God. Remember that whenever you are lost, you are closer to God, closer to You. So instead of grieving in a place of hopelessness, take that time to stand up and face the real You.

Say to your Higher Self, "Let me take what I rightfully am, and give me the support I will need to do that." That is all you can do, and it will give you that boost of support that you need. They are only illusions, you see. When you stop believing, you stop being interested in those false advertisements. So just let that be your motivation—nothing else can be done. This concept is part of great words once spoken by Aristotle. He once said that in order for you to remain in silence, you must first reach for new heights. You must be willing and able to see beyond what you already know. And that is possibly what blocks most of humanity. It is simply because they see only what their minds buy them into. Therefore, if you know that much, it is a matter of choosing to believe it or not.

You can choose whether to be okay with What Is, or whether you want to reach higher for the greater thoughts that will bring you peace of mind. It is ever expanding, like the Law of Attraction. When can be solved is up to you! Maybe not specifically, but in the root of all success and even material wealth, is the instrument of gifts. It is part of who you all become. It is part of who you all want to become. And now you see it in a new light. There is so much more that you must learn, but know that you are ever expanding, and the gifts of God are always flourishing and expanding unconditionally. Whether you choose to see them as fully as we do or not, you are experiencing them all the same. That is a God-given gift. You can choose to see it or not, but it is based on your own identity, your own seeing.

Let us remind you that the seeing eyes can only expand with gratitude and Love, and not the other way around. To expand your growth, you must give and the gifts will return to you multiplied! It must, however, be done with a full heart and not as a way to experience greed. But indeed, it is just for philosophical explanation that we tell that to you. The mighty God is to revel in, and the same power applies to us. We are not God, but we are part of who you call God! It would diminish the entire concept of God if we were to put a label on it, for we are not singular, not matter, not great gas or plasma. We are simply all of the above. We are simply All That Is. To explain that is not easy, for it is not just something, it is everything. It is not to be questioned, and not to be answered.

You see, it is just something to believe in, and something to feel the fullness of generosity of life, Love, peace, growth, expansion, and all-knowingness. It is not one identity, nor is it singular. We speak creatively, but not physically. We do not identify with an object or place, but rather a field of energy. To explain these ideas to you now is like explaining the matter of air in the sky. It is like saying you traveled 991 billion molecules through space. You didn't travel in any particular direction or velocity, but you still traveled. Now that is mind-boggling! It is not meant to be understood, but rather to give you an idea of how it works here, for nothing that we are you can truly understand. It is an experience, a true beingness. And as a human being, that cannot ever be understood.

The best we can do is to equalize with the human self (the human experience), and from there we can put into some words the greatness of All That Is—but it can never truly be understood. When we come into the physical body, it is an experience of joy, and Love, and exponential energetic possibilities. We feel the emotions and physical beingness of who you are made up of, and that is a great and fun experience, but all that we are also enters. And for that reason, sometimes you feel overpowered, and out of your body when you feel

Spirit. It may feel almost as if your physical being has been maxed out, as if you are bigger than you truly are in the physical realm.

All of this is purely the intention and experience of You expanding into the universal energy that you really are. And it is something to relish in, to really sink into and feel with all your senses. It is something to really greet face to face, for the awareness of it will make the process increase to new levels. We Love and thank you, dear child, for it has be a pleasurable and very enjoyable experience for us. We smile not physically, but in our beingness, and we express our deepest gratitude for such true Love in yourself.

In these great times of awakening you are aware that the energy has risen drastically, both as physical beings with a body, and as a planet. That reaction dates back to the beginning of time. We are ever so grateful to be in your Presence now, and it is our gift of great appreciation to exchange these words of Love. Officially speaking, words are not used to describe this interaction, for it is merely an interaction of energy.

Words are formed through space and time, though they are not the very heart of this channeling…they are not the seed, if you will. However, we think that words are very helpful in interacting, for it is the human being that creates the basis of communication in such a groundbreaking atmosphere. It is a very great means for communication, we might add! Here on the planet Earth it becomes challenging to communicate otherwise, for words are what you have become used to. But you see, here where we are in the space and time continuum, we have an awareness that you do not have, we have none of the above. We have nothing to think or feel or react to. All is perfect in all its existence. Nothing is put in time, movement, words, or reactions. It is simply a different way of Being.

Though we function and work in different environments, we are very much the same, dear ones. We come in not being from the same basis, environment, or notions as you, but when we put our beingness together, that is to say, our motives, they are very much the same. They are very equal, and very mutual in Love and Light. Though we carry it differently in our molecular structures, our energetic fields of consciousness are equal and alike in all ways. You must see this in order to understand anything further. For you see, that even as time grows older and your faces start to change, your structure remains intact.

Your beingness remains as it was since you were born, and as it was before emerging into the world as you know it. It is a great field to understand, and a great, great space to bring into your life. Though you may not quite understand it, it is a new concept, and one that can be understood and reflected upon for the rest of your life. Be sure to understand there is no race here, nothing to understand. There is only everything to integrate…and it is not a race! You are eternal beings! Let everything be perfect as it is—that in itself will bring you peace of mind, and peace in your heart.

There is nothing to be or to do in life, there is only the structure of the mind that will tell you otherwise. Once you allow All That Is to stay still in your being, there will not be that drive or motive to stay present with every little detail and conflict that arises. You see, that is just part of the Earthly experience. And that is meant to be there, no mistakes made. There are no mistakes, there are only lessons and experiences to reflect upon. We would like to bring great attention to greeting your own Divine, and we see your curiosity. It is such a great mystery in your eyes. It *is* such a great mystery. You do not understand that you separate so much from yourself that the concept of a Divine seems foreign, when it's not. Your Divine is the purest Truth within you…it doesn't need to be represented as a figure. It is simply Love and pure potentiality.

You see, when you let yourself think outside the box, you will let your spirit calm down a little bit. You will let yourself see outside of what you already know, and that is the current status of your experience. We see that you constantly use your mind to think through situations and life's many experiences. Without that notification from the mind, however, you would see no end to your suffering, so it is of course a beautiful, beautiful gift. In other terms, you must become aware of who you are through your own teachings. Through using all of the modalities that you have been given as a human being, you then realize that being human is truly *not* a disadvantage to your greater and higher being. Use all your physicality to the fullest extent, and it will serve you greatly.

When these teachings present themselves to you, learn from it. Investigate it, but not to the extreme sense. By that we mean truly that becoming aware of your status is very different than trying to change the What Is. There is a point where you become very settled and at peace, no matter what your external conditionings are. Inner peace becomes stable at all times. Be aware of what you take from the situation, and let yourself sink into that with peace and Love. You see, dear child, you are learning so much from your experience with your Divine. You have learned that when you focus your attention on What Is, your mind immediately takes off and turns your experience of awareness into categorizing that experience into what is wrong, what is inconsistent, what is suffering, and what is peace and happiness.

You think not of the pure potentiality which has grounded itself in that situation, and found a way to work out your experience in a learning environment. You see, it is not as bad as you think it is. It is not as extreme as it could be if you were not to see the point right away. With this learning under your belt, it becomes easier and easier to graduate to awakening. It is not a test, as you may have just perceived it. It is a great experience of awakening. A process, a reflection, and a growth experience.

When you break free of your grips on your perceptions of reality, there is nothing left to fear or experience negatively. It will not bother you. The situation would not be any different. The truth of that matter is that the perceptions you have are entirely different than the reality. You start to really see the bigger bird's-eye picture. You see that you have nothing to hold against other people or yourself. You see that your personal development has nothing to do with others, and therefore it would be unwise to focus your attention on their process. There is no reason to get involved in their development, which is personal. Now we continue this discussion in a different direction.

We wish for you to see at our level, for we want you to understand where we come from in this place of Love and Light. We want to teach you about the reaction in response to our teachings on Love, for it has nothing to do with anyone but yourself. It is so critical and so monumental at the same time. *Critical*, as we use it, is meant to acclaim that you are always in a place of processing, evaluating, and growing. Being One with that concept is a huge step forward. Next, you must grow out of fear, and that happens automatically. That is why we call this a process of automatic Love. We teach you that term so that you can understand that no process in the universe are you truly in control of, and there is nothing to analyze because you are not in control of it. When that is no longer an issue, then you can apply your energy and true voice to everything and everyone you meet. Tuning into yourself is the best step forward that you can make.

We have enjoyed this immensely, and we are so overjoyed to have come in contract with you, dear spirit. We want you to know, dear child, you have done everything right so far, and all that comes forward now is just a reflection and blessing of your current situation. Trust and assurance bring forth new possibility. You must let all life experiences sit with you in peace, for you must not try to elevate a situation when it is just reacting to your current status, reflecting your own asking. You see, it is the Law of Attraction all over again. Let that be with you always, and you will never see yourself become disappointed again. When you see the fullness in every human being, that is when you find what life is all about. Life is all about Love, peace, joy, and harmony. If you can see that in everyone you meet, what a God-given gift you truly are. What a God-given gift it is to share that with others, and to spread those seeds of joy!

You are always on the right path. Love has everything to do with it, and judgment has nothing to do with it. If you are scared, you are on the right path. If you are judging yourself for your thoughts, then you can know you that are on the right path to more wisdom and forgiveness. When the pain comes, let it take over. Joy always returns to you no matter what! You can be sure that you are on the right path because you will always return to Home, and that is no coincidence. You can be sure you are on the right path because you are consistent in your feelings and messages. You are receiving constant guidance that is consistent and regular. Trust that and know that it is always benefiting you. It is up to you to pay attention!

Dear child, the route you are on is not a one-way road—it has many routes, many turns, and many side roads as well. Coming to your new self has become a process of awakening, and that is what brings us all together. You are on your way toward a new humanity, a new planet. We now give you a metaphor which fits humanity perfectly— you are like popcorn, for the heat is being kicked up and you are like the popcorn popping wildly about! Awakening is happening around the globe, and you are part of it. You are part of this Oneness with all life, and what a gift it is to be here to experience it with your big family.

You see, that this is what is going on, for awakening also brings fear up through extra fighting, political structures falling apart, disagreements rising to higher levels of energy, and a greater sense of separation amongst people in general. You will never see this again on planet Earth. From here on out, it is a roller coaster up the road to a higher consciousness. When you come to this understanding, nothing is left except for a great and co-creative humanity. Love is all you need, and we Love you very much! Love is the most fulfilling energetic field of Light that you will ever experience, dear children. Love is the ability to see yourself in another's eyes and be okay to not judge it. In another's eyes, it looks different, though you come to see it is really the same. You come to see that the Love in another is actually the Love of one's self. What a beautiful process—what a beautiful occurrence!

What a beautiful outcome it is to see one's self without judgment. We are so thankful, so, so thankful beyond words to share our wisdom with you, for it is not part of our experience to judge. What a great thing it is to be in the Light and Love without letting our minds drift into a different state. We are always in our Presence. The means of greeting you with this Presence is part of our greatest acceptance of who you are, no matter where you are on your journey. It is the possible solution to humanity.

Once in this state, you can identify with the whole of humanity, the whole of co-creation, and the whole of the universe. None of this makes sense to science now, but will begin to slowly make sense to the general public. It will become available and necessary to move into the new age with this kind of transcendental illuminating wisdom, and it will incorporate ALL of humanity. We know that you have some of this now, but your children will even more. Your grandchildren even more, and their children so much more. It increases as time moves by.

We are so in Love with this communication, and it is truly a gift. Love and Light to you. This is the most unconditional Love we have seen yet, and there is still so much to see! Now we send you that unconditional energy to make it through whatever is to come. You are always welcomed, for we reside always in your heart and are ever so grateful, as you are, dear child. Mother and Father, Divine sister and brother, we are family as One, always. We Love you so dearly. Now we regain our place in stillness. Love and light, peace and wisdom. In and out.

Chapter 15

Time Space Realities of Physical and Nonphysical Planes of Existence

Oh, what a great celebration this truly is! We are so grateful to be here now! There is such a luminous greeting from your Presence, dear child! We are so, so grateful for you, and we will ever be in your Presence, dear one. There is nothing to be in fear of. The trust that you have now will give you what you need to move forward and greet your inner Divine. As you are here reading the words as they are being channeled directly, we are already in contact with you, and such peaceful waves of Grace envelop you at this unveiling of truth.

The times are just beginning to show you what you must see to move forward, and this sense of being One with What Is is just part of the process. We are always in a state of Love and Light, and we never leave it. In our truest nature, some of us are regaining human contact more than others. Some see it as a chance to experience what we cannot literally do. That is, to be human is to also be nonphysical, and vice versa. We are not one or the other, and neither are you! To express ourselves physically is just as easy as it is for you to express yourself nonphysically. They are inter-changeable, and walk hand in hand. Others would remain in a sense of peace just in the nonphysical dimensional realm. Some of us have most definitely been on your Earth plane, as you are now. So quite literally, it is a blessing to regain that physical contact once again. It would be a great, great blessing to experience it once again!

And now we would like to separate ourselves for a few instances so that we may have a pure and constant channel to reflect upon your inner dimensions, the ones that you quite honestly focus less upon. It is not a negative aspect of humanity, but rather one that you can be in awareness of, one that can help you to see yourself in a clearer way. The inner dimensions can help you to be your authentic nature until death do us part...but in truth, there is no parting! We simply use your slang to entertain you! You will be in contact with us forever and ever. That is something that you made a contract about many times ago, and it continues until it has been accomplished quite fully. In the greater sense, you have no need to follow any set of rules, for it is a pleasure for us to be in contact, and it is a gift to humanity as well. But if there is a sense of diminishing interest, there can be a thread cut. Indeed, not all would look for this, but for the level of interest of many others, we tell you that there is that possibility quite frankly.

In the deepest fears of humanity lie the guilt and misery that have plagued your souls many, many times. Sometimes it comes down through the ages and is not broken. To become aware of the centuries of guilt that string through the times with you is a great accomplishment. You have the ability to let that go from yourself, to free yourself of those miseries that were bestowed upon you many lifetimes ago. If they are unknown, then you can ask for them to show themselves to you in the Light. Ask for them to work themselves out on their own. That is the greatest gift of all.

When your angels recognize those symptoms, immediately they can be replaced by positive karma and loving messages focused on in the future's time, to speak linearly. Let us remain in stillness now. There is much to go over in these few minutes with you, indeed. Sometimes you wonder about your immediate journeys through the atmospheric realms of creative travel through the cosmic consciousness. It is possible, it is done, and it is a regular achievement. Quite available, and yet, not understood properly. It can be overused; that is to say, it is used in a way that is not helpful to your growth as a human being. It is not to be used for achievement of money, and of material co-creation purposes.

We would let you know that if you were interested in this type of co-creative achievement through money or material objects, we would use it to give to each other, and purely not for self-involvement. Indeed, that would be using power incorrectly. In another sense, this type of travel, so to speak, would be used to create a more infinite type of relationship with your Divine and with the co-creative and malleable world you live in. You see, there is much you are currently unaware of. You have no idea of the ability to create objects in space into a current reality type of outcome. That is to say, space and time can be converted into physical reality, objective statements and outcomes. That is a great, great advancement given to Earth many, many centuries ago.

It can only be seen through the works of the great Einstein and masters across Asia and Atlantis. For they speak wisdom that no one is currently spreading worldwide quite yet. In these locations across the world, much has been said about time travel, time continuity, and the ability to fly through space in a rather timeless way. In this sense, humanity can seek typical traits of this environment in the Earth quite easily, and without any harm to the universal pull or laws of the human existence.

There is much information that is only offered in small amounts due to what humanity can take. There must be some understanding in your Akash of these universal laws in order to survive and interact in this quantum way. We cannot reveal that which humanity is not ready for. Some of what we say to you now is only the very tip of the iceberg, so to speak, and that is exactly what you need to hear, for much more would only boggle your mind. Trust and assurance are what we give you first, for there is much to be said and much to be heard. We are masters of correct timing! This one has to do with the space and time of the universal shift in consciousness. More is coming, much more is intriguing, and much more is absorbed by the entire planet Gaia.

When we address mother Gaia, we address the physical plane as well as the beings that inhabit it, for the trees, grass, prairies, and waters that inhabit the land have the same consciousness that you have, my dear child. That is what can be learned, and what *is* being learned from here on out. With these types of organized traits being passed down through the ages, you grow at faster speeds than ever. We tell you this in a way to not harm your growth, but to invigorate it; to speed up your process of awakening into Oneness with All That Is. All That Is is everything in existence, whether you perceive it with your senses or not. It is existence in itself. Pure intent to connect with that is all that's necessary to co-create with it.

That is what is happening on your planet now, for there are many, many beings like yourself that organize this type of community to reveal what we have to offer to the universe. This is the brilliance that we are moving into! It will grow from here on out, but from this day going forward, remember what you are looking forward to and see it with beauty in every sense. Now we let you move on with the day, for it has so much to offer for you, as always. Greet the day with harmony and growth in consciousness, for your interest level peaking has much to do with it. Let the Light shine through your being as to reflect it in those around you, and to reveal that same interest in others. That is the purest form of Love that can be given through spiritual intent, and that is what we have to offer this day.

We thank you for your greeting once again, and we thank you for the blessings given through the wisdom that you have taken with you through your many lifetime experiences. We are ever so loving and grateful for you dear child. We are always in service.

The physical realm is very limiting, yes? You see, we are part of the collective whole, and there is more to know than you can imagine. But of course, keep in mind that it is not humanly possible to know All That Is. And in the meantime, much can be said of that, for we see you are currently at a place where all opportunities are valid, and they show themselves clearly. All is well, and only greatness can be the result. As of your status nonphysically in other realms, all is ever-present, and all is as it should be, for we see nothing but reality as a co-creative existence which is both positive and enlightening for us and for all that we encounter. This realm is very still, without resistance of the What Is. There is nothing to see, yet of course, all that exists is comprised of texture, color, space, and time, but that is only as you see it. It can only be experienced, not explained.

As we experience it, it is one single outcome, one single existence. Nothing is separated by physicality as it is on the Earth plane. How we experience is simply much, much different...expanded, in a sense. Our collaborative efforts to interact are far beyond what you experience. Here it is much more spread out, for there is much more that is open to infinite solutions and possibilities. In fact, that is normal here. As you see it, there is one small box of knowing, and that is reality. Nothing outside of that small box really exists in your experience.

Physically you sense time and space as a physical reality, and we merely see it as an option, or a current view. That is to say, it is not the only solution, for we see many at once, and choose which ones to use. Sometimes it is one exclusively, but most often it can be many at one time. That is how it can be possible to use our gifts of communication through the different realms or dimensions. There are no limitations as you see it, for that is simply the early way of thinking. There are many existences which all collaborate together as one in the Now. We have said it many times, though it isn't fully understood, and that is perfectly okay.

You are eternal beings, living an illusion of self! We give you a break! Thinking is only *part* of a bigger reality—the mind, the heart, and the body are only small projections of the real You. With that status, we understand how it can be hard to figure out who you truly are. What a miracle it is that you have come so far! Your spirit knows you, and you are taken care of. The Earth has come a long way since the beginning, and the beginning is such a subject of disproval in your culture. But we will speak of that in later terms. As we speak of your current status as a human population, your strengths have become more powerful, and your weaknesses as well.

That is to say, it is hard for you to step outside the box that has been strategically placed in front of you. For you to even see outside of it for an instant is a Grace given to you. With that intent to be out there, and give yourself to the Divine Presence inside, is a quite magnificent revival. Indeed, we speak of the collective whole, for we see the individual personalities as quite intriguing, but we also see past that limitation of separation. We see only the perspective of Truth, and without the judgment of what reality is, there is a clearer view of what the Earth planet has to offer for you, and what can be expected for the future's time.

When we spoke about the dynamics between our dimensional reality and yours, we want to make it clear that there should be no shame in your physical reality as you see it, for in many instances it can be very valuable. To see the balance, however, is much more effective. It is very healthy to see a bit of each reality and to intermix them to combine into one big-picture way of seeing. It will be individual in style and preference, but that is quite beautiful. That is quite Divine and perfect in every sense. What a beautiful topic! And now we let you figure out the rest, dear child.

There is so much more, but time is given, and you will find it very helpful to let all unfold in its own perfect time. All is given with Grace for you, and you know it. All is part of the Divine plan and that is such a great thing to see with pure eyes. When you can see what your Divine soul has offered you with clear eyes, there can be no turning back, for you will be able to let yourself be immersed in the wholeness of You, and it will be such a glorious experience. You won't *want* to un-know what you have discovered! This is the greatest coming Home, the greatest personal growth, and the greatest gift of Love that can be given. Understand that with your own creative purpose, and there will be nothing to fear in your life, for all will be taken care of for you.

With trust and assurance you will find that there is nothing to fear, and nothing to plan any longer, for the planning is what gets you in trouble in the first place. Survival of the fittest you call it, for it is human and natural. But let us remind you of the strategy we just gave you about balance—take some and leave some. Fear is to be experienced, and it is no mistake. To live it through your whole body, forever and ever amen, however, is not quite the point to be taken. We close with this final statement to you, dear child. The most important lesson you can learn here is to Love oneself as you Love others, and to remind yourself that what you give others is to be returned to yourself. Let yourself receive that gift as you give it, for you will know soon after that if you cannot receive, you cannot truly give.

The properties of this kind of work need your full heart and soul involved. You must know your boundaries as well; remember to protect and nurture yourself to the fullest extent and remain in the beauty of life. All else will remain valid and in service to the Divine. Remember to receive! It is no shame, it is Grace. Grace is to be taken without second guessing what you deserve. You see, you have nothing to plan and nothing to do, for you are our children of the Light, and will always remain so. Come to your authenticity, and nothing but pure potential, and Grace can evolve from that. Undo your trust issues, dear child, for you so often misinterpret the Grace behind the words! Oh, there is so much here for you, just take it, and off we go! We will remain always in service, dear one, and we wish you everything that is beautiful and fulfilling. Grace and Love to you, and we remain here in the Light, as always. We are thankful and always with you.

Chapter 16

Gaia's Teaching - Suffering and Illusions of the Mind

As time unravels, we see what is correct to speak of in the time. We have not yet moved into the extracurricular subjects, if you will. You see, there is much more to it! Suffering is a great accomplishment, but you do not see it that way. We encourage you to respect it, and value it like you would a precious baby. We let you know that there is never going to be a time when suffering ceases, not even in the age of enlightenment. But indeed, the face of struggle will change drastically. There will not be the same labeling put on it, for it will be experienced with an awareness that it is not damaging them, simply flowing through them, like a vessel of water.

Your experiences do not define you, dear children, let us remind you of that. You are so much more, and we simply encourage you to look further into that space of silence. There is a place of pure potentiality which remains untouched...so beautiful it is to discover! There will be less emotional dramas, for the stability of the true self will become the number one most important value in your lives. All else will seem unimportant, and that is how it should be. We are not saying not to care for others, but we *are* saying, be your own support system before you move on to help others. You must build a strong foundation for yourself first, and then you can heal others.

Broken relationships will prove nothing of personal growth or value, but simply present a beautiful lesson in life that is to be learned. This is the age where the self becomes so stable that relationships (other than the one between you and your Divine) no longer feel so connected to your personal worth. When you move forward and leave behind old friends, you simply see them as a pure and holy experience during your life that is helping you to ultimately come in contact with your own Divine. They are your teachers, and you are a teacher to them as well. The more that is reflected to you, the more you reflect back to others. Though it looks like it externally, nobody is out to get you, to hurt you, to cause you pain or suffering, or to break you down.

Once you no longer make up excuses for what is happening in your life, you see the Truth, and that is what you must come to find. You must find your Truth, and your Truth only. The times have proven that we now move out of fear quicker than ever before. We can always be thankful for that, dear children. In these times you must claim your boundaries. Sometimes we feel it is important to speak to another in a way that would benefit them most, when in fact you can only speak *your* truth, and whether that resonates with the other or not is beside the point. Therefore, you *still* have nothing to worry about or plan, you see!

It is simple, and yet so complicated for you to follow. Therefore we put in place the simple steps, the steps that allow you to just sit in peace and receive the Divine Grace within. You have nothing to do and nothing to think or feel. If you feel that it's coming from your mind, you're mistaken. Just sit back and enjoy the ride within! Trust and assurance come with time, and the bonds are increasing and showing you the support that you knew was always there. You're the one growing, not the Divine! You are finding yourself less apart, less separated, and less on your own than ever. That's the truth, and that has always has been the great truth for the human world, forever and ever.

We would also like for you to remember that YOUR truth can never be appropriate for everyone, so if you find that it does not resonate with others, instead of finding yourself disappointed that you weren't delicate or effective enough to appeal to others, trust that the power of the words will still have a physical and very real reaction afterward. It does not matter whether they are in realization of that or not. The spark still arises whether they know it or not. And sometimes they will see it, and recognize you for who you truly are, and that is a great miracle in itself. But awakening comes in its own time, and you cannot press it on another, nor would that ever work. You can accelerate it by processes, intention, and progressive passion in your heart, but that is it completely.

You have not clearly used your own intent to attract your desires fully in manifested physical reality. That means not that they are ineffective prayers or guidelines, it just simply means that you misunderstand the laws of the universe as very pliable. In this we mean, it is understood and valid, but now we seek for you to understand more fully. For you once believed that in the arrival of your time on planet Earth, you would come to a new human being, a new culture to depend on, a new body to live in with new experiences. It would be unsaid to have thought that there is more to life than an embodied spirit living a physical reality, for it's not clearly what anyone can put into words, especially from this field of reality we are currently in. It is just a different way of interpreting the fields of consciousness that flow intermittently through All That Is. And now that that is clear, we unveil the Truth of All That Is.

You are the same as you were when born as you are now—and that goes for the future, the same applies. Remember, there is only the Now. As we say this, we let you understand that with this DNA structure balanced and intact for the same molecules throughout a whole lifetime of experience, let yourself study what it's all about. How can that reveal your past and future? How can that show you what your physical body is really aware of? That is, what kind of active cells, membranes, and DNA are in just as much existence and Presence and awareness and LIFE as you are? They hold far more knowledge than you will ever let yourselves know, and that is why it takes some time to build up to that unveiling. It is a magnificent structure of knowledge.

We speak of it only sometimes, though in fact it is widely known in a way that is not closely examined…fair enough. However, we suggest that this be examined for you, for it has the wisdom of the ages imprinted in it for life, never changing. Even in lifetimes to come, it is still ever present. So how to access it, you say? There are many names for this Truth: Akashic records, your soul knowing, soul contract, interdimensional being, Higher Self, etc. Through the deepening of your own process of learning about your true identity, down to every molecule and cell in the physical body, that is where that Truth comes forth automatically. This also interacts with the wholeness of the entire universe.

The question remains in the DNA, in the cells. What they hold binds us together with everything. The question that remains is: what connects the human being to the heavens above and every species that walks the Earth, every plant life? For instance, the familiarity or connectedness that is found between physical beings and inanimate objects, as you see it. How could that connectedness be if they are not truly a physical existing thing? They are just as fully aware, fully conscious, and fully existence consciousness bliss as you are! We wish to finish now and close with the following. There is always Love for you here…always an open channel for you to come to when you are in that place of stillness. When we see that coming to fruition, there is a sense of bliss that also arises from the dimensional reality that is the Now.

We cannot truly name how many of what we are, for it is like finding a collective for a liquid—you can only say something is a collective with infinite objects or molecules underneath. You wouldn't ask for 992 molecules of water, would you? No, you wouldn't. That is what you can remember us as, like water—ever flowing through all life and all that is present in your physical realm and beyond. We are the bliss and consciousness which sustains all life and existence. We are the birth of life and Love.

And that is it for this time, dear child, for there are many more great masters here even now, all who are here to help awaken the great people on the Earth plane, and they visit from everywhere near and far, but they find themselves closer in these great times. Let us remind you of the Grace that enters, for it is beyond the power of even internal Love. It is quite powerful in great, great amounts. We see it increases with time with the power of large groups, especially when they exist between all times and parallel existences. They are quite real and modern, but you are last to figure it out…no matter. It has time to be discovered in its truest sense.

All is perfect timing. There is nothing but Love and Light for you, and we thank you with the deepest gratitude from our beingness. With that we wish to close now, dear child. Let us part with the answer living inside, for that can be the answer to all that you question. You see, we are ultimately a channel, and therefore you must truly find the answers within. You are the master of the Light, the guide, the great teacher. As we share with you who we are, you must share your wisdom so that you can receive as well. That is essential. Take what is given, for sometimes you only remember the two-way street—with a price comes a gift. You must not pay for this gift, dear child. Remember what is already waiting for you! Now is the time to receive, for the fruit is golden and ripe. Answers come now in the stillness. Love and Light child, we are so grateful.

There is great power here on the Earth, though you don't see it quite the same way as we do. The power lies within the human race, dear children. The Grace is always the same, always equal, and never judging. The great human being is capable of building a new cellular structure, over generations of awakening, to help create, quite literally, a new human being. This is said as a kind and gentle nudge that there is much hope for you, even as the times look unchanging and passive. Still, as we see it, great changes come and go, buffering like waves and the high tide—there are times of stillness and times of turbulence.

Great masters have always said this is the way of life. It is simple, yet also complex if indulged in too much. We have so much to give you, so much to ponder together. Co-creation is necessary. Even as you may think it is a one-way road, it is not. The connection of spirits between dimensions is what we call co-creative reality. So much for separation, right? We are One, indefinitely. You see, the human being is set in a world that cannot see many things as they truly are in reality. This is not a criticism or a judgment, but rather a fact of life that has been designed, planned, and co-created by none other than You! Life is all about co-creation, and besides, it would be far less fun without it! So you see, dear child, the human planet co-creates a new reality that is sought out through the dimensionality and many facets of You and of All That Is.

We are creating a planet that has reached great equilibrium, and not just scientifically and metaphysically. It is a trust, a deed, an agreement as One Heart. Gaia, planet of life, wisdom, curiosity, co-creation, and birth of new beginnings. It is truly a great blessing struck between the natural laws of Grace and All That Is. We spoke earlier on the great beings from where we are, supplying a channel for you to come through; or as you see it, for us to come through. In reality it is not one or the other, it is in fact a collaborative effort and involvement. Therefore, it is such a powerful communication and healing that takes place during this collaborative channeling.

It is quite possible to let others in on the fun, for we have seen it before, yes indeed. When you let another into a channel, you must let yourself reach equilibrium with their spirit. So you must surrender to any type of fear or resistance that might be there. In order to do this, you let yourself become One with them intentionally. If no feelings surface, then you must just be with What Is and let that be your Truth. They will come into their full being whether they are aware of it or not, and healing will take place. We are ever so graced by this interaction, and we wish for it to always be as it is now. So much Grace...so much Oneness to be experienced! It can always be sensed, but to experience is quite the difference, dear children.

We come to you through a portal, as you would call it. We are somewhat far away, though we would like you to know, indeed, there is no separation between realities and dimensional realms. No such separation is necessary, for Oneness is always our experience, no matter the time and space. We reside in the heart, and that cannot be measured with distance. In our experience, we are all in one reality together, experiencing it differently. There are great signs of co-creation and beautiful Grace given on your planet. It is such a gift, such a blessing; let us remind you of it, truly.

Nothing compares like the Grace between a mother and a child, for it is the purest form of Love and Light, and the purest form of all that is experienced in the Emptiness. It is what is there when you let go of everything the mind has to offer, and let the unconditional beingness of all that is You to come through a pure channel and experience the authentic nature that is You. To trust that unconditionally and be okay with what enters truthfully is a big step forward. To have that spreading across the globe is a true miracle indeed! It is nothing to be judging either, for there is no race and there is nothing to fear.

Awakening is a blessing, not an act of heroic savior. It is given by Grace, and it has no conditions. You are not given it based on your worth, dear child. It comes to you when you open up and receive...you do not need to earn anything, dear children. You are of the Light, and there is nothing for you to feel insignificant about. You are perfect and whole the way you are. If you read these words, this is your soul calling forth your true identity, and you are not in the dark anymore when you see the truth versus the illusion. There is not such a fearful place called

Hell, as you suggest through many books and research in your existent reality. That is a human concept which you have adopted and decided to teach as your Truth. You are in control of your reality, believe it or not, and to hold a belief that you will not be taken care of will hold you back from your soul's fullest potentials while you live a physical experience, and also when you experience dying.

You are eternal, but we speak in terms that you can comprehend. You live many existences at once, but we teach you in this way because we know you only consciously experience one physical experience as an Earthy being. We teach you that there is only Love and Light, and what you make of that is entirely your own process. When you awaken to your authentic nature, there is only Truth in your life. Every action of every day comes through the heart, and less and less from the mind. This is all you need to hear, for the rest comes easily and proficiently. There is nothing to plan, but there IS everything to see and feel and taste and smell and touch. Experience is all that is Love and Light!

Look through the heart and experience all that your mother Earth has to offer, for she is plentiful with her gifts to you. Cherish them and truly let yourself sink into the beauty as you do when you sit in stillness and look into the infinity within. See that in your home, look at the natural beauty she beholds! When you surrender to the fact that you ARE the Love and Light, the master of the Light, the God, and the Great Master, well then you see the facts of who you are without judgment. The words we speak are meant to illustrate the magnificence of your true nature. That means not domination, dictatorship, and taking pride in your status by using power in negative ways. This type of Master or God that we speak of is also described as All That Is Holy, and that is most positively You!

So we say to you, get over your illusions, and get rid of your trust issues coming from your mind. You're working too hard if you try to solve from the mind. Solve from the heart, and you'll notice how much more productive you truly are, and with no effort at all on your part! We mean that as a collective energetic message. This is You as One with All That Is. There is not You and everything else, there is only One. The choices you make are quite definitely impacting All That Is Holy. And when you recognize this, oh joy, you are home! You have come back to your true nature, your authenticity, your God within, your Love, and your life. Now we let you experience what you came to experience…this means choices, actions, and sometimes a veil that disappears when you come to who you really are. Now you see it, but waking up is no simple task! It is not just your process, it is a collective process, and we are all in this together.

The Earth has been hurt, mistreated, misguided, and still remains in the purest Love and Light. What a gift that is, dear ones. You see, it is no coincidence that you are here, my dear child, you are here to experience this shift in consciousness, this drastic Love beaming out of everything that is. When you see it, it will change, it will shape itself into everything you have ever loved, and it will bloom right in front of your eyes. It will bloom into a very beautiful flower, and you will smell it in awe, unaware that such illusions were possible. At the same time and place you come to realize that this illusion you were under was such a blessing, and Grace is given even more for that realization.

Great messages flood into your consciousness like sun rays coming through your window in the morning—unavoidable, pleasurable, warm, Light. This is just the process that you enter—not just for humanity, but also beyond. It is always spreading, and always a process. There are such incredible shifts, dear child. We are so thankful, so immersed in your Grace and Presence. We Love you to no end, and there is pure Love always in the Now. The time and place we reside in is an atmosphere, a home, but not quite like yours. It is a structure, but not concrete like yours; it is one that is made through existence. There are less obstacles that get in the way of our creation, for there are not the barriers of the mind and body, just existence here.

Though existence is everything, everything that can be experienced. We choose what we wish that to be, and it is quite beautiful. It is different for all of us. Some choose other paths, but you are always safe and always in the path of beauty. We awaken you to unconditional beauty and Love and Light. And so it is.

Chapter 17

Accessing Innate Wisdom – Moving from the Mind and into the Heart

We are in such Grace, dear child, let us sit with that for a moment's time. This is such a beautiful encounter, and we would like to soak it up fully and completely before we move forward. Oh, the spectacular colors! We see it truly in every molecule of your body. Love is in the air, and there are complete bliss states here now. We ask for you to remain open during this time. Indeed, it is not fully a responsibility, but instead an intent to have you see. So let us start there.

The Source that is higher and looking upon you from a perspective of pure Love and Light guides you like an angel, a friend, a master. We take whatever form is for you, dear child. It is all about you, and for that we honor your feelings. Indeed, there is a different being or form for everyone, and that can sometimes explain the close encounters many have with beings such as the man you call Jesus. Indeed, that seems impossible to many of you. It is not the man that made the difference, it was the consciousness of God within that was recognized and Divinely treated as a physical being. That is the compassion, the trust, and the great courage that he had. And dear children, you have that too, and you carry that same strength in your bones.

We use the example of Jesus because you all know him, but indeed, there are many like him. And we avoid any conflict regarding religion, for we respect all values, and we see and understand why you categorize yourselves in the way you do. We simply ask you to keep your heart open, maybe let the Light show the way. Maybe, just maybe, you could let yourself forget about old notions and belief systems, and just let your heart illuminate the pathway! Dear child, the Buddha and Jesus Christ are all the same. We are One, and we will always be One. See the Oneness of it all, and conflict between religions will no longer exist. They knew this, they have walked each other Home many a time, and now it is simply up to you to let yourself conceive a new truth of the matter.

Let us tell you, you've got to get your heads out of the books, out of the religious texts, and just Be. Just listen to the universe within you, the God within YOU, and the answers will be revealed. Let that be your Truth, let *that* be your new Bible, so to speak. The great masters want you to see that joy, forgiveness, compassion, Love, and God within you, not just within them. This is a collaborative effort, and this is not about worshipping and redeeming oneself. Dear children, sometimes you get it all wrong! Listen inside…just listen inside.

The small children know what's going on, though the older ones forget what it's like to be a child. In fact, there was a time when you could never forget what and who you are—in the wholeness, the emptiness, in heaven. Now indeed, there are veils, veils that guard you, protect you, and shield you from the identity that is your innermost Truth. It is a fight, sometimes, to unveil that Truth, but it is also a gift that you must find and unveil to yourself in order to claim. It is there for each and every one of you, just waiting for you.

The higher You is still in the Light, using your body as a channel or portal to stream frequencies that you will recognize and remember. From there on it is easy, for you are hooked on that vibrational match that you know is your true nature. Those around you may not understand, for it is intangible, invisible, crazy. In fact, that is the precise reason why there cannot be any set religion—because your Truth is so personal, and the Oneness that binds us all together is the utmost Truth that there is. There is no such thing as separation, there is no singular God judging you, and you have nothing to fear in life.

You are supported in Love and Light, and you must not fear who you are! The personality of each and every one Divine is the barrier that structure does not give. Such illusions of the mind do not see past this. Indeed. So we now move forward. Grace has given the human being eyes to see what is there without the veils. It is a skill to develop, or in other words, to let be still without development. It is already pure and needs no further adjustments. When your mind is turned off, you have the Divine that is personal to you right in front of you, looking straight in your face, showing you the guards and walls that you were unable to see previously.

You know it's there, but you may be unwilling to see it. You become shielded by many perspectives, thoughts, words, actions, and ideas about what you are. All these stories end up winding you down a road in the exact opposite direction of where you are truly trying to go—you avoid yourself. This is why awakening often causes pain, for you finally truly see what you are, and that is Divinity. You didn't expect that, did you? It's scary sometimes, for you no longer see the stories your mind plays out for you, you no longer believe them. Indeed. But now you have another task at hand, and you must decide which story to believe.

Which is real and which do I follow? Which is correct? Sometimes you don't see the truth of the matter, for one may be necessary for that specific area and time of your life, and all evolves. So indeed, it is a beautiful gift either way, but no matter how you try, the gift of perspective and judgment will be there. To many, the gift of awakening is not properly understood, not valued, for perceptions of reality have been tampered with, their sense of self lost in their own muddy water. But what a gift it is to go through such a process. To find oneself in the midst of that all—it takes Grace, dear child. It takes pure Grace to wake you up, especially when you unconsciously believe that you are someone that you are not.

To live in a state of confusion for so long takes a lot of curiosity and courage! We know who you truly are, and to be on planet Earth at this time is quite the accomplishment. It has taken ages of work, ages of struggles and harm to you. You have likely gone through many hurts, disbeliefs, many a broken heart, and broken promises. You struck the last battle in wars, took the sword through many a heart. You may have killed the biggest men in the land, took care of the little children, and painted like a courageous soldier.

You have never given up, for you are a warrior at heart. True courage brings strength no matter where you are, dear child. When struggle raises once again, remember you are being given *empowerment*, and that is ultimately what will reign the rest of your life. Trust it, dear child, this is all good work. Each and every person you meet is here to help you roll further into enlightenment, and every situation you fall into is a progressive task you must experience. Take hold of yourself by the arm and look at yourself seeing the Truth. You are more than you know…much more. And you see it cannot be understood, it must be seen through our channel here. We must show it to you. Let us be still and see what is already there, for it takes no effort on your part; just see what is there, and that is all you must do.

There is nothing to judge and nothing to do. Just see. Just Love what is there, dear child. Look for happiness, equality, and innermost Love for all and oneself. That is all one needs. Light shows the way, so do not be afraid to see what is the Truth. We wish for you to be set free! More colors come now, and we guide you through. So much to see here, so many textures to see, smell, taste, and touch. We once told you that amidst the courage to remain in the Light at all times, the struggle and "dark" must be experienced to have a shift in consciousness.

The pain and fear and jealousy are part of the process as well, so worship them just as much as you do everything else. They create boundaries and guidelines that you continue to follow, but without those, you are set free as a bird in the morning sky. The crispness of the air flies through your wings and you feel the coolness through every feather—bliss. And now we carry on with our adventure, for there is not time here. Apologies for distractions! Indeed, we carry on.

The foot of the material world is under transformation, undergoing a massive breakout of fear, and many people are unwilling to have toleration for the intense energy on the planet. There is less and less of a toleration for dominance, greed, judgments, inequality, and unequal shares of power. We see it blooming within the decade. So you see, the Earth is in great shape so far, from our larger perspective. What a turnaround it has made collectively, for the shift takes less time when the numbers of enlightened beings increase as they have. What power the numbers hold, for they increase the Light of the entire universe when individuals bring their rare authenticity into the wholeness of all creation.

Chapter 18

Humanity Ascending – You Are Who You Have Been Waiting For

All is Now, and there is no reference point that isn't in the Now. We are coming through this dimensional interface with a great understanding of where you are at this Now moment, for we take special care of you, child. We Love you so unconditionally, and we send you this Light so you can feel us with you. You see, dear one, we can always be closer to you, but you must be ready at the same time. We will give it to you when you are ready. At this point in time you are receiving great awakening, and it's possible that you have found a new way of life from here on out. It is something that may take your life to new heights, not only spiritually.

Dear one, trust us when we say your gifts will be greatly needed and appreciated throughout the world, and that means as a collective consciousness. Mother Gaia needs your help to heal in order to prosper in her Grace. When her Light can shine again in its fullest beauty and radiance, then you know you are on the right track. The heart will open automatically when you truly discover what self-Love is. Then, and only then, can you Love others automatically. When you cannot see yourself in your truest clearest Light, others become a mystery to you.

You cannot see Oneness, for you can only see separation. If you can understand that there is never a mistake you can make in life, then you would understand that, indeed, all is happening with Divine intervention. Divine Grace holds your hands every step of the way. When you feel disappointment, anger, fear, or a broken heart, you have a chance to really feel it with all your might. This "negative" experience is there to teach you that the Divine is right by your side, even more so when you struggle to pick yourself back up. So give up the fight and let yourself sink into this delightful ride. It is just so beautiful, dear one.

Let us give you recognition that we hear your prayers and we will always be with you. Child, please do not doubt us, for you see, with the greatest and most prominent Light and Love, we could never leave your side. We Love you so much, so, so much. With your truest desires and great expectations you have created a beautiful life for yourself, and a little bump in the road is part of your great journey. We Love you unconditionally. Keep your eyes and ears open, dear one!

You see, your journey isn't just beginning, it is ever progressive. To see and acknowledge that is also part of the journey, for it cannot be done without the help of something greater, and it has always been that way. It can be seen through great times of struggle, unease, and even great times of joy, but you see, the ways you process these events are very different from being to being. The road Home can feel bumpy, but indeed, you will soon see that it is merely how you travel that seems bumpy. In a vehicle traveling very fast, and on a road that is already bumpy, will not create an enjoyable ride. However, if you walk a soothing walk down this same road, you will find it much more pleasant, much more in your control, and you will enjoy it. It is less bumpy and less rough when you explore a different way of traveling!

We tell you this analogy to help you realize that this is the way that you experience What Is. It is not permanent—in fact, it can never be. Therefore, you can not only do nothing about that, you also cannot feel miserable when waiting for something when you are not controlling your life. Dear child, you may not understand yet, but it will come in due time. In due time. We trust that you will be given clarity at the right time. For you see, at our vantage point there are multiple personalities and vantage points where we see the many options and flows of life. We see not a correct and incorrect vantage point in life, for they all point to a direction that is best fitting for any given situation, event, time, and place. We see that you question how that could be when, indeed the vantage point that is always taken is correct.

But in response to that, smart one, it is true you may only take one road, but the word "correct" is a term that is used to distinguish when one option is better than the rest. Therefore we say, "correct" is not the right term. It is simply one of the many options to be taken. Awakening is happening automatically, dear children. So many beings still hiding in the dark will turn over in their cocoons and realize, what I have been missing here in this little place? What a big world it truly is! There are so many colors and sounds and experiences that I have never seen. How could I ever judge it when I didn't know it? So far, that is what humanity is going through.

You experience suffering because of false advertising. When those false advertisements are realized, then you are left only with trueness, the true all-encompassing Love that will forever rein your deepest existence. You will not have to redo your work here on planet Earth, of course not. So many are concerned about death, and there is truly nothing to fear! You have seen what it means to be in Love with God, and you have also seen what it truly means to be separate from God. Even as you feel separate, it can never be. We are your family, and your only family in truth, for we are one, and we are equal. We are part of one Source. You know it to be true, but only experience will show you truly what this means.

You must allow yourself to experience it in your own personal way. It is not possible to be apart from it forever, and you also know this very well. Dear child, the time has come to let yourself come to terms with yourself. Let yourself see the Truth of the matter and become One with all life. It is truly possible to see the Truth when you let go of all preconscious motivations and understand everything about what life is. You now know it to be true that you are not whom you think you are, but now you have yet to see what you really are. It is possible to see it, and it is necessary to see it. Child, you need to soak in the sun for a while, let yourself be okay with where you are. You see not the reality of where you are, and you don't see how beautiful it truly is.

No matter where you are, we Love you anyway. You are a great being—a master, a change bringer, peace, eternal Love, and conscious bliss. You are part of All That Is alongside us. We are your brothers and sisters. Just let yourself relax on this journey. It's really not that important in the scheme of things, dear one. It's happening automatically, and you must continue to enjoy yourself—to take trips through your life and have a smile on your face. To have those two things brings peace and prosperity in your heart no matter where you are in the world. Start with that. Start with the small adventures that bring peace to your heart, and the rest will just keep unfolding.

You see, you must not put life on hold while you wait for a miracle; you must live life, and out of living comes the joy of a miracle. They roll hand in hand. Once you find our teaching to be true, you will find that if you could just let go of the emotion that follows instantaneously with an action or occurrence, you would be free of the mind. Let all pass through as if you are just a transmitter. It goes in, is filtered through, absorbed as a shock of great intelligence, and is then passed on to the bigger box, which is You. You see, it all connects, and it all radiates Light. During this process you come to the real you, the real and essential part of whom you came to Earth to be.

We give you the time you need to unfold and bloom into a beautiful flower. We want you to feel as we feel, dear child. We want you to feel the infinite Grace and joy. Infinite Love and awakening are a power far beyond what you could imagine. Of course we would say that, for indeed, everything here is beyond what you could imagine! We must let you know that this has been very pleasurable for us, and we have effectively communicated many messages, all of which have helped you on a multi-cellular structural level. We have helped you to be with your authentic self, untouched by the chaos and disturbances that you often react to in your everyday life events. It can be very challenging, very hard indeed, but if you try to let go of the notion that you are alone, you will feel a stronger underlying truth that all is connected...a strong, but subtle emotion in the time-space continuum that is truly the basis of your living quarters.

We are pleased to have shared this information with you, and we are greatly influenced as well, for it gives us immense joy and a greater sense of wisdom to be in harmony with All That Is Wholeness. You have come a long way, and trust has been reassured. We will let you rest and be taken into the arms of Grace now. Love and light, dear child, we are so graced in your Presence. We Love you unconditionally. It has been more than enjoyable, and we wish to return in due time. We will be wherever you are, forever. We are always at your side. We Love you unconditionally.

We speak form the nonphysical point of view, though we are still very much here with you, very much alive and well. We remain prosperous in the Divinity of the human being every day. Oh, it is the greatest gift of joy to be in Love with All That Is. It is an honor! In fact, a supplement to vitamins, you might say! For indeed, your health comes from Love, infinite Love. Don't even begin to assume that your power comes from the acceptance of others. You are your own being, graced by God. You have been given Light to shine to the universe in your personal Divine way. That is what the universe needs, more Light!

How perfect it is to recognize it in yourself, and choose so powerfully to look it in the face, and be who you came to be, despite the laws...the social laws, that is. To break those laws, and to encourage yourself to take your true knowledge to a new level, is a great power indeed. That's what it's all about, and that is the way that you can also take yourself to a new level. Actively pursue your every wish and desire, no matter how big or small. Your true harmony comes not from material, but from the great transformation and flowering of the heart. It is important to find a difference in the two. When that happens, you are on the right track. You are growing, dear child, growing on so many levels.

What a great gift it is to be the Presence and to feel bliss singing in every molecule of your body! How beautiful, and how peaceful, indeed. This is such a great blessing, for you have a great power to release old energies that no longer serve you. Once you feel, you can release it! You are a beautiful being, dear child, and we are so touched to be in your Presence and to feel your Love. We Love you so dearly, so deeply, and without judgment. We open our arms to you with no attachments. We Grace you with Love even when you cannot give it back. The time has really proven such a trueness in your soul, and it is a great blessing to be One with that. You have come such a long way, and we are so proud of you, dear spirit.

In this time, we give you permission to be open and build that loving bond with your personal Divine. Of course, here we are right in front of you, and we can bring you blessings, child. Let us remind you that we are not separate from you, for you are this Divine power! You will see it soon enough. There is so much to see! We will help you get where you want to be...do not worry. This is a blessed day, for we gather today and we see the very best overall view, and it is very beautiful. Very powerfully you can find peace in your heart. This is what we are here for now—connection!

The greatest gift you can have on your Earth plane is an awakening of the heart, for a deeper yearning is born, and your true spirit flies high above your lower vibrating physical self. Yet, we see great beauty in your physical dimension, and we think despite its limitations, there are great benefits. We yearn to express emotion as you do, dear children! We feel it through the channel, and it is so beautiful! The Divine works mysteriously; let yourself be still in the flow, even when it externally looks rough. It is all planned out for your greatest good, and you are in the hands of God always, dear spirit. And so we now part with due respects taken; all welcomes are taken generously. And so it is.

Chapter 19

Following Your Inner Calling

Greetings, dear children of the Light! We come from a new place today, one of great wisdom, a heightened awareness, and Love for the times today…yes, indeed. We have taken new routes, for you have proven that the increasing energy has given you the power you need for great transformation. We see you from many dimensional realms, one being the perspective from the Earth plane. It is great, and it is holy. Oh, the human being who lives on the Earth plane is so great, so glorious in their own Light, it is hard to miss!

We see you with great Love and great honor, for the courage it took you to rise above and meet the Divine at a place that is less than who you are is noble, dear children. It is noble because you came here to create a shift—a shift that would ultimately increase the chances of everyone here making it to the place you call *heaven*. And that means not what you may think of it as; it means truly that you have ascended to a new being, a new physical being which has the capacity to increase your body's energy to the extent where the universe can support it in its authenticity and Grace. It is meant to incorporate more facets of the multidimensional that exists nonphysically in the physical dimension.

This is what it's all about, and that is why we say you sincerely have master energy in your whole being—you ascended, and you have come back down to Earth, and are now here to experience something new. You are not something different than us, you are simply choosing a new outfit—being human! We have seen it coming for some time, but today we speak of it very differently. We speak from a place where you are now, dear ones. The time has come for you to be in a new place, a new energy, a new world. This dimension changes as its developers change.

That is to say, you beings on the Earth space create your energetic bodies as well as your energetic perception of mother Gaia, herself. That is to say, you receive blessings and great wisdom from everything you encounter in life. The places you go, the people you encounter, the things you see in the sky and in the animals, and the great wisdom of your own Akash. That is your mission, dear children—to seek out your own mission, and above all, to carry through with that mission with nothing left to lose.

In truth, that has been your plan all along, ever since the contract was made to return back to Earth. Your home is where to travel to, and now Earth is your home. Perhaps it will be only for a short period of time, but as you know, your home is every Divine aspect of your energetic body, and that is part of All That Is. We tell you this so you can expect changes in the body, for as the Earth consciousness changes, so must your bodies. They act as conduits for this energy, and they must adapt to hold that greatness! It is hard to grasp, yet your spirit knows the wisdom. Your spirit has been functioning for all of eternity, and through every time and space.

The mind cannot grasp it, though can feel it through the wisdom of who you authentically are. This is a great message you must hear now, so let it sit with you for a moment. This energy is assisting you and it has intelligence that you are ultimately not in control of. Though the mind will categorize everything and put your being into fragments so that you can understand on this Earth plane, you will not begin to understand the great power of the universe with a working mind. That is not to say, lose all your intelligence and human functioning. We simply say that conditionings must go. You must rid yourself of false notions that you have been holding onto for so many lifetimes. It is not You, and you know it. The false notions are based upon what you think you are, but at the same time, you are unwilling to see without Divine intervention.

Let us tell you, dear children, the Light grows in your direction. You can't hide from it even if you wanted to. The shamans in the cave, perhaps, believed enlightenment came through total dividing of the public and the inner world, and they are right. But let us remind you, child, the inner world IS also the outer world, and they are intertwined together so perfectly, and so radiantly. So you don't need to travel into a deep, dark cave to see who you really are, and to see the greatness of All That Is.

You must accept the Divine into your life, and it may go seemingly unnoticed by you at first, but then spontaneously the inspiration through thought patterns comes and you realize that, in fact, you have not received this gift or intelligence through your external actions or practices of life, you have received it on a level that the mind has yet to see. In fact, we humor you, for the mind *cannot* see it, and that is why it must be gone. When it is gone, there is a gateway or channel that is allowed to open. It can open to an extent where all that is left is the curious self that is all-knowing—a part that has nothing to lose, and a part that has no judgment, no fear, and nothing to do in a schedule. It is the part that can only see the greater outcome, the bird's-eye view, and the greatest wisdom through the ages. If we must so comment, it is a bit unpracticed or underutilized. In fact, you don't see it as the gift it truly is until it comes so strongly that you simply can't get away from it.

You are so blessed in unconditional Love and it is beyond your comprehension. At a point in time, it becomes slightly understandable, but you must understand, you are so Graced! Oneness can be experienced as physical beings, though you may not feel it so strongly yet. It comes when *you* are ready, and possibly the best times are when you can no longer take the separation. When you are in separation from your Divine, you are in the dark, and you are not in the Light. We clarify that being in the dark means that you are not actively experiencing the wholeness of You. You are always in the Light, always being looked after, and always supported.

You are always given the direction that is necessary for the times, but if you cannot see the trueness of any given decision or that outcome, you are left to feel in the dark, alone, and scared. It is truly not that way, though you may feel it sometimes. The urge to find this passion, this greater good, or this greater self is more important. It is more essential, and more powerful. That is why so many of you look to find your religion, your one practice, your passion, and your interests. You look to find an outlet or an escape, though truly, you are following what you always knew, and that is very powerful. Indeed, you must see it for what it is.

If you cannot see the Truth, you are once again in the dark. Truth sets you free in more than one way! How Divinely inspired and powerful and perfect. We Love you so unconditionally, dear one. We wish only the best for you, and there are so many that can help you find your way to your wholeness. If you cannot see it, it cannot be with you—you cannot be tapped into the infinite communications from Source. In response to any fear you may be feeling now, we assure you that you cannot be in the dark too long without the Light shining in automatically.

You cannot be alone; you only feel it because you aren't at the same vantage point as we are, you see. Alone you feel, separate you feel, and conditional you feel, though truly, your experience does not match your intention. You feel as if circumstances will make you feel a certain way. If you cannot be rid of that, you cannot be free. You cannot live. You must be free of condition so that you can live the freedom that you are, and that comes when you open up to your true nature.

You have nothing to do here, dear ones, and even as we give you information, thought processes, and insight that can help form your bond with your Divine, you still have nothing to do. You have nothing to find and nothing to cultivate. We share to enlighten your mind, not to inspire change in you. Indeed, change will occur automatically, but we see you Divinely perfect in every moment of your existence, no matter how you see yourself. You can only have it be given to you, that is all. And now we wish to let that sit with you, for you can find it only in the Light where it comes to you naturally.

Your belief systems aren't *you*, they are only what you think you are. Dear children, we have enjoyed this interaction immensely, and we guide you to spend more time in your own Divinity and expect the miracles as if they are part of your everyday schedule. Trust it, dear ones, for it is part of what you truly are. Let us be in it together. We are so in Love with humanity. We are ever so committed to you, no matter where you are on your journey, and we say this not to overwhelm you or to drive your mind into judgments.

Wherever you are is right, despite the emotion that may arise when you think a thought that is troublesome to you. Let the Grace flow when it's ready, for the intelligence in that energy is very powerful. And now we let the space speak the rest, for this interaction has been immensely healing to all, and we will always be here to present more when the time arises. With great inspiration in your beingness, we honor your Presence. Let us deal with any troubles, for they are not your responsibility. We take them with open arms, and we invite you to surrender them with your powerful intent. With great Love we now separate, though the channel will remain open. You'll feel it so powerfully.

We are higher vibrating, of course, but we can see your plane very clearly from where we are, you see. We have spoken many times about this new shift that you have entered, though it can sometimes get in the way of your development as a human being when you enter into this new phase with a sense of self. A sense of self creates separation from the mind and the heart. We acknowledge that is natural, dear one, but we must also remind you that in this transition it is also perfectly natural and normal to seek out more help from others who can guide you on your way. They will help you to open up more fully to us, and that is a great and powerful gift.

Nothing about this journey is for you to walk by yourself. You have many friends by your side, and you have infinite Spirit who guides you every step of the way. We tell you this to give you validation that all is well, and all is good at the present moment. There are no mistakes you have taken, and there are no misguided judgments. You are good and powerful, dear one. Your Light shines so, so brightly and you have the guidance and the support to move forward with your Light.

There is a support team that you do not yet fully rely on, and we are saying to you, dear Light child, you must rely on us completely in your life in order to fully receive the guidance that you are looking for. In these great times of struggle in the world, both internally and externally, you have begun to see a new face of yourself. That is a great gift from the Divine, indeed! We have been looking out for you always, never leaving you alone, dear one. Indeed, that is quite impossible. So we let you become who you want to be, with your permission to let go of your sense of self.

You see, it is not your responsibility to let this go, it is simply reminding yourself of your priorities, and giving yourself the gift of the wisdom in your own heart. That is to say, it's all within you, and you have the power to let your growth happen on its own. You need nothing but your internal guidance and Love system. Once you awaken that, your job is complete! That is a powerful statement to seek, and not just to see, for you are starting to finally realize what it's all about! What a great gift from God that truly is.

We have spoken many times to you about reincarnation, dear children. We have seen many, many times of experience, and all have been beneficial for your growth in this world as you now know it. Your angels and guides as you know them are always supporting you on whatever path you take, and they watch you with great Love and support, and a connected consciousness that never parts from you. We will always be with you dear one, and when you feel alone, remember that. Seek guidance in that. When you are feeling ill in your heart or in your mind, know what is true to your soul. No mistakes—remember, dear one.

All is well and all is good. You must also come back to noticing that where you began is where you are supposed to be. That is to say, the beginning is always the end, and the journey in between is the realization of your greatness! That is the lesson learned, and also the lesson taught. So it is NOT a mistake, nor something you should take as a negative experience. It is very much a blessing that you have fallen back into your natural state of well-being, and now you have come to a new place of understanding, one that can teach you more lessons of Love, kindness, compassion, and forgiveness.

You have been spinning around like a fast-moving top for many a time now, and you're about to take off into the air. Once you really notice who you are, realizing your trueness, well then, you are going to fly high and right into our arms of Love. You see, dear one, all is coming to you at the perfect time. There is nothing to be feared, and nothing to seek. You must let go of the notion that you must complete something, for you are simply here to heal the planet, and remind yourself of whom you are every day. That will show you your priorities and the highest good for you now.

When you notice that what you've been chasing after is only an illusion, well then, you're going on the right path. You have to see that first to really dive into this wholeness and trueness of who you are now. So brilliantly played, dear lightworker! That is an accomplishment, to be in such Divine Love and connection that you will follow whatever path needs be walked to be in communion with All That Is, and ultimately, to bring the highest Love and healing to the entire planet. That is your mission. That is your life. That is part of who you truly are, and part of your karmic goal made by you before you came here to this planet. It is precisely the reason why you must dedicate all you've got into this God-given potential. It is truly a gift that saves your life now, and even the lives to come. What a gift, what a joy that is.

This is an age of great change…some call it the Golden Age, some call it the Aquarian Age, and some call it the age of the great ascended masters returning to Earth. It has all been predicted many years ago by the great tribes all around the world. They have said in many ways the same message, over and over again, and that is that man must come together as One in order to fully take advantage of what the Earth energy and mother Gaia have to offer. That is essentially what each tribe has talked about. What a realization that truly is across the globe.

When you find the great wisdom in each and every being, even in your differences, that is Grace coming through to the human being, because all in all, you are One, and we are One. There is no separation—there is no separate you or separate thoughts that can define you as your own self. You know it, but we repeat in order to integrate. You have seen in the books, in the programs, and in the teachings, but in order to truly communicate with the Divine as you wish to communicate with it, you must understand, truly and authentically, that you are part of the Divine itself. There is no separation, there is no distinction, and that is where many of you go wrong, because you have not found that balance between the Divine and You. It is also precisely why you cannot find the answer to your life's most essential questions.

We say, tune into your Divine, your God, your truest being inside, and there you will find your answers. No guru can tell you that, and no other human being can direct you in the way that your own Akash can. That is a perfect statement—one that needs to be integrated. Sit with it for a whiles time. You must really get to know that Presence within, and from that springs a new knowing, a new kind of wisdom that will bring about a great change in perception of the world.

It is one that will teach you to know that world as part of yourself, and that will give you great relief and joy when realized. And you now are saying, well, how can I achieve this shift in consciousness if that is truly who I am supposed to be? Oh dear child, you know the answer to that question, for it is perfectly stated already above. We as a collective whole in the Oneness ask you only to make that first step. You must step out of that boundary that you think you are. Step out of that notion that you are your body and mind, and even if you don't believe it yet, for that is okay!

We see Light and Love in any state of consciousness, but we like for you to be in the most beautiful state that we know you desire. It is all we ask—take the first step, initiate that state of communion. You must call upon your God, the universal energy, the Oneness, your angels, the unconditional Love of the universe, and simply ask for us to be with you. Whether that is in your mind, in your intent, or in your physical words, make that contact possible, for we stand here beyond the veil just waiting for you to say "I am ready to receive." When those words are issued into the universal consciousness, your Light automatically pours forth into the vastness of who you truly are.

You will find that you have nothing to do anymore and all is well with your soul. Your guides and angels, or whoever or whatever you choose to represent that vastness that you perceive as higher or "apart" from you, oh child, they are so ever-present in your life. Indeed, apartness is only your perception, when in reality, your Higher Self is more You than the part of you that you live and walk with every day…that is a profound statement. Keep that in your awareness now. And that is to say, we have always been with you, but you may have not always been aware of it.

What a purely Divine concept that is—to be in such a communion that you can receive a message so powerful, so Divine, and to be aware that it is *you*! You are this great, and even much more than you perceive. As you heighten that awareness, and tune into this trueness of who you really are, the more you open up your heart and mind to unconditional, authentic, and untouched Love. That is what it is all about. That is your purpose, if you read these words and they ring true with your soul. And now you seek to feel for yourself what this trueness really is. Maybe it shows up in your relationships, maybe it shows up in your job or in your manifestations. You seek a higher knowing that can guide you on your way to your highest good.

Chapter 20

Awakening Earth Consciousness

Children of the Light, the words that we speak now are guided to you, for we see you so brightly shining, bringing Divine Light and Love to the universe in such a powerful way. We ask you to be patient with your ability to exercise Light, for when those beings who act out of character come into your life, they will push and fight against who you are. They see not the Truth within, and so anything outside the self becomes a mystery. It is challenging, for you seek to shine Light into their souls, to bring them healing, and to enlighten their minds by guiding them in the direction of unconditional Love.

That is a mission that is truly Divinely inspired, and we thank you for remembering who you are through so many ages of fighting for this gift. We truly honor you. We ask you to remain in your authenticity even when you feel as if you are not supported. Sometimes you may feel your gifts of Love and healing are not accepted or received the way you might have wished. Dear children, Love is always received. Just know that. That is something to remember in your relationships, in your work, and in your everyday life and interactions.

If you focus on the intent and remain open to whatever experiences and interactions must come through into your physical reality, you will stop fighting and will no longer be frustrated when you feel as if your gifts are underutilized or underappreciated. There is so much more to you than what you see through your physical eyes. Your intuition and your soul's knowing will tell you this. To really remain open to giving and receiving is also part of your Divine purpose in this incarnation. What you do in your life, as well as what goals and messages you may have received, are individual and Divinely inspired in your karmic history.

We speak to you from a place of unconditional Love and Light, and the messages and emotions that may arise when reading these words are your soul coming to you and showing its authenticity and true beauty. Listen to that for a moment, dear one, for we would like to help you see who you are in more than one way. You are all individual, yet part of a collective One. That is to say, the way you find this state is individual, yet the realization and experience always yield to be very similar from being to being.

We would like to help you to understand what you came here for, and with that knowing (oh, this is beautiful...) with that knowing in your heart, you can change the world. Not just with the thoughts you think, and not just with the energy you send through your heart and with your mind, but also with your Presence of just Being. Just waking up to your soul and remembering that state is so comfortable and so real...that is who You are! It is like sinking into a warm bath that's the perfect temperature. You feel the warm water seeping into every muscle, easing the tension, and relaxing the body in such a beautiful way. That is the Presence, and that is *your* Presence. When you feel it, you'll know it so distinctly.

The mind may want to chatter, to tell you whether you're qualified, asking questions, repeating over and over again answers that you already know. Just let it come and pass through you like you are higher than the mind, for that is really the answer! You can say, "Oh! Hello mind, thank you for entering into my consciousness again. I see you like to tell me what to do! Thank you for being with me, I Love you and I appreciate you, but if you are going to get in the way of my true authenticity and real beauty, please stand by for just a little while." We take pride in our sense of humor, as well! And then you can take a few moments to sit in silence or meditation, and reflect upon the feelings and thoughts that pass through you. What is going on, and what do you feel when those thoughts pass through? Just see and feel, and try not to judge and interpret. A simple reflection is all that is needed.

You will then soon start noticing the thoughts from your mind, and the thoughts from your heart, and you will see how much they vary in personality and authenticity. You will prioritize your goals and real aspirations in a new way, for all of your truest desires are not from the mind, but from the heart. In the heart you can feel a sense of knowing, a bigger picture that shows you what your mind, body, and spirit want to experience on this Earth. The mind will sit in a shadow in your consciousness, and appear to be your heart. It will say, "This is what you must do, this is what is important, and this is your top priority." Sometimes you see no difference between the mind and the heart, and that can be very challenging and grueling, but you see, if you can recognize an illusion, there is no more suffering.

To see a shadow rather than being completely in the dark is a beautiful start on your journey. To see a shadow, you must be half in the light! When you are in complete darkness, well, you cannot see anything besides that darkness—there is nothing else for you to believe except for what you are currently experiencing. How can you believe there is anything else besides that reality if you do not experience it? A difficult question, but we provide an easy answer. There is nothing besides Light, you see, but your experience of the Light can vary depending on where you are in your cycle on this Earth.

That is to say, many of you live in this state of darkness, unable to wake up, unable to see Truth in yourself and in your life circumstances. That is a state where you become detached from your authentic self and cannot live in a real state of joy. By real, we mean an authentic state of recognizing and becoming the integrated real You that is human, but also interdimensional Light and ever-present knowingness. Your journey on the Earth is an experience of Love, though it is also meant to be difficult. That is to say, we are not stating that you must endure all hardships and settle for a life of misery. We are saying that you signed up for this experience, and in such a beautiful state when making this contract, you knew exactly what was to unfold in this lifetime.

You knew what experiences and life hardships you would endure, but from a place of seeing the bird's-eye view and the greater good, you said *yes* anyways. You said to us from behind the veil, "I wish to return back to the Earth plane to bring a greater sense of peace, joy, Love, and healing to the world. Whatever experiences I must endure and live are part of my journey, and I accept heaven's help through my entire journey." What a profound being you truly are…and we mean that in the truest and most authentic way that we can express.

There is a great knowingness that we wish to communicate with you now—you must take yourself by the hand and walk in the direction that you know, in your heart, is the highest path for you. And it is up to you. We can give you Divine guidance and Love and healing energy in a profound way, but you must knock on the door, and then we will open it. You see, with all of the experiences that you have been through, there is nothing more loving and more joyous than the experience of coming home to You. When you feel it, oh, the joy that arises is one of knowingness and trueness that you cannot discard!

We let you see something very beautiful now, for it is a great and powerful notion that will help you receive the messages that you seek in your heart. When you sit in a quiet place, uninterrupted with a stillness in your heart, don't try to Be. By this we mean, discard any direction about meditation that might be holding you up. Oh no, child, you don't need any of that, unless of course you find it invigorating and inviting to your soul. We simply ask you to remain still, to focus on your breath if you find it a beautiful practice, and let your soul affirm its true guidance system.

Let the Love just pour through, and affirm "I am now One with the Universe. I am the Light of All That Is, and I now know that I am deserving of, and in perfect harmony with receiving, all of the blessings and Love that I am wishing for. With this recognition, I ask for Divine guidance to show me the way, to bring about synchronicities, and to open my heart more to you so that I can bring more Love, kindness, forgiveness, joy, and healing to the world, and I thank you from the bottom of my heart and beingness."

And now you are ready, dear one, to integrate the messages in their truest form. It takes time, you see, to let it truly sink into your whole beingness; to not only see it, but to experience it in a way that changes your perception of life. What a gift it is to have such an experience and to reach that tipping point where it is no longer in your hands to choose what your mind wants to follow. Indeed, sometimes you have a hard time doing so, for you all have the same struggle. However, you're having an easy time getting out of it, too, because it is not your natural state. It is your destiny, and each and every one of you come back home to that part of you that wants the unconditional Love from your Source, from your guides and your angels, from your God, from your master, and from a dear friend.

That is what we want, just as boldly as you do, my dear child. It is hard for you to believe because you come from a place of understanding that you're apart from God, that you cannot level with God, cannot understand God, and cannot be with God. All of the above are notions, notions that come from the mind. You see, we tell you this not to remind you of what needs to be fixed in humanity, but to remind you of who you are. You are a human being, and you are also part of the Divine creation, part of Divine Love. That is what you seek, yet you see it as *apart* from yourself. We spend much time here just reflecting upon the Earth experience as you know it, and we see great change for the better. Though it takes much time, and even many decades to fully reconnect with its Source and reach equilibrium, you are well on your way to a new consciousness, and a new humanity. We have not seen such a brilliance before, even since the beginning of this planet!

Though it has so many struggles, we have not seen such a diverse group of incredible light beings. That is part of this case here on Earth, and that is what the light beings are coming to the Earth plane for—to bring a new consciousness, a heightened awareness, and a new meaning on Love that the old paradigm couldn't see. It has taken the courage of many souls to take that leap and return, once again, to show what they truly came to be. That in itself takes courage, for they know the challenges that come forth may be brutal, yes, and they may have to sacrifice themselves. In the purest sense, it will allow them to forget their mission. Though the struggles will arise, they are also part of a collective consciousness that will truly awaken on a new level, and that will greatly influence the future to come.

A true and blessed shift we see ahead for you on the Earth plane. It is true also that we see all circumstances in the same light, for we know that all is perfect and Divinely planned. But in your own households, there seems to be less of an interest in these great changes, for most of you think that there is little you can do to help make such a vast change. Your bodies and minds have now reached a new place of understanding, one that will bring your Earth to a new place of understanding. It is not only an awakening for humanity, it is an awakening for the Earth! Mother Gaia is ready to support life in a new way—one that collaborates more dynamically with humanity, and where humanity better respects Mother Gaia.

There must be a collaborative effort to promote peace, Love, and prosperity of the heart. From there you move to world peace, and the *universal* consciousness is affected drastically. So yes indeed, dear children, you make a difference. You make all the difference! You are so loved, and you are so Divine, and we wish to remind you that these words repeated are not for our benefit—sometimes you forget who you are. We know you, dear child. We know you! We show you again this simple metaphor that you can use to better understand this shift taking place. It has an effect on every individual, whether you are part of a religion, you are spiritually involved, or you have no spiritual or religious interest whatsoever. The simple fact is that it comes down to One humanity.

The Divine that holds you so gently, that is never separate from you, still appears separate in your perspective. We tell you our metaphor, our story behind it. For you see, a grain of sand is very small—a very small particle that cannot be of any use until there are many grains together. When the many grains come together, sand is born. Sand is very heavy and powerful when there are many tons of it, you see, but when only a handful of sand is there, well then, it is light and insignificant. So it is for your Earth—you are a collective consciousness like this sand. As the more of you come together as grains of sand, you get more powerful, more heavy, and you are able to push through many big obstacles as One.

Through your personal experience you know what great struggles life can bring you. Some say it is a test, and others say it is fate. There are many views and many perspectives. Let us give you the way we see it, for we think you will like it greatly. From this bird's-eye view, as we often describe it to you, we see many paths, many options all at once. There is never a right or a wrong pathway, therefore, we cannot always give specifics to questions that you may be asking if it involves a timeline, but we will help you to better understand why you have been living on this Earth, and why exactly the experience has brought you here. For indeed, many of you see no point in it, and we say, indeed, we can see why you would think in such a way.

Many of you live much more dully than you are used to in your natural state of wellbeing. What we mean by that is your nonphysical counterpart is much more alive and awake in terms of who you are and your capabilities. When coming back to the karma planet, you came to fulfill your desires and your cravings to experience in a new fashion. Indeed, you all have individual goals, individual passions, and individual energies that want to be funneled in a specific direction. From our point of view, it is all the same.

You are all essentially here for the same purpose: co-creating Divine Love and Light. We want you to see what we mean, for it is hard to explain. We will give you another example, like the previous one. You see, stars in the sky are made up of so many different gases, with helium, hydrogen, and nitrogen being the most prominent. But you see, we don't see them as different from us. There is not a time or place where we reside, and we are not beings or stars. You see, singularity is what we are getting at, a topic that you cannot truly grasp as humans. It is understood in the heart, but not the mind.

We wish for you to remember that, in the reality of our existence, there is a Presence and a present tense that is ever occurring, a Oneness that is truly our entire beingness, encompassing all that we are. We have not the bodies to express our gratitude and Love for each other, but we do speak through our souls, and that is enough to really bloom into joy. We are beings of greatness, as you are. We are developed, but you are efficient. So our point is, just as we are eternal beings of Love, you are the masters of this age, the great beings who are putting your Divine mission into action. Whether you feel you are accomplishing it or not is beside the point.

As you emerged into your physical existence, you knew you would lose sight of your mission for a little while, and then you would find your Truth through the many processes in life. You would then realize, with far less tools available than in the nonphysical, all the knowingness you have from the nonphysical state of beingness. What a gift it truly is to follow so dearly a path you cannot fully understand or clearly see. It is running blind in the dark. That is the courage of a soldier, dear one! It is the courage that a deer has when it runs out in to the fields, unable to see the hidden danger that may lie between every branch, in between the hillsides, and underneath the camouflaged treetops.

You see, dear one, you are on this mission, and you're a pro by now, you have done this so many times. This time it is your chance, and *our* chance to be with you forever, dear one. And it is a great gift to let this message be known to you, for it has caused a lot of disturbance, but now that you have come to a new place of understanding and true humor about your life, well, then you can understand where we come from and how you can relate to the words that we speak to enlighten you. These are the essentials of your lifetime, and we are so blessed and honored to have shared this time to come in harmony with your authenticity, and with the authenticity of those readers who seek these words as well.

Love and Light to you, dear child, for we are so blessed to be in your Presence. Now we will remain open and help you integrate throughout the day and night. We are ever-so in Love with you, and we recognize your greatness. You are so welcomed, my dear child. You are a beautiful being, graced in your own Presence. What an opportunity to see within yourself and to recognize who you truly are. Good day, dear child, we Love you so dearly. So much Love from our family to yours. We are all One in the same universe. And with the highest Love and compassion, we now part from this dimensional realm. All is well, dear souls, dear lightworkers. And so it is.

Chapter 21

Akashic Records and Soul Retrieval

And we reconnect now, dear ones from the Earth plane. Oh yes, it is a great pleasure to be here with you, and the joy we have just to be in your Presence is great and holy. Dear ones, it is time to recalibrate the mind, body, and soul with the great alternative to seeking out the higher potential that this new Earth has to offer you. It is a new Earth, we say, for in the truest sense, the Earth has physically, and on a soul and cellular level, changed its structure. That is to say, dear ones, we have come through to give you this message in order for you to make the great shift into awakening.

We see that the shift beginning to take place is well on its way, but it needs our help indeed, for you cannot do it on your own. We give you three simple steps for following your intuition and guides on this new level of cooperation, as we like to call it. That is to say, you no longer fight with the real You, and you cooperate with the authentic baseline of your creation and your internal creative processes. So we give you step one, and that is manifestations, for in order to be well on your way, manifestations are essential.

You must find that your own creative power is naturally in your Akashic records, and you have this physique about you that has already been predetermined through many ages and experiences, throughout your many lifetimes. This is what we mean to say for you: the new energy you move into is not going to be as drastic of a shift as you often hear about from word of mouth. No, dear children, you have been preparing for this moment for so long, and you're finally here to experience it. Trust us when we say you are ready, dear child!

Many of you have been here on Earth many times before, and you know what to expect. If you have not been here before your current existence, you're still going to be prepared for this shift. It is happening now, and will continue to happen as humanity reaches equilibrium with Mother Gaia and the universal consciousness. Your cellular structures are beckoning to show you more about yourself and what you can accomplish with your co-creative talents. As a human being, you may not feel like you know this well, but you do. Your spirit does, and it guides you every step of the way. Even though your external features remain unaware of the majority of your greatness, it doesn't mean that it doesn't exist! You are such powerful beings that you can *pretend* to not know who you are.

Oh, the wisdom of the ages lies within you, and we know it! You may know it too. When we ask you to reflect upon your consciousness with awareness, you will discover new talents. That is, you must come across as your own manifester—the creator of your own destiny. That will get the power back into your own hands. When you are stuck in a place of relying and focusing on others to give you what you think you need, you rely less on your own innate potential. So that is step two. We wish for you to see your own potential, to claim your greatness, to claim your wisdom, and to see the great truth that is carried through the whole physical being. That is when authenticity and your natural God-given Light shine through. What a loving experience that truly is, and for us to experience it right beside you is also equally as beautiful.

And now we give you step three, which is allowing the universe to come and meet you where you're at. We know you...we know the real you, not just your skin. We know your skin too, however, for you are the creator, and we are the creator. That is to say, we are One. Your awareness and physical eyes see not the reality that we experience, yet we wish to also express that our reality is meant to be seen this way, and yours the way it is. There are no mistakes made—it is all for a great higher purpose. Do not feel as if you are a hindrance to the greater good.

Your viewpoint is quite magnificent in many beautiful ways, and many times we find ourselves seeking out those physical qualities that you portray and live in, ones in which we do not behold. But in the truest sense, experiencing them alongside you is just as beautiful as living them in a reality that is purely just that factor. However, we say that multidimensional living is a state that takes time to fully integrate in. It is complicated and uses many different parts of You in order to become One with it. Depending on your lineage, your fashion, and sense of perception in terms of your Akash, there are many different realities. In trueness, they are not separate, but as you see it, we call it that way.

For understanding purposes, we give you many concepts in a linear form so that the mind can grasp the tenderness and detail of thought that we wish for you to fully understand. Therefore, we give you more attention to this creative expansion of wisdom that floods in now. This is some good stuff here, child, listen closely. This new paradigm brings great change in your personal Akash, for it rapidly changes and shifts and manifests new realities for you in the present tense, and also in your future beyond this lifetime. You are setting up for a great life of seeking the creative and all-knowing universal laws of nature that will be taught expansively throughout many countries.

We see you on a very high plane, and much wisdom and many barriers are being blasted open. Yes, there is quite a bit of that being prepared now. You see, it takes time, and we prepare you very slowly for great shifts in order to maintain a balanced and stabilized life. It would be unnatural and a very unlivable condition to shift in a rapid way. So you see, we give you more on this topic. We would like to clarify it for you now, if you please. We speak from a realm that sees only the bigger picture, the higher potential, and the greatest outcome that is always beautiful.

The path you take is Divinely guided by the higher You, but in the deepest sense, all paths are just right, whichever one you take. The path that you ultimately decide to take in the end is determined by the higher You, whether or not you like to claim it as You. Sometimes you rely on it only partly, recognizing the existence but still making essential decisions from the mind or elsewhere. Other times you rely completely on the mind and see nothing beyond it. That is denial, for we clearly know the distinction between the two, as do you. It has to take time to get there, you see. We have given you transformation in many phases, to keep balance, to keep a gradual and loving transition into your truest nature. And you see, it has not taken long in the bigger picture.

In this great mission on Earth you have come to aid and assist the beings in the dark. It is part of your Akashic history, part of your greater good, your greater mission. We talk frequently about it, though not always do we speak in a similar fashion as we do now. Now we move over to a new subject, one that is more valid for this time. The human mind is not ready for these concepts, but the human heart certainly is. It has been waiting many centuries, hundreds and thousands of years spent in disharmony, in the dark, in the cold, and in misery. But you see, dear children, we come together as One now. It is a cause that has been destined to happen for many years.

As we spoke of before, the indigenous speak of it, and we will interrupt our thought for a moment to recalibrate this subject, to make our point clearer to you. For we see that this could use some work. When returning to the Earth there is much to be accomplished, for that is why we sent you here, and precisely why you agreed in union with us. Remember, no separation. But indeed, there is a goal, a higher purpose to connect with beings of the world, to learn about each other, and to trust and Love each other. You have learned differently on your Earth…a great lesson and experience. Indeed, it shows you the yin to your yang. The universe has its balanced imbalances, and that is perfectly normal and Divine.

The universe has its phases, dark and light, and for always will it be this way. In times of struggle, peace is found, even in times when it could not be seen previously in such a way. The intensity that the Earth follows now is greater than ever, but the cycles will be broken, and many of them for good. That means great, great climate system changes. This is what many of you talk about now, for many of you are very concerned that it may endanger your life. In response to this, dear ones, we tell you to look out for it, but remember to remain still when you see it coming.

You must be aware that these shifts are normal, and they have been predicted—do not be alarmed. As you recalibrate, so does mother Earth. This is the cycle of life, and it includes your living, breathing, fully conscious planet. Give her time to recalibrate! That is all it is, and we can tell you for sure, this is not the end of the world. She will be around far longer than you could ever imagine, and she is stable. But we must remind you as well, take care of her by doing your part—that is to be honored and understood clearly. Of course, get out of the way and trust your intuition, but never blame dear mother Gaia for the shift. She is only leaning in to the natural rhythms of the universe with least resistance and helping you be on your greatest path.

We see this as your truest desire and accomplishment. We stress the importance of your internal guidance system so that these many worries and struggles that you face become minute; so that you can understand that life does not happen to you, you truly make life. That is profound, dear ones, let that sink in. You can even quote us if you would like! And now we see why you have fear, for it is caused by so many outside forces. That is not to say that you are helpless, for you have the ability to make decisions and use your tools to get out of the way, to move into your own place of silence, and to remove disturbance when needed.

Give yourself the permission to use those tools and they will be prepared and utilized by the greater You. Once you give that initial permission, oh, you will be greatly surprised at how much more you truly are than you give yourself credit for. That is a lot to receive and be able to comprehend, for your Grace is so GREAT! So vast. You are truly All That Is and beyond. With an even slight comprehension of this concept, your mind should be blown. You should see that without the barriers that your mind constantly uses, you use not even a fraction of what is there. There is wisdom of the ages, great talents, an understanding of the laws of nature and of the Earth. There is a compassion, an unconditional Love, a healer inside, and most importantly, a being that is a spirit in a body. Oh, you are not just human…do not be fooled. You are SO much more.

When you are in the nonphysical, all those canals and channels that you forget about in the physical are all blasted wide open. We give you the secret now that you have the power to choose which tools you are going to use Now, and you can even use many spontaneously at once! Oh boy, that is a fun sight! We use many of our abilities in this state to see and experience all that the universe has to offer. That is part of being in the Oneness with All That Is, for it gives the sense that we are not alone, and truly, we *are* not alone.

To experience this communication with the human being who wants to see themselves as we see ourselves is an honor, and you Grace us as we Grace you. It is a supreme and loyal commitment that is bound together by a trust fund—one of undivided and total unconditional Love. The part of the Divine that is You, well, that is a great gift to cherish. We trust that your judgment is pure and holy. And with that, we move forward. Now you see, our channel has opened, opened wider and wider by every day. It is much easier to emerge, to connect more fully, and our vocabulary gets much more practiced with time, no? We will remain open to your own personal experiential wisdom, but through the communication of this channel there will be a great utilization predominantly by the Grace of the higher energies, of the Mother Gaia's Light, Love, and radiation, and from the wholeness of the universe that gives you this transmission of wisdom and Light through a guided channel.

Through this channel is precisely where we connect and receive a great and powerful emission of Light. Through this Light there is a powerful connection in which the channel receives the thoughts and words in a specific manner. The patterns of thought come from energy blocks that are used to construct into sentences. From there they spontaneously and immediately backfire back into your consciousness to give you the words at the speed of Light and all thought. The correct words and sentences to write come naturally and automatically. So dear children, let us remind you that there are no excuses for telling us that you are not energy workers.

You *are* lightworkers, and you can identify and communicate with energetic fields of consciousness on a very deep level of being. It comes not from the mind, it comes from the wholeness of You that knows and actively practices quantum physics. The correct words and sentences come at an unconscious level, for it is too fast for the mind to process. When they come through, you speak them in your mind with a heartiness that cannot even be portrayed by an actor. This is authentic relationship, and authentic Love and connection. This is what is missing from your lives and relationships that you live every day in your fast paced and unconscious mode.

You are not actively seeking out true authenticity. You've forgotten who you are, and for that, you settle for your lower self, and you also settle for the lower selves of others as well. It is also pure and holy, but let us remind you, child, stay where you're at, for it is good and pure. It is holy and beautiful. To be on the high-flying disk is always more pleasurable. You will find that whenever you sit in this channel for long periods of time, or you read the words often, there will be great shifts that take place. The channel will continue to open, to grow, and to emote more and more Light to your soul, and to the universe.

We greet you with a new face of yourself, and a new face of your reality. This comes and goes depending on where you are in your existence. When you seek this dimensional realm, it is here for you in whatever way we can be with you in it. Sometimes it varies, but that is depending on where you're at. That is to say, what you experience varies, but the root of Source never varies; God doesn't change, you do. That is what it is all about. You come and go from the Light…sometimes you get stuck in a place of darkness where silence is not prominent, but in the end, it is no matter. It is not part of your overall purpose, it cannot be understood in your mind, but when connecting the dots in the bigger bird's-eye view, all is well. All is perfect and Divine.

The ascended masters know this firsthand, for they have been through ages of turbulence and destruction, crying out for help before finally coming to enlightenment and peace. We are now in a place of pure, holy Love, and that gives the channel a new consciousness, a new life. It comes from your own growth and openness, but it also comes from the universal shift that aids you so dramatically. It germinates and rises and falls with your own seeking, and suddenly it comes to a halt when you find that there is really no answer to life.

There is no more seeking for you to do, for all that you look for, all that disturbs and bothers you, is within yourself—not outside of you. When you look within, you find the answers. You don't even need to meditate to see it. You don't even need to concentrate in a specific way to feel it and notice it. When you seek it and want it most powerfully, the universe comes to meet you, to give you what you're looking for, and then the inspiration will arise…in whatever way is best for you. But you must remember what the goal is: and that is your own personal strength never for others. When you no longer put up with the happiness of others over yourself, essentially your greatness emerges on its own, without any effort on your part.

It is like planting a new tree—when you buy the seeds at the store, you must plant the tree in the right conditions and in the right area with healthy soil. Those are the essential groundwork and factors in letting the universe respond. Next you let it sit, for there is nothing left for you to do but wait, and it takes time always. There is no determined date, no, but it will take time to let the seed sprout and eventually grow up. When there are many new plants together, the energy is very new, very authentic and immature, but with a passion and life in the air that is so very powerful. This is the age you emerge in, and it matures and grows with a new life that was not present before.

With this immaturity, there is a greater sense of knowing and reliance on God, and that is precisely the initial plan, the initial passion that arises out of the curiosity and mere knowledge in the heart and soul of the Akash of the wholeness. That is what gives you the need to seek something more than what you see with your three-dimensional mind. There is still a very essential part of you where that seed remains, and it remembers its birth and its trueness before maturing. And that is your Akash, for it is like the seed of the tree before growing up. As it grows and matures, it slowly dies away from the old notions and lifestyle it was used to as a baby tree. It grows in new beautiful ways!

Now that you see the distinction between the many cycles of life, you can begin to use these parallels as guides to greater awareness of yourself. That helps you keep your passion in the heart of staying young at all ages. That gives you the innocent heart to stay like the newborn seed. Beautiful as it is to grow older and to regain a new sense of energy, it is also essential to maintain a certain amount of your youth, and that is our main point.

So we see you will integrate these ideas now. For today we have given much that will be used in the near future, all of which must be reread to be understood completely, but for now we let the mind rest, for it tries to understand when it should just listen. It is okay, just let it be, for it can also see the truth of the matter, despite its ignorance to pay attention to the heart sometimes. Now we will let the rest of the night sink into the new channels that have just been opened to new heights. It has been a great pleasure, and a great honor to be in communion with Source with a great light being who is so connected so in touch with the infinite Source of God.

It has also been a great, great challenge for you to come into this new energy, this new place of stillness. The struggle will soon (if not already) catch up with you and be replaced by a Light-filled walk through the Earth experience this time around. So we reconnect on a daily basis, for it will be much easier to shift in that sense. Now we part, greeting your innermost soul with respect from our side of the veil. And so it is in the greatest of the great God and Holy Spirit, a great communication once again. And we part.

Chapter 22

God Recognition and Living the Essence of Truth

And now we return with great excitement for this coming age and time, for commitment is now here, and we see great transformation not only as a personal adjustment, but also within the greater whole of your family and your ancestors. To be even more specific, we show you the ways that we see this greater transformation from within. Through the ages of this great transition there have been many struggles, the majority of which dealing with identity. We speak not only of identity of the self, but also of the identity you hold in regards to the world you live in.

This great time has shown you, dear ones, that the universe you reside in is a mere optical illusion, for many of you believe and identify with this illusion of self. There is a misconception, dear ones, for there is a time and place for everything, and therefore "mistakes" is not a valid term. All is well, and there is a great spirit that resides in each and every one of you, and that is well known by many. However, coming into recognition with this self-identity—one that is higher than your knowing—is part of a great ascension.

From within flows an outermost sense, a courage that is from beyond the veil. You know it too, for experience has showed you this. Your great and authentic nature has poured into your life in a way that can affect those around you. We speak from this viewpoint in order for you to see the parallel between the *greater you* and the *dimensional you* that you call your current reality. Stepping beyond the veil, we see many possibilities, all of which are held equal and true, and all of which hold possibilities in our greatest good, as well as yours. However, the pathways that you choose to take is another gift, another technique that has been predetermined.

In this lifetime your mission is to co-create for the better and greater purpose of peace on Earth. It is easy to say, for we see the universe in a much greater and clearer sense than many of you, but in reality, you truly see it this way too, you just don't know it yet. You don't see yourself in the clarity that we see you. From this angle or perspective, we can tell you with great honor that you are truly a being from God with a greater purpose, and for a greater mission to fulfill on this karma planet. The name that you often use to describe this place is often diluted with stereotypes and preconceived notions. As we use this term *karma* we tell you that in trueness, the Earth plane is not a place to redeem yourself or to make up for something you have lost in the past.

In reality, your mission on Earth is to find who you are in a greater way, and to experience the beauty and Love that it has to offer you. Karma, as we perceive the term, is to initiate a greater sense of alignment within yourself, to initiate a great and superior awakening than last time around. Karma, as we use it, is not to define that you are in debt in any way, it is to define progress and co-creative change. So you see, our terms differ, and we get used to your terms along the way, clarifying when they do not match up correctly.

This is another reason to study the words from the heart, for if you get caught up in the words, dear ones, you will miss the point completely. This is all about you, and we want you to see yourself as clearly as we see you! You knew it all when you came, and you agreed to come, in fact. You came in with great respect and thanks, for you knew that it takes a great being to have the authenticity and strength to move forward into a new Earth. You were expecting great challenges and blockages to emerge for you. You knew down to every last detail, but it hasn't stopped you, and it won't ever stop you in the future.

Giving up is not a failure, and leaving is not a failure—it is a pathway that you can choose, and for whatever reason you choose it, we see it valid. There is no shame, and there is nothing to be embarrassed about. We tell you that this is relevant for any subject matter, because in whatever pathway you choose, your innate is supporting you from behind the veil. It is similar to a puppet show, you see, for this metaphor is so perfect for this analogy. When we see you, and how we experience you, is in Oneness with all creation—with God.

When the show called life goes on, there is a curtain that blocks the hand, or the Creator, from the innate object that dances in front of it. It is completely unaware, and not in control of the movements it produces in the body. You are the puppet. We say this with Love, for it is not a manipulative relationship, it is one of great respect, kindness, and super power. You see, it is a bond that you created respectively. We care for you with the utmost respect and Love and kindness. You can choose to perceive it as a manipulative relationship, or you can see it like a parent-and-child relationship.

As a young child, you depend on your elders or your parents to care for you and fill your every need. We are those caretakers, and we have *unconditional* Love for you…we really do. And now we tell you what you want to hear from this channeling, for in this time that we speak there is a stronger connection than you are aware of. We stand behind the veil and we move the hands, connect the brain tissues and the connectivity channels that use the brain though their fullest potential. Parts of the brain that are utilized are not prepared to be utilized on your own, but they are there with our assistance! Yes, indeed.

In the trueness of who you are, there are so many potentials that are not utilized to their fullest potential. And you know it, for you practice the thought patterns, but you don't seek to find it within the self, and that is the first problem. In fact, answers lie within, and there you find the same Oneness, the same kind of interdimensional bond that is greater in strength and Love than anything that the outer world can teach or try to transfer to you. You see it now, and that is important to truly hear now. It has not always been valid to share, but now it is, for the times are proving it necessary to share the human potential.

Receiving these blocks of thought at rapid speeds is only the beginning, for the potentials on a much higher level will propel you further into whatever possibilities are conjured up. For the record, they are never a mistake. No pathways chosen with a passion and trueness in the heart can be a mistake. Rather, it can be seen as just another rendezvous that has propelled you further into the greater trueness and wholeness that is You. And so we say with gratitude to you beings who are honest enough to accept the Truth of You, we thank you for your brutal honesty. To respect yourself enough to see who you are without the veils takes a true and courageous warrior. To see it in order to accept and see the world in a new fashion takes a true and courageous warrior.

It takes a warrior, because to see not only with acceptance, but with a great sense of mission in yourself, and to have a clarity to bring it to others and to the world means you must have unconditional Love for oneself first. It is a mission that changes the future of DNA in the human being, truly, and it happens now. It has already begun! It is indeed a slow process in terms of the amount of human beings on the Earth plane, but we move fast across vast places, and we spread this message amongst many. And they hear it, as do you. They are on this Earth, as are you, for the same mission. For this great responsibility to hold true, to be held with respect and honesty, it is essential to hold, in the highest regard, all that is authentic and true as your only guide.

It is important to not reflect upon the rights you feel controlled by and tied to by others—especially of those who feel the need to control others. That is the mind…that is the outer world, and that is not the authentic human nature that co-creates. In the bigger scheme of life, you are the creator, and we are the greater picture in which you seek to find yourself. Indeed, it is that way, but we say, make the connection to see yourself as you see us, for it is truly that way, and you do not see it. Part two of this assignment is to greet yourself in this way, not just understand it.

They are very different, and in respect to yourself, with this you can open the doors of forgiveness and kindness to yourself and to others in a new way. It is an openness that will lead you on your journey of giving without needing to receive. That is, in a material way, for we must tell you this in a very specific manner. We do not mean to not receive at all. In fact, that is contradictory, for we wish that you are open enough, at all times, to receive all that the universe has to offer to you.

Receiving is very important…for you to understand in every cell of your body that you must be able to receive if you want to give. It is the yin to the yang, and it is necessary. You are often taught that receiving is something that is useless and greedy, but in fact, we see it oppositely. When the mind and heart are closed off, nothing can flow in! That is not your fault, it is simply part of a bigger journey, one that is coming on its own time and that must be honored and respected. Just let it be when that emerges in you, or in others that you come across in your life.

This time of great peace also comes with its challenges, relationships being a big one to reflect on. We see that this conflict arising is from an increased amount of internal conflict that projects outwards in an attempt to conclude or decrease the amount of stress that occurs in your body. Some that struggle with this illness in the body have been struggling for many, many ages beyond their awareness. The hurts and struggles come through in unexplainable ways, and most often in sickness because it gets your attention very quickly.

We see you all with great Love and great honor, for there is no shame, wherever you are at. And from your perspective, you don't see an innocence in each and every being on the Earth plane. You see only good and bad, but you see, dear children, we have no judgments for you. We see you as the pure essence that you are. That is simply a process, one that is not to be realized yet, and that is okay.

The human being who wishes to bring about evil in others is fighting with ages and ages of emotional hurts, struggles, and painful deaths. This may be both in themselves, and in their closest family and friends. It is a great journey to be with you now and change this thinking with these words.

It is a blessing to have your thought processes change through a simple realization that we give through this channeling. It is simply why we have made such communication possible. It is exactly true that In God We Trust—that is what is stated on your currency, indeed! That is the greatest basis of the life purpose, not only for the Earthly beings, but for the universe as a whole. *In God We Trust* means, in great simplicity, "I believe in myself, and in the Oneness of All That Is. I am God, and in God is me." That is a realization that can bring you into such a blissful state of wonder and in peace.

Great, great understanding and learning come from within, and the simple, yet very powerful, act of channeling a message in this fashion beyond thought, and therefore, it takes time to cultivate. It is a state that is very much subliminal; that is, they are not thoughts of your own, but rather they are monitored by the self, so they are filtered often. When in enough of a relaxed state, often the mind will jump to a new place and time where an emptiness lets you sink into peace while the letters flow, one by one, into the greater sense of You. That is the simple explanation for the messages behind the human being, that you see in physical form, making the messages come through.

In reality, there is no forceful action that comes from the human being; it is an act of letting go, of receiving without the need to interfere. It is a letting go that only comes from an understanding from within that all is well, then, and only then, can there be a letting go into the hands of a graceful and loving force that takes them in a benevolent and careful way. Some call it God. In its truest form, yes, it may be called God, but it may be called anything you like, as well! This is precisely why you create religions, to access the creative mind that knows its personal God well.

But indeed, you hit a bump in the road when you decided that everyone else sees that way, as well. You became too literal in the mind, following scriptures and the written words. You are studying them, making significant changes to them even, and calling it the one and only God. When you stop delivering these messages that you are separate to others, then you will be seeing and identifying with the wholeness and Oneness of You. We come to a new understanding even now, with your greater self that identifies with the words spoken. They ring true, and they even call out to you and catch your attention with the energy they hold to co-create with you.

Whatever you decide to call the wholeness, there is a Oneness that binds us all together. There is a great friendship and great understanding with you, one that all can relate to in their own way. What a gift it is to have a personal God—one that can be your own, and one that feels no pressure to be the God of another. How often you come to judgment of another without letting them be themselves. There comes your ego again, showing up in the false identity of the self. If you let go of the notion that you must follow the rules, you'll free your mind in ways that you cannot imagine.

That does not mean break rules in ways that are harmful to yourself and to others. It means do not get blocked into stereotypes or labels that attempt to judge or change who you are. You *know* who you are. That must ring true, for if you read the words spoken here, they do. For those who do not read the words, they still ring true. Whether all beings choose to see the truth of the matter or not, their higher spirit, their God, their true nature sees the truth of the matter without needing any nudge or convincing. You see, wherever you are is just perfect, so unique, and so beautiful. Let it be still with you, and let your inner guide come through when it's necessary and perfect timing.

With the intent to be in a higher place, in a greater understanding of yourself and of the universe, well then, you automatically unlock the doors to Oneness. You will begin to see a new awareness within, one that allows the mind to gradually step back and see a bigger picture that humanity cannot always identify with. You will see the mind contradict, and that is what we tell you to expect at first. To know this ahead of time is helpful in unlocking that invisible door in less time.

The first guy may not have known that, but what a brave soul they were to try it out and be the guinea pig for the rest of you. That is how it goes. So they signed up for that mission, just as you signed up for your individual mission to be here now. So we say to you, do not pity the human being that struggles, and do not pity yourself. Though it may be hard in times of struggle, you remind yourself of your greatness, of your truest strength that brought you here, and of the courage that keeps you alive every day, no matter what blockages and great walls come up right in your face. The great struggles mean nothing in the end, for how you endure and persevere in the big picture is of far greater importance and value.

With the utmost respect, we remind you that even in times of struggle, you need not even try to control the situation, for it is really not in your control. Indeed, we introduce a new concept, one of vulnerability. It comes when you find yourself out of options. In times of struggle you need to reach out just a little bit further to receive new guidance. What if we told you that this level of vulnerability is going to be the new normal? We see that in the coming years; very soon, in fact, there will be a new focus on co-creating in a way that is greatly connected with this teaching of letting go of self-control and being vulnerable.

You have fought for so long to maintain control and to find your own way out of problems. But now you see, in these heightened times of struggles, you can't, and you won't—you will never survive that way. So from now on, you are finding new pathways, and new opportunities to come together and co-create in a harmonious, beautiful, and joyous manner. You see it—the angels are reappearing on Earth, and they greet you with an energy that is vaguely familiar to you. You'll find them from time to time, so keep your eyes open. But not too open, for then you'll miss the obvious.

There is so much Love for you here, and we are ever grateful to be in your Presence and to co-create in this way. It is not only beneficial for you personally, but also to the co-creation of the wholeness of the entire universe! We are grateful for a connection with the human being who is coming back to Earth once again after many thousands of battles on this place, only to come through to a new era which is finally, finally, finally the awakening point. And what a relief it is for you, for who would want to miss it now. That is why you came, to participate in the fun! You must enjoy it to your fullest potential.

Growth is coming, and growth is already here, in fact, so bask in it! We would now enjoy to part in these great timings, and it is a good time to close the channel with Love and Light. From his plane we send great Love and a heightened energy for transformation. We close with the following statement: and with God we trust, you must trust God. In the end, you are partners in crime with God. We say that not literally, but in a form that you often say. We mean, truly, that we are co-creators of the same reality, and you must treat yourself in the same respect that you treat us. And so it is.

Chapter 23

Tapping into Your Internal Guidance System

Support here comes from your Source, from your unconditional Love and joy that lies within. Trust that own guidance you have, dear ones, for it is essential in this growing age, and this time where many of you become similar to a small child lost in a grocery store. You are confused and scared for your life, often times running around in circles and struggling to find your way out. That is what you go through in this new age—though it is a blessing, for it brings you to the Truth.

That is not to say that you have nothing in life to accomplish, or no purpose. It, in truth, means that with this new age called the Aquarian age, there is a new Light and power that resides in each and every one of you in the very epicenter of your beingness. It is transcended from the great place which you call heaven...what we call the interdimensional unseen realms. They are very much part of your reality, but you see them not, for you underutilize your innate tools.

You seek not within yourself—you seek outwardly to churches, religions, and masters or gurus who supposedly show the way to your truest nature. Yes, they are beautiful beings graced by God, but indeed, so are YOU. You see it not, because you see a small and inferior being when you compare yourself to others. We tell you this, dear one, for those words ring true with many of you. You cannot find the truth within yourself, or within the circumstances in which you live in every day. You ask yourself, "How is this me? What is the real me, and how can I live with this mission when my real life does not match up?" Oh yes, a good topic, and also valid for most of you.

We speak from this realm with great honor and joy, and we must say this as we open up this question. It is beyond your imagination to see beyond what you can imagine. Oh, that is a great one, let us restate it in better terms so you can feel the resonance. You see not the truest potential and power of your own co-creative abilities. They were born with you, with each of you who walk the planet Earth at this time. You feel you aren't here for a purpose or you were a mistake or accident? Oh dear one, you are so funny sometimes, for you cannot see the big picture as we do. You cannot see what great expansiveness and pure unconditional Love and consciousness you truly are.

If you feel you are a mistake, you are in the dark, and not greeting your authenticity. If you read the words spoken here, you have the drive and intuitive nature to move out of darkness and find joy in your own self. That is the greatest gift we can teach you, for your Divinity and the Divinity of all that is lies within you, just as much as it does the great Buddha. What a powerful statement! Wow, you must think about that…ponder it until the greatness and authentic power of that statement hits you. Dear child, you are that, each and every one of you.

To be here on this Earth at this time means you are that, and there is no question in your Higher Self what you are here to do. Once you clear out that static that creates a barrier between your living reality and the real You, man, you will be living the high life! We use your terms wisely, for it is a new vocabulary that we have picked up humorously!

In times of struggle you find yourself unaware and incapable to focus your patterns of thought in proactive ways, and as a result you find yourself in a frazzle to come back into balance. This is the human way—a powerful, yet negatively based practice that seems to be habitual. We speak not these words to have you feel worse about your actions, but rather to enlighten you on your so called "mistakes" so that you have fully and co-creatively come into balance in the fullness of who you authentically are. We like to think of you as a small puppy, one that is just starting to learn his or her new role in this new body.

As a newborn there is a resting period; a period of integration that must happen in order to come into this new place with strength. Once you've learned the ropes and found what works and doesn't work for you, well, you start to have fun! You climb around, jump up and down in new ways that weren't previously possible for you. You may have found that when taking these new fun steps you often fall down, but you always shake it off fast enough. You see, a young puppy is quite resilient and tough to get taken down. They may have accidents in the house and often run into objects, chew up household items, or create other troubles, but they find their way through those mishaps! You see, you are like a young puppy, but on the Earth plane.

This is a process to Love and bask in, for it is beyond your vocabulary for us to express to you at this time, but we wish to emphasize your greatness in as many ways as we can possibly deliver. Though these words you read on the paper, you may experience them in more ways than one. As you read the words, you are receiving this new philosophy, or new enlightenment, at the present moment. That is to say, when you experience these words as you read them, we are with you, speaking them in the present moment. There is no time, no location, and no order in which we reside.

We are nonphysical, but very existent beings, which are comprised of the fullness and illuminated beingness of the entire universe—galaxies, planets, supernova, and all the fluff in between. We are All That Is, and beyond. Through a great illumination of the mind, and through these words, you may find yourself in the Presence all around you in your own way. We speak through the computer for some, others through the mouth, vocally, and for many and most, we come through as feelings. Some as spontaneous thoughts, and others as positive and co-creative actions that lead you to your greater good.

We hear you, dear child, and we feel you right alongside us, for we work hand in hand. Sometimes when you feel alone you cannot imagine that you have a partner-in-crime—you can't even imagine the hopeful resolution of there existing a greater place, one with such beautiful emptiness and infinite peace that is beyond the reality that you call Earth. Oh dear being, we say to you, see yourself in the trueness of who you really are—who you REALLY are—and you'll find so much knowledge. You'll find so much greatness, so much openness, and so much growth and wisdom in your soul that it will be impossible to doubt or not feel completely at peace, in Oneness with the Mother Gaia and All That Is.

You have been brought to this loving place to experience yourself in a new fashion—one that is brining your transformation, and continues to teach you new lessons. You are bringing about a greater purpose by living on Earth and playing the game. We know it can be difficult, and that is why you need support, Love, and friendship. But please, dear souls, don't take it too seriously, and definitely do not take it personally when you fall down.

The new puppy, small and fluffy, pops back up and runs back into the same wall it just hit. "Oh," he says, "there's that wall again, I didn't think I could do that. Let's try something else, cause that hurt!" He then turns around and runs into more stuff in the next room over. What is his conclusion? He says to himself, "Looks like I'm in the wrong place, because I can't get anything right!" That is similar to you, human being. You give up on yourself, and beat yourself up for not getting it right when you're not even mature enough to be able to understand it all! You can't expect so much from yourself when you have not had the experience to learn the lessons.

We tell this human being who is still the small little puppy, let yourself fall down! Instead of telling yourself how stupid and uneducated you are, let yourself laugh at your mistakes and try to see a little bit more in advance where those walls and obstacles are so you can avoid them. Sometimes you won't see them coming because you're looking the other direction, and you'll hit it hard. Is it your fault? Maybe. Should you keep thinking and reflecting upon it after the experience? No, definitely not. It is a waste of your energy! Our policy is experience and release—that is all! Make that a conscious effort so that you can relax in the present moment.

Sometimes you get confused in a way that is a distraction from the present moment, but we tell you, it is your natural state to be in the present moment always. To this day it is something that is very important for human beings to recognize in themselves. It is essential, for you often speak from a direction that indicates that you are unwilling or unavailable to live in your highest good. Dear ones, move out of your judgment, and come back to the real you. If you don't know what that is, it is the one that feels authentic, easy, and at peace.

You ask now, so what is that for me? Where is it, and how do I find it? We say to that, it is not hard to find, and you look so hard for it. You openly discuss what you don't have and the gaping holes in your life, but you seek not to discuss the beautiful and golden bits that you have experienced and been offered to experience by the greater

You. So we say, if you cannot find what makes you truly happy, stop digging, because that will be unproductive.

Instead of focusing on what you feel you do not have and what is causing you to be inauthentic, focus on the qualities of your being that separate you from others. It may take some practice and add some time to dedicate to yourself, to be generous and really grateful for your existence, and just to show yourself how Divine you are. It may take some acquainting, for you've been separate for so long. You'll soon find what that passion is for you, and the pathways will illuminate. When you follow that greater good, the authentic, lighted pathways will show the way and you will know it so definitely in your heart. From there on out there is nothing for the universe to do but conspire and co-create alongside you.

Your job is not to plan your life—it is to *follow* your life. You don't give us credit for much of what goes on behind the curtains, we must say! The show continues to go on, and we are like the backstage managers that are producing everything for you and the crowd, the rest of the universe. A great production it is, and of such high importance, for without the backstage managers there cannot be a show! If this movie came out and no credits were rolled, can you imagine the confusion and embarrassment? We are saying not to worship and praise as you are often taught; we are saying in reality, *experience* that behind-the-scenes action, and that will take you further into your great existence. That is who you authentically are.

If you make friends with, and give credit and acknowledgment to, the backstage managers, they will be very grateful and even more willing to participate and help create the next show. It is similar to your life experience. When you co-create with us behind the veil, or "curtain" as we used in the above metaphor, you are creating more power, more resilience, more gratitude, and a much more supported lifestyle. You will feel that you are not alone creating your production; you will feel more relaxed and less stressed out over the little details because you know that the managers are taking care of it all. This is the process of your existence, truly, and we welcome you to see and experience it as we do.

You may find that it feels very strange, almost like you are retraining yourself, and that is exactly what it is. Over many years you have found that there is a lifestyle and way of being that is socially accepted in every country around the world. Some, more than others, widely accept and speak about the notion of co-creating your own realities, and not following the set-up notions and groundwork that are supposed to be the "right" and "successful" ways of living. Truly, it is one mission, one experience that we are all on. With this great mission, each of you with one that is different and unique, we guide you and ask you to really step back and see the bigger picture.

Is it worth fighting for this socially accepted "normal," or is it really encouraging you to push and fight away from the greater self? When we see you, we see you with great eyes, and we are in wonder of your strength and power in the universe. We are in wonder of the strength you have within yourself to be able to focus such intent into form. To have power and eagerness to jump into any venture, no matter where it takes you, is a beautiful trait. That is every human being who walks the Earth, and we are in such awe of you.

We say, focus that intent in a way that supports what you want to accomplish in this lifetime. We see that there are struggles with material and social needs, which get in the way of your logic in the heart, but truly, see the big picture. Stop evaluating from the mind and go into the heart. If there is a drastic change of events that needs to come about, so be it. Will you suffer? Maybe. Will you find peace? Yes. Will you make a drastic lifestyle change that exceeds your expectations? Will it greatly serve your greater mission and life purpose to co-create in this way that is individual and specific to each purpose? Yes, indeed!

If you follow your heart and step into co-creating with your Source, with your inner God, you will find a great, a powerful knowledge that is a guidance system, and it *will* show you, with clarity, what must be your next step. Trust the universe, and the universe will trust you. You sometimes say, treat others as you wish to be treated. We modify this verse to say, treat God as you would like to be treated as God, and with that comes a cooperative manifestation and wonder which will surprise you so much that you will have no choice but to believe that you are God. It sounds conceited, you say, for I cannot be God! God helps me when I need it, and when I fail to live correctly. I am apart from God. God is only there when I need help. That is what the human being sees sometimes. We say, no, you seek God when you need it desperately, but if you were to focus on greeting God in every moment of every day, as a true form of yourself, then you would see a new face of God.

You will see a new face of God that is more personal, less subjective, and truly, one that is easily accessible inside yourself. Prayer and devotion through rituals are a path, or technique, that's given to the human being to help them feel closer and guide them on their way, but it is not necessary. It is not even THE way. It is *one* way, and again, it is with the individual guidance system where you will find the necessary practice or creative stillness which brings you into union with your Higher Self—your God, your angels, your master, and the universal Love which is you.

Oh children, we are so in Love with you, and we wish you all felt it in this way. It is such a gift, a gift that is yours for the taking once you bring it into your heart and sit still with it. We wish to let you sit in stillness with this now, for it has been an opening and very profound channeling tonight, and we thank you, dear ones, for having an open heart to let the words pour in and be in great union with the wholeness with rings true with You. And we now let you rest and hold yourself in this great vibration which is so, so beautiful. And so it is.

Chapter 24

God Is...

Oh we thank you, dear ones, for gathering here now...what a great gift it is to greet you with such Grace, such harmony, and such a trueness in the heart. It grows and prospers every moment of your existence. We Love you unconditionally...in a manner that you cannot understand, but can experience. You see, when we gather in this way, we ignite our consciousness to bring about the seed of growth as a wholeness, as a Oneness of the Divine aspect that is you—and that is the universe. Oh, great souls you are, gathering together and awakening into your authenticity and being Divinely guided by that Source within. It is a great responsibility to hold that trueness to yourself, and to bond so greatly with it that you are not even slightly tempted to waiver.

We are Graced in your Presence, dear ones, and we speak to you each individually as you read these words, for they hold true to each one of you, and they are growing in your heart each time you reflect upon them. When you hear the words they sink into your innermost depths where your soul resides, where the memory of your greater and Higher Self resides. We tell you this now for it is important to recognize, if nothing else, the greater You that is interdimensional, ongoing, never dying, loving, and pure Light of the universal Love. You see, with every breath you take in the Now, you are always this infinite Source—always abundant, always the same. And that is God— never wavering and never changing.

The human being changes, and that is why it appears that God changes, for your aspects of God may change, and you may grow and develop your experience of life and God in a way that lets you fully experience what life has to offer you. But indeed, you certainly do not understand the works of the universe, and cannot attempt to with the mind. Dear ones, when you look inside, in that deepest space, which we call the Akash or Akashic records, there is a knowledge, and an infinite Source which remembers you. Your mind won't see it, for it cannot pick up on the multi-cellular structure and interdimensional ways that your Akash can distinguish.

You see, it is designed that way, for it has an element of protection for you—it keeps the heart safe and allows for you to start seemingly anew each time you come back to reflect upon your existence. You choose it, and each time you experience it in a new way, learning new lessons and completing new aspects of your Divinity. When we say completing, we mean that you round out your capabilities to live your innate self to a fullness and capacity that is beautiful, whole, and inescapable.

You may find that you are apart from it for some time, lost and alone, with no direction in your life. That is the process for many of you walking the Earth plane...but not for long. You will all come across your Divinity at one time or another, and it may take you by surprise. You may not welcome it, and you may push it away when you're not ready to see the Truth with clear eyes. Dear ones, if you read the words, you're past that, and you've come to a knowing and a wanting to feel and experience life and the joys of life. And if that is appealing enough, try the idea of giving that to others.

Spread this joy and Love, and what a great, great calling this is for many of you. You may find that it feels like a mission, like a Divine purpose, and you may be right. This is another way of your innate coming up and waving their hands in front of your face saying, "See! See! Look at you! Look closely and see who you are! How beautiful, how giving, how generous, how Divinely inspired!" And you may come to find that you surprise yourself at how generous you have become, for your soul is so flowered that you cannot imagine a life without giving and receiving from the Divine.

You cannot imagine not being in the communion with the Source—and that is what allows you to be so in Love with humanity. Oh, how beautiful it is. How marvelous it is to have this experience...and we know you so well, dear one, and we Love you unconditionally. It is your Divine purpose to seek out your mission, your passion, and to find what makes your heart sing with joy. We know you have hang-ups that prevent you from seeing the bigger picture. Oh how nice it would be to play more, to quit your job, to write a book, to be involved in more artistic activities, and to sing with joy doing these yummy things every day of your life. Oh child, you see beyond the obvious. You're so trained to look at the details, to solve, to conquer, and to use the mind to get through life. It is the opposite, for it is the reason why children often show you the way more often than your spouse or boss can point you in the right direction.

If you want real feedback, real Divine guidance, go to the small innocent child who knows nothing but unconditional Love. They are so beautiful, so Divine, and so prosperous in the heart and soul. They see the big picture. Some of you have trained yourself to see it also, though you may be older. The old soul comes to it easier than the younger ones, for they've been around to witness and experience what life has to offer. They've made mistakes, they've conquered their minds, and found what may be more important—the logic of the heart. As contradictory as that may feel for many of you, the heart is so much more intelligent than the mind.

In times of struggle, it shows up even more because you tend to seek out the most guidance when you are weak. You find your way out through the heart. At a certain point the mind fails to understand and evaluate, it runs out of plans. Once you've been through plan A, B, C, and D, and still you cannot find your way through this tough problem, then what do you do? You say, I'm going to follow my intuition, and maybe I'll pray to God. How foreign it feels to you when you are so used to depending on the mind 90 percent of the time. And we say to you, dear beautiful being, if only you were able to focus in this way, with this intent to use your tools all the time, and not just when you have run out of options and you feel alone and helpless.

We tell you that there is a Divine guidance system that is here to help you run your body, mind, and spirit in a more efficient and joyous manner, and with it you'll feel so loved. You will feel so at home and peaceful. Dear ones, we are here for you all individually, and we are so blessed to be in your Presence. You see, many of you see us in a misguided light, for we are not separate from you or floating in the sky with wings. That is a representation, a symbol just for you. The beauty of the picture of us gives you a sense of Divinity, a greater power, a role that you often perceive as separation since this representation is apart from you. This is natural, and we say don't try to change what is already in place. Love it and appreciate it, for there is nothing wrong with it. But we also love for you to come into harmony with these principles so you can feel less boxed in and apart from us.

We are the infinite Source of God, of the universe, and of the Light. In other words, we are the wholeness, which is indeed part of you. We are in an existence of Oneness, of pure potentiality, and of great service to the universe. This includes all creatures, beings, and energies that assist the universe. The human being is in very close contact with this energy, and therefore we are accessible to you clearly and easily. It is a great gift to be able to exchange this gift of communication so that the words can be shared and spread around the Earth. And they are spread in each country, for there are beings who represent the true authenticity of Oneness, and they shine Light on the trueness of You and to everyone else who struggles in the dark.

Your soul knows it; it recognizes the words here even if the mind isn't able to step aside enough to let it in. There is a Divine recognition that will show up for you, and if you are courageous enough to let it shine in with pure potentiality, a knowingness will pour in that is beyond what the mind can evaluate and register. If you can do that, you are succeeding in carrying through with your co-creation and living your Divine purpose. It is a process, dear ones, so let go of the notion that you fail each time you struggle. Struggle is experience, and experience is learning. It is beautiful, even though you may perceive it differently.

We see your confusion, for you have come to planet Earth to evaluate a new mission, to fill in the grid, and to re-stimulate any holes in your existence that you feel need to be experienced again. Truest knowing comes from the life experience on Earth, for mother Gaia shows you that sometimes imbalance is the truest form of blessing. It is challenging, and that is why you are a brilliant warrior, dear light being. You came here at the most difficult, and yet, most sublime moment in all of history. It is the most remarkable shift in consciousness that has been seen in history, and it will continue to progress day by day.

You wake up to a human evolution, a new human way of interacting, living, and being that assists each and every one of you on your Divine and individual path. Some of you still fight hard, for you've been through ages and ages of grief and struggle, which are still deeply imprinted in your Akash. Don't blame yourself, and don't beat yourself up, for if you see the Truth in your action, you let a little thread loose for you. It is like walking a dog—when you really want to control your dog, you hold tight on the leash and let out as little rope out as possible, holding it taut. That is what you are doing to yourself! You are holding the leash so tightly that you cannot move, because you've taught yourself to be strict. That has been both a blessing and a curse. For it gives you empowerment to feel in control and in a structure, which can be very good for some; but in the long run, you are deceiving yourself.

If you put all the cards out and decided to see the Truth in yourself and not be afraid, what could you hide then? If you know the Truth in yourself, you can see the Truth in others and in your life events. Problems that once caused you so much pain, misery, confusion, and struggle are no longer issues. It no longer becomes a matter of wasting your energy, but rather a matter of following the answer that lies within. Once that becomes your mantra, you'll find that your life unfolds so automatically in such Divinity and Love that you cannot even suggest to us that you are not what we tell you you are. That is God, that is Divine, and that is pure unconditional Love.

We love to remind you of this because you forget it every day—in one ear and out the other, as you say! You hear it, but you dismiss it because your reality and image of yourself do not match up with the words we speak. That is where you're at, your present focus and consciousness bring you to experience life in that way, versus a being who lives an awakened life. What is the difference? The difference is that you could be able to see the Truth in yourself, and have the deep courage and strength to feel and experience whatever blockages need to be blasted open. It takes courage, dear one, and that's why you resist, because it causes pain.

You think it may be easier to live in false identity instead of even suggesting a new way to live your energy system. This is to say, you would rather be in denial of yourself than face yourself head on. But you see, though struggles come about, you have such Divine Love and connection with your Source, with your God, and with yourself, and you know all parts of that Oneness which is God. God is not singular, God is not a He or She, and God is not a specific person or being. God is All That Is, and the greatness and wholeness of the universe and beyond.

God is you, is All, is unconditional Love and Light, is potential, is energy, is beingness, is thought and wisdom, is ages of incarnations of beings, is the words of the great masters, is the animals and the flowers and plants, is the ocean, and is the rolling hillsides. God is the blue sky and the white puffy clouds, the singing bird, the paints on a canvas, the sweet music flowing through the air, a small rock amongst many big rocks, the small fragile hummingbird, fire, and Earth. Child, you see, God is great, and God is many. God is not singular. If you continue to put labels on yourself and your universe, which your mind cannot recognize or understand, then you are pushing yourself further into denial of who you truly are.

When you decide to consciously come into Divine harmony and knowing of who you are, you roll the dice, you get the ball rolling, and the game begins to unfold automatically. Without taking that first step, Love and heaven cannot pour through. It is simple, and it is a God-given rights that you all hold true in an individual way. And it is up to you to take the first step into guiding yourself where you want to go. It takes nothing more than following your heart. From there, your Divine guidance takes over, bringing you harmony and unfolding the perfect circumstances right in front of your eyes.

You will be pleasantly surprised, and in such Love with the Love of God, when you realize that the universe conspires *with* you to fill in every want and need that you come across and ask for. When you surrender to letting in that Divine healing and help, you open your heart up to so much more in your life! It can be so much more than the mundane ordinary gifts that you often ask for. Yes, we can provide those for you too, but so much more is available when you let heaven do the work. You know, dear one, it is up to you to take the first step, but after that, it is not up to you. You step back and don't fight the universe, for if you truly want Divine guidance, don't attempt to try and solve it on your own. You ask, you receive.

The receiving is hard for you, dear ones, for you're trying to transition from a life of proving for yourself and others to receiving as if you were a small child again—asking and receiving. You needed your basic needs met: clothing, shelter, and food. We are your mother and father, we are your providers, and you can depend on us, dear ones.

We never fail you, and we cannot leave your side as long as you make the commitment to keep us in your heart and in your everyday life.

You don't need to get down on your knees and pray. You think that these practices and rituals are for us, when it makes no difference to us. However, it certainly does for you! You seem to have definite preferences and ideas about how God sees you. Dear children, listen closely, for here is the Truth of the matter: God sees you as infinite Love, expansions and extensions of All That Is, and in a Oneness and wholeness that is labeled with the term called *God*. Those labels are manifested by you, dear human beings. We wish for you to understand that you really have no concept of God, and you must move out of the notion that you need to learn it from others or from books. This is about you finding God within—and that cannot be the same for everyone, dear children! We sometimes have to giggle at your practices, and we are not being offensive at that. Simply, wake up!

If you choose to see God as a big man up in the sky, one that grants you wishes or rights depending on how successful and innocent you are, how can you possibly see your own Divinity? If you do that, you are again placing great barriers between yourself and God. That is not what we want you to see, for we want you to see God as You. We would love for you to be in harmony, like family, with God. Come back to the unity with your fellow Light beings who surround you with Love and Light and greet you with their smiling faces. They touch you with their shining Light and illuminate your soul. It is so beautiful to converse in this way, for the trueness of your soul interacts and corresponds almost synergistically with the greatness of All That Is in the universe. The mind doesn't see it, but the heart does. There is great wisdom in the heart.

Once you rely on the heart more and more, it starts to override the mind, and the mind will then shrink away in fear, unable to dominate you anymore. This is the ultimate lesson we teach you. Focus on the life experience and co-creating your priorities by living in the heart and not the mind. We have already given you the steps to get from the mind to the heart, but we want to keep on the subject of God and how you must stop focusing on your human experiential interpretation of God. When you are not in the boxed-in human body, you are the innate…the wholeness, beingness, and Light.

You are also all-knowingness, which knows all that is spoken here and much more. That is why reading this now is so essential for the human being, because you can understand so completely what is being offered when the heart is open. If you wish to be in harmony with God, start treating yourself as God. This means not that you should strut around with an ego and call yourself superior. This means that you must start remembering your Divinity. This means you must greet yourself with Love and Light and see yourself as extensions of the universal Love.

When you feel so connected and in harmony with this notion, you can begin to feel comfort in spending time with other beings, whether they are alike in personality or polar opposites to you. They may be in complete disharmony with you, but you will be able to see the bigger picture in them, and in yourself as well. That may be a process of realization, for it takes time to be able to Love that which does not feel harmonious to you. But dear ones, trust that the words we speak are true and holy, for this realization does come with intent and practice of holding that positive vibration in your heart. It is something that cannot be realized with force, but rather an automatic process. Dear lightworker, your time has come to shine. This is why it is essential for you to really let yourself see the Truth and the authentic nature of yourself. This will let you relax a bit more in this life experience that has its ups and downs. It will help you feel clarity and very connected even when the mind sees loneliness and separateness.

It will greet you in a way that will not let your mind interfere, in a way that is a conscious effort to get your attention. And it works! We are so graced in your Presence, as we say often, but how true the words are. It is a great, great gift, and a relationship that is so precious. Dear ones, we are your greatest gift, your greatest relationship. This is not said with judgment or with emotion, but rather as a statement that is to enlighten you in another way that cultivating a bond with your Divine can help you to sort out everything else with ease. It becomes so easy to feel Grace and Love in life when you feel you have a partner-in-crime that is so personal and so easy to interact with.

We always listen, we are so giving, and we will never cease to listen to you and provide support and unconditional Love and Light to you. It is a pure and unmoving relationship. We are always the same, even as you evolve and grow. When you grow, we are able to come through in new ways, but we never change. The channeler may notice changes in personality, and in how the writing comes through, but this is in response to the changes within you personally, not the changing of God. You see, the angelic beings that we are known as are simply features of the Divine that are projected into form for the use and integrity of the human being who finds comfort in this projection.

We are so in Love with any concept or projection, as long as the human being continues to find it valid and helpful in their evolution. Once you reenter this plane where we reside, you will see us in this pure Light. You can only experience it to understand. You know it, but we cannot fully explain it, as you are human beings that see only a linear and very short-sighted view of what you are really comprised of. It is the nature of the mind once again, and it serves its purpose, but when you are rid of it, you will see much clearer. The Earth evolves and grows day by day, finding new pathways to open the consciousness.

The new babies help the planet exponentially, for they arrive with an even greater consciousness than the beings decades before them. It is quite profound what the young children have to share, for their wisdom and trueness of heart are the purity of Love and Light, which is the basis of our teaching here, dear ones. If you were to Love us like your baby, so pure and so unconditionally, you would see the way we Love you. So in that light, you can see us as your parents or your Divine caretakers. We are always there for you, and it is the purest form of Love we have for you. We have never-ending joy that we transfer to you.

You can transfer this joy to others because you are each extensions of each other. Fighting, disagreeing, and killing on any term of misunderstanding teaches you separation of the self and separation between You and God. Once again, you learn from your mistakes, which are truly hidden blessings. You learn that you have been deceiving yourself for so long, and now it is truly time to come back to what you know is real, what is Home, and what is undeniable, and that is that you are God. Your mantra today is: I am God, and God is me. I can Love myself now because I accept and am willing to see with clear eyes that I am what I am.

This is the power of affirmations, for your cellular structure will begin to regroup and revaluate what your mind turned into reality for you. Now your mind starts to re-wire because it sees that what it thought it knew has a flawed premise to it. There is nothing wrong with it, but it no longer serves a purpose. In the Aquarian age where you are waking up so rapidly, you are fitting into a new energy that is ready to take this new thinking style. This includes new learning capabilities, new laws, new practices and ideas on religion and God, and incorporating your own Divinity. It is understood that when you follow structure, you come away feeling pressured, feeling insecure, and unnatural in the circumstance. When you find yourself singing or painting, being creative, dancing about, speaking your Truth, and practicing things that come easily to you, you have found your healing abilities. You have found what your great gift is. When you follow it, evaluate your purpose and how that fits in with what the mind may try to tell you to do, and you'll really start to live authentically in a way that illuminates your mind, soul, and all the beings around you.

You are going to be so happy to feel the Light growing and illuminating those who are still in the dark. Don't worry about 'em, for they are just as taken care of, but if you can see the beauty in their process as you see the beauty in yours, you are well on your way. Do your good, do your part by strutting your Light and healing the Earth, and don't focus on the responsibilities of others. They will follow their innate senses, and that will lead them in their own way, which will bring essential Love energy and wisdom to the Earth planet.

Let us remind you, authenticity in your personal nature is what brings the balance of the yin and yang together. This is the answer to the purpose and meaning of life. With that you will find a real resonance with God and with the Source, which is You. You will see, yes indeed, I am God, and God is me. Those angels that I thought were in the sky are truly me, in my heart and soul. We thank you for being open with us, for receiving this infinite abundance and Love which we have to offer you, and with such Grace in your heart to receive and greet yourself and your true self in a new light. And so it is.

Chapter 25

Channeling, the Infinite Golden Toolbox, and the Human Experience

And we now return, dear ones, to this circle of Light so deeply engraved in your soul. By that we mean that in rituals, this type of communication has been a deep and ancient practice for you all. It is so natural for you, so, so beautiful to come back into this existence, and return to your soul and greet it in this way as you once did before. We ask for you to return to this place of silence as much as you can.

Dear ones, we have a very beautiful message today, one that is for great sharing. We will touch upon the subject of channeling, for it has come to our awareness that it must be better understood. We greet you from a place that has no time or space, yet it is full of existence, similar to your Earth plane. However, we cannot even call it a place, for it is simply an existence in the midst of deep energetic alignment. With this alignment comes a communication; a beingness that is mutual between all beings here, if that is what you like to think of us as. Universal energy is what we truly are, though even this concept frightens you a bit.

That is to say, you need concrete singularity in order to feel at peace with this idea. It is for this reason that it is hard for you to surrender and unconditionally Love a power that is not exactly as you see it in singular and linear three-dimensional form. That is not to say that you never accept it, just that you have a hard time moving in and out of this perspective of beingness when it is not your current reality. That being said, you have a great awareness for all that is beyond your existence…or you think you do, but it is not encompassed to its fullest degree in your lifetime. You may feel as if you concretely understand what needs to be known about your existence, or the heavens above, but in reality, you only have a sliver of a knowing, and not even that much. We tell you this not to make you feel inferior, unnoticed, or small, but to let you know that greatness does not fit inside the box. Manifestations do not occur from within the mind. There is so much more out there that encompasses and utilizes all of the tools of the universe, and of You. Some of you use powerful practices, such as channeling, or the use of crystals to communicate with the innate, but those are only two tools out of thousands and millions. They are not countable, but for your reference point we make it understandable.

It is like when you are building a house—you use many tools, not just one. You can't use a screwdriver to build your whole house—that would be impossible! There are many boards and bolts that need to be put together in different ways. It makes your house diverse, more stable, and much more reliable. The universe is this way too, for it utilizes the many tools that are available, and with that skill set, or in better terms, reliable sources, it can become stable and very accurate. That is to say, the human being dialing in, so to speak, can access a variety of energy sources, all of which are available to the human being. But with the tools that they use, matched up with their innate skill sets and the tools available by the universe, they can locate the energy that is the best fit for them. Simply stated, the energy is the same, but the process varies.

If you want to locate a different part of you in the bigger picture, go back to your innate in your Akash and locate what skill sets you are using. Are you using the screwdriver, the wrench, and the hammer, or just one? If you consistently use one, you will get consistent and invariable results pouring back at you. We use this metaphor for you so that you can dive deeper into your connection, or if the case is appropriate, your channeling. We wish for you to use many tools, for it is more reliable, more stable, and more FUN! With the right tools, you can feel confident that your results will come back just as accurately as the effort you put forth to build the metaphorical house.

You see, not only are there a variety of tools used, but there are a variety of materials used. For that reason, it is necessary to be efficient and flexible, using many different resources. With this knowledge and ability comes a practiced mind and experience. With experience and a practiced mind comes stability. With stability and confidence comes the ability to integrate information and to teach it, if that is your calling. It can be with anything—with a new project, with a subject in school, with a major life event that has taught a lesson, or with a practice that you feel the need to teach.

You must come through to the other side of your own journey before you have the capability and readiness to teach it to others. It is part of the journey of the human being, and it is part of the journey of the bigger You that is interdimensional and present across many planes of consciousness. You see, the small little sliver that you experience as reality is such a little, tiny projection of who you are. Most of the time you are in the dark through that experience, for you have lost your identity…your true identity, that is. You may think you know it, but that is the mind showing you a false projection and filling in for the absence of the misplaced. You see, that is the journey you are on, for you eventually come to find who you are through many ages of looking, experiencing, and growing. And that is no mistake, for it was designed collectively as one whole, and brilliantly planned.

So we say to you, dear children, don't feel that being in the dark is always a negative experience, for we see it quite oppositely. When we come through, you focus that aspect or memory, as we call it, to the plane that you are still living on in that higher realm of consciousness. It is very much alive and well! Just because you live a reality that seems to be the only one present doesn't mean you should live there fully and push aside the bigger part of You that has a higher understanding. That means don't try to jump between realities, but use your tools, dear child. Use them and don't forget you've got them in your shed. If you don't remember, you'll keep buying more at the store and wasting your money. And what is our response to that? We say, you do it every day. You've got the shiny new tools at the store that are so tempting, and the crummy old ones you already have you wish to forget. We say, they're not crummy, they're rustic!! We laugh at our humor indeed. So funny we can be, and some appreciate it more than others.

Of course, sometimes it feels easier to walk away and buy those new tools because they are shiny and so beautiful, but what you take away after you buy those tools is *my inventory is now getting larger and larger, and money is getting low.* Why not use what you've got stored up and clean them up if you're unhappy with it? Use your tools that you've got and take a look at your inventory if you're unhappy with what you see. What cleaning up do you have, and how can that be done with integrity in the heart? For we say, it cannot be done with fear, and that holds you back from taking that courageous step of looking it in the face. What is the worst that can happen, dear ones? So we say, if you wish to go buy the new tools, that is your choice, but at least see your inventory and take an honest look before running in the dark and wasting your time and money.

You see what we're getting at? Honesty; seeing the Truth of the matter and taking a step back to look at the big picture. What do you miss when you don't do this? Everything, because you run blind in the dark when you fail to slow down and see what you are doing. You act so silly, for the obvious steps in life become such a mystery when you fail to take an honest look at your inventory. This is so appropriate for you all, in your own ways. We direct you to take away from this what you will in your own way, and we give you permission to take that honest look, without judgment.

We ask you, what is the fear that comes up when you start to see what's going on? Are you running away from it because other options may be simpler and easier to access? Yes, many of you do it, but only the brave souls will look at it in the face. You think you are strong and powerful, but dear ones, your definition of strong is mutilated. For we say, the real warriors are the lightworkers that look in the face of fear, and go forward in it BECAUSE they are so willing to experience it, and bring upon the challenge so they can move through it. There is the great motivation to seek transformation.

If you decide risk is too high, look at the mind...take a look at the mind and see where your fear is coming from. The mind will raise its hand shyly, and you'll begin to see with clearer eyes where the importance lies. Decisions cannot come from the mind, or you will be always deceiving yourself, running in the dark, and unable to utilize your tools to their fullest extent. So what are you waiting for? If you read these words, you are willing to claim your greatness, to jump forward in to the life you are made to follow, to greet harmony, and to assume your true wisdom that you never knew you had!

Fear comes up, your past comes up, but they reside in the mind, and they can be conquered with the heart if you are just willing to LET GO. Dear ones, let us remind you who's in power here, and it's the universal Love and the Divine in you. That is said with great care and Love, for it is not intimidating, but we say it for you to realize you're playing the victim almost without realizing it and it holds you back from utilizing your tools. When you decide that it's not worth it to hold back any longer, you won't put up with whatever other people want to tell you is right for you personally, you will stop settling, and you will certainly stop agreeing to demands which are keeping you back from living your highest potential.

That may not be what you think it is, and your mind tells you what you're capable of and not capable of. "Well, you don't have that background...you can't do that...it's too late...you'll never make it." That's when you can very politely remark to the mind, "Yes, that is your reasoning. However, in my great experience, through many, many more ages that you have been alive and well, my conclusion is that you are deceiving me, and what you aren't clued in on is that when I bring my tools from the ages beyond what you're aware of, then what I can do is beyond what you know." That is the heart telling you what is Truth. Truth is identity. Mind is not identity. You live mind as identity and not with the heart as identity. Very different.

Clarity can't come from the mind. The masters spoke it, but your modern day lives don't speak it, for they tell you to work from your mind. You were likely raised this way as well, all in the head. It only comes down to the heart when making a personal and very essential decision in your life. So the misconception here is that you're not utilizing your tools again. If you only came to clarity through the heart, your fears would become much smaller, allowing you to see what you're truly capable of. It grants you the confidence to move forward in whatever tasks or life changes need to be made to claim your greatness.

That is part of the process—fearing that which is seemingly not available to you. To push it away and instead go buy more of the same new, shiny tool that you've been trying to use for every material on your house. You struggle because the screwdriver doesn't put a nail into the house, and you try forcing it in, but it simply doesn't work. It is the wrong equation, and you can't see it with clear eyes. When you try to see from the viewpoint that we suggest, it will become clear that your silly actions have led you into destruction, self-destruction, for so long. You're in the dark, and you see it not. But we tell you, you're not alone. We say it every time, because you forget every time how close you truly are. You don't ask for guidance, and you don't ask for Presence because you feel you are alone.

So get out of the head, feel your authenticity and your Divinity, which is part of us, and you'll see that you can so easily communicate in this way, to help you, to guide you, and to encourage you through this process and experience on this beautiful Earth place. You're not here for long, and you will return with the all-knowingness that you had before you came here in completion. Soon after your birth back into the physical realm you were bombarded with conditionings and notions, which quickly drove you away from who you truly are—and you are star seeds, the Earth's great gases, the plasma in the sky, the heat of the sun, and the universal Love all bound into a body. You appear to be singular, but if you see how we see you, you are not at all singular!

You are part of a great whole, as are we. And we say, we see you no different than us, but we see there is a difference in consciousness levels based on what you consciously invite into your experience on the Earth plane. When you decide to let in more and utilize your tools, then the more powerful and greater your beingness becomes. *You* must initiate it. Once you decide it is for you, then you let the universe pour in with its unconditional Love and Source energy, filling you up in every cell in your body.

You see, we are in awe of the human being who has focused their energy in one direction, perceiving a linear standpoint when you are so much more—in fact, you are exactly the opposite of order, singularity, and directed linear thought. It is so powerful to be present on the Earth and to bring this new consciousness to humanity. We tell you that it assists us, as well, for all aspects of the universe are greatly impacted. It is more than the Earth place, though that is where the Love and protection are most needed. We greatly assist you in these times of transition, though they are very hard to incorporate into your experience when you are so used to a different form of being.

The Earth place is often a shock to you when you arrive, for you cannot even imagine such an experience when you have been in the Light for so long. All of a sudden the sounds, smells, and loud chatters fill your body. There are now sensory details that weren't present before. You had communication in the nonphysical, but in a much deeper way, and it is not one that is vocal, for we have no physical bodies, as you do. Or as you think you do…for truly, the physical body is only a manifestation of thought process, and as a result, your DNA structure and cells order in that way. That has been your choosing this time around.

But indeed, that is a big subject that we will not get into now. We see such a great, great opportunity for you to start to incorporate your innate abilities into your life experience today as you know it. When you start to uncover abilities and passions that you never knew you had, wow, you uncover a potential that you can be whatever you want to be, with true greatness! There is a super human power that you cannot imagine! If you trust this innate to take you over with Love and peace and harmony while you follow your guidance system built into your physical bodies, then you can fully and physically start changing your DNA structure. This will be incorporated to work with you in your favor when you utilize the tools that you've used before—and they will make you successful.

The knowledge you have been storing and utilizing over many ages and many lifetimes has gotten you much farther than the mind will know in one lifetime, for it sees only the linearity of your current experience, and that will get you only so far. When you uncover the mystery and the story behind your many existences (all which happen in the Now), then you can remember what you are truly passionate and talented at. That may lead you down unexpected roads, ones that you would have never ventured into before and, at first, may feel out of your comfort zone, but soon enough you will have the confidence to venture down that road with your guidance system.

Your angels will be by your side to assist you and remind you of your greatness, and you will start incorporating these abilities and talents into the physical linear reality that is your present day experience. Now you know, dear children, this experience is very precious, and we encourage you not to try to change all that you have become automatically, for the life experience is so beautiful. But there comes a point where you have come to find that you are more than that, and you seek more than what you have found automatically through experience. You will find that following your guidance system will take you the rest of the way, and that is what we guide you to do, in your own way. Reading these words is the first step to start the ball rolling and to get the molecules and cells to listen up as the words of Truth start to wake up inside. Once you recognize the Truth of the matter, the cells will start to exclaim in joy and gratitude that you're listening, and you're awake!

When they think you are dormant, they will start to relax and also remain dormant. When that spark of knowingness of your greatness hits by some great chance, you know you are on a path of waking up, and of growing your passion to see who you are with clear eyes. That extends much further beyond what you believe you are through the current life experience on the Earth plane. It dives much deeper into the wisdom of the universe than what the mind has to offer, and even what other beings try to offer you through their wisdom. Let us illuminate your mind, dear one, for this is part of a co-creative effort—one that cannot be unseen, cannot be un-experienced.

Once you have come to the knowingness of who you truly are, then you will refocus your intent on what your real goals and missions are in your life experience. When you start to come to the realization that it is not as you think it is, with every living molecule of your body, you start to mistrust what goes on around you. It feels like it is all a dream, like a conspiracy against you. It may feel like that in the beginning, for you're still midway in the dark of the true story that is playing out. In reality, the true story is that your mind gets in the way of the real story. The real story is individual, but if you try to put labels and religions on the face of God, you miss the point completely. You miss the most essential point, and that is that God is you, and you are God. So how would religion work if that were the case, when all you know completely stabs churches in the back? Because whatever knowledge came to be in your lifetime now is not the fullness and all-encompassing knowingness of the bigger bird's-eye view—not the You which sees the truth of that matter. That is the point where you realize what is truly important, and what isn't as important. You begin to sort out your priorities and come into valuing the trueness of who you are without the deceiving anymore.

We like to send you all the guidance you can handle, but you must be willing to see it. Don't play the games of the mind, for what you know to be true in your heart is what you must rely on. Forget all the rest that is not useful. And so we part with one final conclusion, and that is that you must start focusing on this step of relying on your Divine. With that comes the focus that is more directly on the notion that you need no other guidance than that from within, and the knowledge that you bring to the table from the Higher Self is personalized, greeting you from a place of such personal Love and history in a way that no other master or guru can point you to. If they are truly who they present themselves to be, they will tell you it lies within, and that is indefinitely and truly, a great, great mission. And so it is.

Chapter 26

Moving into the Light

Greetings to you, dear children, from the eternal Light and Love of who we are. This is a great age of transformation and great, great prosperity in the heart. We channel through this great space to give you a great exchange, a great glimpse of your trueness and your potential when you come through to the other side and see just how much you had been missing. We give you the time in this space to channel so you can see, without the death experience, the greatness of You and live on in an existence that so different in perception. And we greet you with so much Love and Light, for you are so blessed unconditionally.

We are so graced in your Presence, in such loving harmony with the greater You. When you see us for who we are, as a piece of You, you will see, for sure, that what you once knew as small children was correct. And you were so innocent, a little baby, a small child with wide eyes and a smile always on your face. You were so eager to get out into the world, to experience as much as you could with your senses, and despite the changing consciousness that is You now, there is still a big part that comes from behind the veil that proclaims with such definiteness, I AM LIGHT, and I AM LOVE. And I am in such harmony and Presence with the greatness of my ancestors, and I am the history of Mother Gaia. I am the Source in its truest form.

We speak now from a dimension that can help you understand this complicated subject, as communication can often be very difficult. We speak through the letters, and through the energy threads that connect us in this way. As we speak, we feel each one of you individually on this thread, on this powerful vibrational wavelength that is all encompassing, including the bigger part of You that wishes to be seen. You see, dear ones, this is a great opportunity, a great gift to bask in your own Presence. And you see it more clearly now, for you may have once felt the need to cling on to others. You may find that now, perceptions slowly shift to one that is more focused upon the greatness of the self.

You can now see that when you focus your intent on going inward and following the guidance of your own Akash, you will see a power, feel a power, and experience the power of the bigger part of You that so wishes to be integrated fully into this existence. That is all that is to follow. We speak linearly, though as we know it, this impact of awakening inside extends and integrates into every time period…and that, my dear ones, is precisely why you won't have to worry about doing it all over again. As if you had a choice in the matter, right? For truly, it is all a process, but death is one subject that is greatly feared among the majority of human beings. And we say to you, we see how fear can take off, causing you to become very unstable with an idea that you cannot fathom. It is one big reason why we are here to help you move past your insecurities and move into your authenticity.

When you come into that aspect of your Divinity, then you will see the Truth of many, many fears that once were inescapable in your mind. You will see, "Oh yes, there is me, there is my mind, and there is where they part, so distinctly." There will be less of a focus upon prosperity in material objects and possessions, and more in the heart. Prosperity in the heart is a wealth that cannot be taken away from you. Death is one of the greatest gifts, for it is one experience that means coming back to the self, the true self. We have learned that you see it oppositely, like a punishment. Why is that, you ask? Because you live in your heads and cannot see past where your heart and mind make judgments. When judgments characterize thoughts and actions into good or bad, they do not come from the heart. The heart is pure and always shows you the Truth and the best outcome for you.

But dear ones, we speak on death, for it is a great and holy subject, one that is bigger and more vast than we can put into linear thought blocks. But we will summarize, for the great and vast ideas cannot be understood clearly. The process of dying, as we speak of in terms of the body preparing itself, can be either very sudden or spanned over a long period of time if it is natural. Indeed, you have fears around how death will occur, for many of you would rather it be natural, rather than an accident or crisis taking your life. We tell you again, it is not what you think, for you are so fearful of being alone and losing things. We must remind you again, it was when you came to Earth plane that you first created the notion that you were alone.

The previous time was when you were in complete unison with God, in a unity consciousness that only you can experience. But indeed, you are that still, no matter where you are on your journey. When you remember who you are and feel the unconditional Love and Light from behind the veil where you reside in a parallel bigger picture, you have all you need. You have your family, your joy, and your greatness all at the tip of your fingertips. You are so powerful, in so many ways. When you utilize your tools (and you'll start to uncover what these are when you're designing what kind of house you want to build), you'll uncover what kind of support you're unconsciously asking for.

Many of you start to realize you feel alone because you don't have the honest and uncanny behavior to ask for it. You are designed on Earth to be independent, to find resolutions to your own problems, and to fix what you deemed upon yourself. We say the opposite, for there is nothing being put upon you, and you never came here involuntarily. When you arrived, you knew the guidance system that was there, but you started to forget as time passed, getting caught up in the life process. We like to remind you, dear ones, this is one great process of life, and whatever You had in mind for you, it is great and it is personalized, and there are no mistakes ever on your part.

Even if that is your experience, and the fear and hatred overcomes you when you start to think about asking for help, start to remember being a young child, and go back to a time when you were too young to care for yourself on your own. Remember that vulnerability you had, especially to the world outside of your immediate family. Small, fragile, very distant, and often shy. You depended upon your family in many ways in order to help you through your life. They provided the essentials for you, but also taught you, through conditionings of what they learned over their own lifetimes, about what is the right way to live. Now dear ones, we let you know, to let them think and grow up to be their own individual it is the most natural and loving way to help a child up.

But let us remind you, the young parent may or may not have the intelligence to let their child be their own thinker, and sometimes they try to disengage the creative unit in your brain, putting you inside the box. You become confused and feel out of place all of a sudden, because a new life experience is entering your consciousness. You previously had no embarrassment or feelings of being out of place doing your own things, being yourself, and not caring or even seeing the out-of-ordinary actions as strange. Death shows you to that place of vulnerability, to a trueness of being a small child and depending on the universal Love and greatness of All That Is. Let us tell you, it is far from loneliness or aloneness!

For you are with your creator, your parents, your big family, and even if you wish, your family that you knew on the Earth place. They are in the nonphysical plane, as on Earth, all at once, and so it is for you as well. It is that way for every being, they have many attachments and parts of them. That is why we refer to you as You with a capital Y, because you are so much bigger than you see. You are so much greater, with pieces of the puzzle that you often wish to not look at. It is part of the process that you are in doubt, in a state that allows you to blind yourself from the Truth. But at some point you are to wake up, each and every one of you. It occurs naturally, and we help you to uncover what really goes on so that you can get down to the root of your existence and uncover the Truth behind the seed of your beingness.

It lies in the Akash of each and every one of you. When you move out of the body and into the Light, you see, you feel, and you experience, spontaneously and at once, the fullness of who you are. Not only do you experience the fullness of You, but you also experience the fullness of the universe and your guidance system that has been with you ever since the beginning of your existence, which is for eternity. You are eternal beings, and death is not the end. It is but another beginning of your long, staged existence. So you see, don't fret when you hear the word *death* anymore, for it means nothing more than reentering into the space where you are most at home, most comfortable, and most at peace, in order to decide and re-evaluate what you feel you are to do next—and it is your choice. You will find in trueness what you feel you are here to do, and if you want to reenter into the Earth plane, you will do so.

It is a most beautiful process, for it occurs when you and You are joined together in One consciousness, no longer needing to communicate from two ends of the same string. We are looking at the big picture together, finding what you truly are, and basking in the real energy of who you are. It is part of what you are here to do, and you will find it so true to your soul. It is so beautiful and pure when you see that this is part of a long and very mature span, all of which is in your control. You are part of the bigger whole, one that assists the evolution of humankind by reentering as linear human beings inside a body.

This, indeed, greatly reduces your expansiveness. You will feel with such reassurance that even as you are in a body that is so small and compact, you have so much infinite Source within that remains the same, untouched as always. You will move into a new space, a new frequency, and a new evolution of beingness when you come to your own conclusion that you can move into such a profound state of Oneness without the great master's teachings telling you what you are—and it may astound you at first. You'll start to value this connection more than one that would be less personal. In the viewpoint of another, what's truly taught is their own personal experiences in a way that better acknowledges the audience, or the bigger picture, which is humanity.

Sometimes teachers help people see themselves in a new light, help them accept what their mission truly is or what their Source truly is. But you cannot imagine, not for one second, what you truly are without experiencing your expansiveness from the inside. We encourage you to see it within yourself and stop relying on the direction of theirs. And we know it is helpful, but it does not point you into the deepness and personalized memory that you can find in your Akash. So, listen to your body and heart, and come to your own conclusion. And we say again, use your tools! We know you get sick of hearing it, but we repeat it to help you integrate, and that is the purpose of repeating any teaching.

We love to do it, for it helps for you to find peace in all that you are. We are so blessed to be here, dear ones, in each and every one of you in a personal way, and we will show up in a different personalized way for each of you. That is a great gift from God, and from your honest requests, and we thank you, dear children. Death is not fearful, it is coming Home! It is Love and Light and knowingness with such definiteness that all is well in your soul, and you have nothing to fear. There is no fear because the mind dissipates out of the body and into the expansiveness of the bigger picture of the many facets of You. And it is a blessing to spread this word, for then you can get on the fast track and know what to expect and stop feeling the fear. We hope this assists you in getting out of the mind. It is not hard, dear ones, but once you understand what is in your control when changing your experience, then it can be an instant realization.

It truly is in your control. Start getting in contact with your cellular structure, with your guides, with the greater You, with the universal Love energy, with your ancestors' unconditional Source knowledge, and utilize your tools to their fullest extent. They are eternal as are you, and you have so many new tools that are being replaced by the old tools. Let us remind you how this works. We can only explain it in another short story, for they are helpful for you to see the concepts we bring to the table in a new light.

You live in a time where you are considered the modern beings and the great ones on the fast track to finding a new purpose of the Earth. You reflect on the ancients as the elders, the ones long, long ago, but they are not really in the past tense. They are very much present, but you don't see it. The antiques in the store are old and rustic like the tools in your shed—they are not often seen with as much value as the modern ones in the store that are updated and shiny. The tools that are at the root of the creation are the ones that may be more useful, for they have an ancient wisdom in them, a purpose that may really fit better than the shiny new tools that will be utilized.

We say, if you are looking to really utilize your tools, go back to old faithful and try to encompass what has always been there for you instead of trying to look outwardly for resources that are not dependent and don't have the history behind them. So we conclude with this idea: follow the words as you would a manual. Usually you don't even take the time to look at them unless you need help figuring it out. So we speak to you like this to help you understand that we are not church, we only seek to help you out. If you need it, come to us and our arms are wide open. If your innate speaks to you, communicates, and the wisdom is there in the heart, then you need not feel compelled to seek outward guidance. We seek only to help you find what's inside, so personally.

We are clued in that you may not see that there are many faces of God, and we are not one entity as you may have guessed. We are not a specific personality, though we mold to the channeler based on their life experience, their goals, their wisdom through the ages, and their collective understanding, wanting, and capability of receiving. We are a collective. We are always the same and will remain the same for all of eternity. What changes and varies is the human being. We let you create your own God, one that is personalized, all-knowing, and a great, great friend to all who experience a passion and will to receive. That is who we truly are. You are not meant to be alone—it is not your natural state. When you come into your natural state of wellbeing, the fears and misconceptions will die away automatically.

There is nothing for you to do here but stay in tune and in communion with your Divine so that you can be on the fast track and get as much out of your life experience as you planned from the nonphysical standpoint. Whether you try to play out your Divine purpose or not, we guide you, and all occurs automatically. We want you to know, even if you're not in on it, You are, and that is much more important. We are there for you when you don't even know it. Your life experiences and everyday mundane activities and circumstances are Divinely inspired and planned from a standpoint that you decide not to acknowledge.

We know that the great You sees it so purely, for that is what the Divine in you is wanting to be assured of. There is nothing for you to do. We say it again, for often you feel very overwhelmed with such information and such greatness of You that you feel as if you cannot hope to follow all the rules! Oh we laugh, metaphorically of course, at your silliness. For you see, we say it again, even if you have no plan for yourself and your life, it is already planned. So if you can focus on that, rely on that, and speak from the heart, and that is all you need. Have an intent and an integrity to follow that higher path, and you'll be Divinely focused and directed.

You need not a plan, you need not follow any rules, for there are none—not from our standpoint! In your linear field of thought there are many strange practices that have become normal to you, and you cannot remember what your real normal is! We will remind you that it is freestyle…that is, do what you want, listen to your heart, and be individual. You truly are in every cell of the body, quite literally, very Divinely individual. Even as we are in Oneness and Divine communion together collectively, we are also like water droplets—each unique, but as a collective, they are water. Such a brilliant and magical substance! So it is with humanity and with the wholeness of the universe.

How could you resist or misinterpret God and your greatness when you hear this? How can you fear the death process when you know truly in every cell of your body that there is a memory of You coming into alignment with Source and having such a party that you can never imagine ever leaving there? And yet, you have again returned to Earth to fulfill more by returning to the physical. It was your choice, your Divine mission.

We thank you for your great courage from above and beyond, and we wish for you to have no worries, and to focus more intently on feeling and being in great union with your body mind spirit. If you do this, you'll be just great. You are Divinely helped in every way possible, and you are never, ever alone. We Love you from every part of our beingness, and our experience of your Love is overwhelmingly beautiful. We greet you individually from your time and place. From your standpoint and we wave to you with so much Love and Light, and we wish for you to wave back, if you have the time, for we are so in Love with humanity. We seek the connection just as much as you do. We will reenter in new times, but for now, we close and let the integration begin. SO much love and light, and we will never leave you. And so it is.

Chapter 27

The Human Being – Awakening Star Dust

We are so pleased to return, dear beings of Light. We have descended into the body of the channeler, and we are so graced in your Presence, dear soul. You are exceptionally open to our beingness as we come through from the other side of the veil. It is a great gift to be here, and we are so open to greeting you with new subjects that will enlighten your mind, clarify your practices, and help you regain balance in times of struggle and disconnectedness. We are the great Source energy of God, and we heal you with our words as if they are words of Grace or encouragement from a dear friend. It is that simple—words and Presence can help you to feel as if you are part of a bigger plan. And truly, that's exactly how it is.

You are so loved here, dear ones. We will continue to unveil the Truth of your existence as time unravels in mysterious, yet very planned, ways. You see, all which unfolds is Divinely inspired and was co-created by You in a time and place where You could see the bigger picture. You have chosen to consciously emerge into this existence and body that live this current life on planet Earth. You are here to create a life for yourself that is filled with the greatness and reflection of the greater You, even though you are inside the box and temporarily in a place that is limiting.

Your tools are greatly decreased because you are put into a physical existence. That is to say, it was designed this way, and you are not the only one that often feels disabled in their ability to co-create and see the Truth of the matter beyond a vast haze. You are often put in limits because it challenges you to go beyond your physical existence, and pushes you to reveal the greater You where your tools are. This helps you to start seeing your mission. If you came straight into knowing, the learning and the experience would not be the great and courageous event that it truly is when you endure. You find so much blessing and Grace in the challenges when you go through and emerge as a bigger light being.

We see you truly as these light beings—not in metaphorical terms, but in reality. You are composed of Light and pure potentiality that is made literally of the stars around you in your galaxy. That is truly why we are not kidding when we say that the wisdom of the universe is within, for truly you are made of it! If you have the intelligence and courage to see your own wisdom and experience—the Grace and overwhelming knowledge that is within the human body—you will uncover so much more of You. That is, your past, present and future. Such a beautiful timeline...but we remind you, it is only perceived linearly. Truly, it will be recognized as a vast time and space that occurs not in a past or future, but quite clearly, as a present moment at all times. Present moment, present moment, present moment. That is your life, and that is existence in its purest form.

This is why the masters teach being in the present moment, because beyond the mind you feel and experience only this dimensional reality, and that is ours as well. It is so beautiful to be in a bliss state without the judgment, the beingness of singularity, and an opposing personality. We are One, and even on the planet Earth there is Oneness. Oneness is the root of all existence, and it only takes waking up to this realization. It is already there. Your outside reality may not reinforce this idea or notion, but if you seek Truth as a very conscious and regular practice, it will become a very powerful mantra and teaching that will get you to that place of understanding.

You are your own teacher, and that is what we refer to when we say it is a teaching. You truly learn it from yourself, from the bigger, vaster You. It is in your Akash, in your physical body's evolution and human consciousness. The body holds the wisdom of the abundance of the whole great atmosphere, but only in such a quantity in relation to its mass and its size. What a beautiful and graced concept. But you see, you do not see it like this ...you see a very, very small portion of yourself, in more than one way. The way you experience yourself is singular with separate bodies, with separate minds, separate dimensions, and separate egos.

All of these notions are controlled by the Self—you are almost functioning from a place that is out of your control. You see flesh and bone, muscle, and lack of muscle. You see different sizes and different weights. You see color and texture, but you see not the atmosphere. You see not the great power of you cells and your DNA structure that we see in you. We experience it in you as if it is part of who we are, for we experience you as us, in Oneness with all creation as one God.

We are God together. You look to God with the hope of feeling more in sync or in union with God because your mind keeps you from coming to the obvious conclusion ...the problem is not that you cannot connect with God, the God which is in Heaven while you are on Earth, it is that you *are* God, and God is within. You can't fathom it because your eyes don't see the Earth plane as Heaven.

If you find that your existence is not matching up with what you know is your true identity, it is time to start claiming that, and not only start practicing new thought patterns, but also making the changes that you know the bigger You would find to support your life purpose and overall happiness. That is to say, you cannot start to experience the way your trueness and authentic nature is unless you have the incentive and ability to consciously choose that as your new way of living. You must accept this as your existence, and practice it through your actions, thoughts, and creative practices every day. That doesn't need to mean any big life changes, but it does mean you must put it out into the universe. You must claim what you want to be returned to you and trust that it comes back, because you are your own creator of your life existence.

If you trust and give in to the mind, it will try to make you believe many things about who you truly are. It will limit you in so many ways, and we know with great assurance that you're looking for more—you just can't find where to start. The holes are showing up in your happiness. You tend to look everywhere but within. You can't find the depth, and that causes great disturbance in your soul because you had never had this very shallow and running-in-the-dark experience as you do now on the Earth plane.

But you see, that does not mean that you're alone, for you can come back into this knowledge of your greatness. You can return to the consciousness and uncover your past and expansiveness through intent ...that is all we mean to tell to you. We do not say that you are hopeless because you run in the dark and you don't have the bird's-eye view, for we know that what you are venturing in in the Earth experience is very, very good for you in many ways. It actually strengthens you from the inside out and creates a balance that you needed to move forward. Your greatness is not limited by the human body, though sometimes it limits how much you are able to remember about the true You.

If you get past the mind's details and labels, you're no longer in the dark. If you see the tricks happening as if you were watching a slow-motion movie, you'll notice them and not fall into the trap of believing them. It comes back to awareness, to seeing without trying to change or understand. Just see, and you'll likely uncover many games that the mind used to let you believe. You'll turn it around by deciding very consciously that you choose for this to not be your existent reality. As soon as those mind games came in, they will be replaced by the greater big picture from You that understands the universal concepts and ideas that will keep the physical being on the Earth place in great harmony with All That Is.

This understanding of the role of the self creates a great opportunity to also put your current DNA structure or molecular memory into action, utilizing anything that will serve your greater purpose in the future. Here we see many of the ideas and experiences of the great masters who utilized their tools over time—consciously putting new information into their Akash and cellular structure and communicating intimately. This is for the purpose of bringing in the information from the old ages, and storing their learning's from their current era for the next time they come through. This enables them to teach a great depth of information, or to channel, or to be a great artist or musician because they are relying on so many ages of experience. It is no wonder they are so practiced, often from an early age! They need no more practice, for it is so natural to just jump in. Their waiting time is over, and their time to capture the moment is ready.

So we say, there are no coincidences to this, and you can use these tools just like the great masters did when they uncovered their own past. So many reincarnations and many times of struggle resulted in many ages of wisdom and teachings to come about. It is wise for you to get in touch with that greater knowing inside so you can start co-creating with the greater nonphysical You ahead of time. You'll be even more aware of what you're doing next time you come through, for there is so much coming that you will not want to miss! We are eager to let the ideas flow naturally in the human being, and this is happening through the great transmission of Light that is happening automatically.

We see many, many beings around the globe finding a Truth within so automatically, one that does not come from the mind ...it is nothing that can be taught in a step-by-step process. We cannot tell you how to get in touch with your innate, for it will be a varying process for each and every one of you, but we give you words of advice for the times where you may feel lost about how to start the ball running. Your ideas and notions on the life process are so undervalued and underappreciated that your communication with the innate and nonphysical realms have become invalid and foreign to you. Though as you truly know it to be, it is the most pure and homely place that you have ever known in the history of your existence.

You are eternal beings, and we will repeat it again, for sometimes you do not see the truth in that. You are eternal beings— never-ending. You will return again and again to a new planet that is ever changing, ever growing with new intelligence, wisdom, and energy that fluctuates as the beings arrive in new states of consciousness. It is determined by *you*, dear ones. Mother Earth will accommodate you, but in reality, the change or shift is dramatically and most majorly in response to the human beings. As a collective, we work together, hand in hand. We are the great ones all together, and so you are never alone.

The Earth will always support its kind as long as there is a cooperating and interdimensional communication to stay in Divine bond and interchangeably, co-creators of the same reality. As long as that is so, there will always be a home for you here, in Divine unison with All That Is, and in the soul of the core of beingness. There is so much for you here, dear ones, and there is more to it than you realize. As you awaken to new levels, you will start incorporating your tools on new levels. These have been stored away for some time, waiting to be uncovered. It is an awakening of the heart, and it seeks to guide and protect you in all the ways that it can.

You'll notice the changes in your behavior, in your personality, and your outward public conversations and opinions. There is less of a focus upon being in unison, being in sameness with those around you, for you finally see that individuality is the greatest blessing for yourself. You wake up to realizing that you cannot see any alternative of beingness than the one which is You and which is eternal. You see that—even though your outward experience may not match up (and the mind will definitely argue)—you are all that you believe you are in your heart. You are the greatest teacher and God that is known. You are what we say you are, and you'll hear it ring true in every cell as you read the words here.

You'll feel the wisdom start to show up, and it may feel almost like the flip of a switch when the wisdom of the ages pours in ...the connectedness of the universe, and your big eternal family flowing in. When you start to feel alone, you connect with the knowingness that is ever-present in every cell of the body, and you rely on it more than you do your mind. That is a daily practice. It will happen automatically, for in due time your experience will shift. You cannot make your experience shift, for an automatic adjustment is what comes from your innate, and you personally cannot turn that switch on and off. However, you can help it along by acknowledging and encouraging what you know to be true about yourself. With that little bit of encouragement you can let yourself accept heaven's greatest gifts. In the truest form that they come, indeed, for when you get beyond the efforts of trying to control, you start to move into accepting the greatness of the universe that sees the higher bird's-eyes view that you do not see.

If you rely on that, you can be sure that the right decisions will be made in your life. If you accept that, yes, you cannot see the big picture, and yes, you can be okay with this, then you will feel so empowered by, protected by, and supported by the universe. We are like your mother and father who greet you with unconditional Love from our whole beingness. We have nothing to give but our support, Love, kindness, encouragement, and guidance—even down to the small details. We tell you this because you know in your heart that it's there, and you may be hesitant to reach out when it goes against the practices the mind wishes to incorporate. See first what the mind has to say, maybe agree or disagree, but look at your inventory.

What are your choices? Try to make a conclusion from the heart space so that you can move forward in a higher and fast-tracked path. This is much different than if you were to focus solely upon what knowledge and experience you have in one lifetime—a very small percentage of the great vastness the mind has to see. It is such a small little area of seeing, kind of like when you look through a peephole of someone's door—you see only a tiny little percentage of the real-life, three-dimensional picture. That is similar to how the mind views your reality, like a peephole. If you were to always look from the heart as if it were the mind, then you would start to see this big picture. That helps you to make honest decisions and thoughtful healthy solutions in your life.

It is such a powerful, powerful way of thinking, for it can so dramatically change your perception of your life experience, and it will greatly alternate your view of yourself as well, dear ones. You'll see yourself in a light of respect and greatness that was not allowed through the mind. Through so many conditionings you were taught to see yourself with a very greatness, for it is better to be selfless—not focused on yourself, but more on others. You were taught that it is okay to Love and be inspired by others, but it is self-absorbed to think or talk about yourself. We say, as long as it is not destructive to yourself or to others, claim your greatness and see yourself as you are, for you truly are just that great and vast.

You are that expansiveness, a bundle of universal knowledge and creative forces. It would almost be deceiving yourself to start acting like you are a simple, small being with nothing but a physical body on a physical linear plane. It is disrespectful, that's what it is. If you want to truly learn a powerful lesson from us, dear ones, it would be to see yourself in the respectful trueness that is You. If you have thoughts that you are just that *awesome*, then don't feel bad about it! You are that, and it is not self-absorbed.

It is self-absorbed if you choose to put yourself down and downplay your role in your great, powerful universe. That is disrespectful, for you may not experience how great you are, but once you leave this place, you'll see with clear eyes. Even those who don't see the Truth now will see and experience this reality as normal. It is explaining it to you from a reality that you cannot put into context that is somewhat difficult. There is still some understanding because the memory is present, but we remind you, you must still seek out the memory and keep it in the front of your mind and reflect on it often. Keep it in your to-do list, you might say. That is to say, keep it on hand.

You are such great beings who easily absorb these ideas that are in your Akash, but you are slow to learn those that are not there yet. That is why we explain these ideas, so you can slowly start to return them into your internal mailbox. It is like we are reminding a patient of his of her life after a memory loss—all is gone, nothing is remembered. This is similar to your situation, but it is partly an illusion. For the mind does not see it, but the Akashic records deep within retain the information so truly. As long as you have enough of your resources to find the memory with the Akash, which buried a bit, you'll start to uncover it naturally.

That is the great process of life. It is one that is a journey, a process that is often paralleled with an assumption of great confusion and strange illusions. It is, however, your conscious decision to stay in that confusion and haze or to move out of it. You are your own creator, your own teacher, and your own representation of God in its purest form. Remember that trueness and you are home free. We have been graced in your Presence during this time, and we are so blessed to have had this interaction so purely and with such smooth transitions that are opening up so naturally. The channel begins to open so naturally. We are returning now, slowly, to our natural residing place, and this has been one great transformational process. We see it happening before our eyes—a process of remembering, of coming Home, and of great, great relaxation in knowing and feeling the presence of God within.

We are so, so joyous in this interaction, and we greet you from the Light with a resonance that is purely a bond between you and You—a bond that is never ending, a pure connection that is from within and also from without. It comes from the universal expansiveness that incorporates All That Is. We thank you from every part of our beingness for the focused intent, and we are looking forward to future connections, for they are beneficial and so beautiful for both sides. We get great, great wisdom and Love from you as well. And so it is.

Chapter 28

Perceptions of the Three-Dimensional Human Being

You are so, so Divine, dear ones. We are so grateful to be in your Presence, and it is of such power to begin this transmission through a channeler who is open to receiving the guidance from a place of Love and Light for all that are to read these words at a later time. It is currently a moment in time that is called the present moment, but we also wish to invite those who read the words later to come to the realization that there is only the present moment. That is how you can feel the words as if you were in the room where they came through, for we are just as ever present with you as we are with the one who channels the words. They come smoothly and very easily now. The message is now being channeled to you from a place that initiates the communication between you and You.

This is for those who are wishing to seek the greater Truth in who they truly are. We wish for you to find the Love and Grace and support, for we are reaching out and handing you a rose every day of your existence. We tell you this symbolically so that you can recognize that we never leave you—we are your undying friend, lover, and true companion. That is a gift that cannot be taken away from you. As you move through the fluctuating waves of bliss and despair in the life process, you will find yourself in places of seeking new ways out, new alternatives and perhaps new solutions. Sometimes it is in response to the loneliness that is on the inside, and sometimes you are at a loss to understand what the heart yearns for when your mind is plagued with fears and resistance. You must first be open to receiving the universal Love and support that we have for you.

You may not draw the conclusion between your life circumstance and your knowingness of the Love and Light that pours through from the interdimensional realm, but you do still seek to find the true answer to life. You are well aware of the gap between your existence and your true reality, which is interdimensional and very hard to grasp. It is often not worth noticing to you because it seems out of touch. That is, we speak of your connection with your Divine, for often it feels as if you may be too distant to do anything about it at this time and point in your life. However, you see it, and there is no judgment on the face of God. No matter where we are, we still hold out our arms with great all-encompassing Love and affection that is undying.

This has nothing to do with pleasing God or acting in a certain way that would give you permission to receive unconditional Love. The young child in you, who remembers vulnerability and receiving without guilt, is what needs to be replenished in the human being who feels selfish about so many things in their life. Let us clear it up for you, dear child, for despite your learning's over your many years of existence, it is important to come back into balance by remembering what felt true in your heart before adapting ideals that challenge the Truth. This is especially true if you grew up in a household that taught a practice or religion that was dominating your authentic nature. We do not mean that there are not many great facets of these certain practices, for in our eyes, all is well with humanity, and time is perfect.

In truth, when humanity rises to a new consciousness, as it is already, you can sit back and enjoy the ride and see the transformation begin, for we are not at all waiting for a conclusion or a solution. We see everything as a journey of great importance. There is no beginning and end, but there is a journey which defines your greatness, and that is what we wish to emphasize more than anything else. Follow where your heart takes you, and if the integrity is in your heart, your personal teaching will come about naturally and bring you to a place of understanding of your true greatness. It all happens so naturally.

So truly, do not pressure others or try to change others minds; let them come to their understanding in their own time, when the time is Divinely correct. If you push against the universe, you are pushing for a conclusion that is not yet ripe, and we know what happens when we taste a fruit that is not ripe! It is sour and unsatisfying. Similarly, if you choose to be impatient with the creative and infinite Source knowledge, you may be disappointed in what comes about for you.

We said before that your life is to be followed, not planned. That fits in with this notion, for pushing will only leave you unsatisfied. You know, you do not see the big picture that we see. Trust your universe, for it is so expansive. Do not rely on the mind and the journeys it takes you on, and do not rely on the mind to try to show you what is necessary for you to do in your life. If you follow Divine guidance, you'll be even more surprised and delighted by what comes about for you. Sometimes it is frustrating to be in the dark, but at the same time you feel extra connected and empowered to be one that will choose to follow the Divine path instead of the mind, which is narrow and shallow. It brings about trust, great trust, and infinite abundance for you.

Choosing to be vulnerable is a great challenge. Stepping aside and following an energy and a wholeness that you know you are a part of, but you feel no physical evidence of, can be discouraging. The mind in the physical existence wishes to have the connection physically, with human touches and spoken words, but we do not see it that way. In the realm of the nonphysical, we are not focused in that direction. We express our sincere Love and gratitude to one another so powerfully, even more fully than in the physical plane. We feel so whole, so Divine, and so at peace with one another. Separateness does not exist. It is part of this consciousness that starts to awaken for humanity on this Earth, and it has such a powerful impact.

It points to the human being in an obvious manner that doesn't let many of them get by without really taking notice. Such miracles are occurring in these times. There are those who awaken, from out of nowhere, to find this guidance system, to find God inside, and to depend completely on this power despite the games within the mind and the limitations of the body. It is truly surrendering, and living from a new plane in the physical body. It is accepting where you are at the present moment on planet Earth.

The next step is to then also acknowledge the strong Presence of the Divine within, and to do this by encouraging it to really dominate you. This is the alternative of letting the lesser part of you take over, allowing yourself to feel lost in your life, purposeless. We wish for you all to feel this amazing Grace of God, but we are in Love with the human being who is in the dark as well, for they are courageous and so blessed to make a transition on Earth. When the switch does flip, it is a great sigh of relief, of super Love, and of such a beautiful Presence. It is like warm sun on your back; it remembers the human being as the human being remembers it. It is the powerful human being who steps outside their comfort zone to seek a power that is beyond their physicality and understanding.

It is like coming home once you've moved past the barriers of the mind, for they are often very thick and engraved in your body after many years of conditionings. The human being will have a long process of waking up from the deep slumber, but they will come back, full speed ahead, and you'll see they are emerging so definitely. Bless them for their greatness every day. The human being who struggles often is experiencing a shift that is exceptionally hard to break, for they experienced many lifetimes of chaos, self-destruction, great crises, and even innumerable amount of human killings. It is quite true that it comes in and stays with your soul.

The triggers of these events are hidden in your life, in your personality, emotions, and behaviors that you cannot explain. This is part of waking up, as well, for it forces you to find the root of the behavior and come across an opportunity for a very blessed healing to take place. It is a great mission that we have for you. In the truest sense, it's already happening for humanity, but you're well on your way to keep it going.

It is beyond words to express such gratitude and peace in our hearts for being present, and being so open to receiving, for it has been a great pleasure. We are so, so happy to share our infinite wisdom, and we are encouraging you to reflect and think upon the great knowledgeable teachings that are so beautiful when they're incorporated into life. You have infinite intelligence inside if you are willing to take an honest look. You are there, as is the whole of the universe, and together we are the Love of God, you see. We are ever so in Love with humanity. It is from this place of such Love and Light that we greet you now. It is beautiful to settle in this energy while we integrate the messages. Reflect back and try to see what your story is, my dear ones. It is different but the same, for your personal circumstances will vary, but the universal laws behind them are always the same. And we leave now with a closing. In and out.

Chapter 29

Illusions of Separation, Grief, and Honoring the Human Experience

It is a great pleasure to return to this sacred space, dear ones. We are here with you all in your own time and space, for truly, it is the present moment always. Time and space make no difference, for the linear patterns are nonexistent in the bigger picture. Earth has created that dimensional realm that has its boundaries, but it is such a great gift to be able to see beyond the laws set in stone in your biological field of consciousness. We see you each individually as One with us. We experience you as our children, as well, for we are here to assist you in your Earth time on this mission that is being carried out through the goodness in your heart. This is about co-creation with your fellow family and assisting this shift in consciousness.

Each and every one of you is just as important and powerful. Those who feel disconnected from this are feeling the mind coming through, categorizing themselves in this way that depletes their greatness inside. So we share with you now from a place of great and honest judgment: you are loved unconditionally ...that means without conditions. There is nothing on your physical plane about your actions, your appearance, or your faithfulness to God that determines how much Love you receive, or how much you are loved. You are God, and you are part of the whole. Truly, no matter what your outer circumstances command you to believe, you are always and never-endingly part of God. You are always loved to the same extent that you were when you were here with us in the nonphysical realm.

You came forth as a small baby in the womb, greeting Earth with new adventures ahead of you, and with the knowingness that all is well despite what you may encounter as obstacles. You knew that they may be challenging at times, but deep within you knew with a sense of great accomplishment that you came here with a mission in mind, with a true purpose that is so important, so essential, and just as important as those around you with a mission. You are equal, despite the materialistic and physical differences that may set you apart. We see you each as Divine aspects and projections of the same Source, and that is God.

We tell you that nothing can take you away from that. You are always co-creators and always the same Divine aspect, but you may be seen as different creatures...you may focus your energy into different forms and existences based on your soul purpose and journey. It is completely up to you—you choose what you want to do when you reemerge back into the nonphysical. Sometimes you will focus entirely as nonphysical, and sometimes as physical in the shape of many different bodies and creatures alike. You are all assisting the shift in consciousness that saves your planet Earth. It does not just have to do with humanity.

With one heart, one beating force, you co-create, bring shining sunlight, and great, great Love to the universe and all that reside in it. It is much beyond the self and personal fulfillment. All beings are on their own journey, as are you, and they should not be judged for what they endure, even if it is destructive to other beings around them. It is difficult, and know truly that at one point you may have been a dictator. So know dear ones, if you truly try to bring unconditional Love to the universe you reside in, have compassion for each and every one that you meet and come in contact with.

This compassion will lead you to see, without judgment and without fear, that this is a process that all beings are on, and it is different for each and every one of you. If you see separation between yourself and another, remind yourself that they are waking up in their own time, and leave it to the Divine. You went through the same struggles, whether in this current lifetime or in one previously. You fell apart and you came back together through Divine intervention. It was all planned out, and you're still supported even when you've supposedly lost yourself. It is all within the Divine hands, so do not get too caught up in everyone else's journey. Just see it for what it is, and try to go on your merry way. And if there is something that you must learn from it, trust that it will show up for you.

If these words ring true for you, you'll have the directed attention to manifest and keep your ears perked up, so to speak, when the time arrives that a lesson must be learned. There are no accidents. All is Divinely planned—even the circumstances which are experienced as chaos and destruction, for out of the ashes raises the phoenix. Even in these times, see the blessing, and if that cannot be accomplished, go inside and feel your connection to the Source. Feel your angelic beings in your heart, and feel that all is well.

You don't need to escape from What Is, but try to go beyond the mind, see the big picture, and put your reliance on the Divine. Trust us when we say that will make it so much easier to move through pain and suffering without letting it grow and integrate inside you. You can experience without letting it plant a seed inside ...that is all we mean to say. For letting it pass through, though it may still be no less painful, is crucial. The awareness of what is going on sparks a hope and an appreciation through which gratitude can move in, and healing arises.

Death, especially in the family, is one great example of how the human being goes into seclusion inside when they feel vulnerable. Not only do they shut down, but they go into all of these unfamiliar emotions, symptoms, and characters which bring out all the stuff that's been trapped inside. That is why you all experience these crises in different manners, because you have different backgrounds and history behind you that create a certain reaction that has been so deeply engrained in your cellular structure.

There is no need to change, for that gets you back up in the mind. Just see what is going on, if possible, and then you can let the heart move in automatically. The process of life is not one that you control, but you can assist it with your co-creative abilities if used wisely and efficiently. You see, you are creators of your own existence, as we often say, but that is deeply associated and teamed up with the notion that you must co-create with your Divine, for you need to rely on your Divine to see the big picture. With the mind in full working order, you cannot see it without help. So we say, get in contact with your Divine and trust it to show the way for you.

Be personal, be honest, and ask for the connection to come into your life. "You" must bring "you" into unity consciousness ...to make your heart alive and deeply bring you to a new understanding of compassion within and without. You first must move into yourself and work through what is within, and then you can see what is without with a greater understanding and compassion. We teach on death because it brings up vulnerability to a whole new level. When death walks in the door, there is such great misunderstanding and loss in the heart that one simply bows down, without questioning the mind. This is so powerful, but it only happens in times of struggle. And we say if you had this type of communion always, you would be in such Divine communication every day of your life.

We are not saying it is simply casual and unimportant to lose a family member or close friend, and we do not diminish your feelings towards this loss, but we simply point you to seek out the Divine within so that you can feel a sense of support when inside you feel so ripped up and hollowed out. When you are vulnerable is often the best time to reach out ...and most of you do. Take that opportunity to feel Love inside and feel the deeper connection and quest that we all have. It may just be the reason for all of this disorder in the Earthly realm. Death is not easy on the Earth plane, but when you see it from the perspective that we see it, it is the greatest gift, for it is a gift of coming home and recognizing ones true self—limitless, all-knowing, super powered, and with a heart of Love bigger than the universe itself.

You are in all-encompassing Oneness with All That Is, and that is the composition of the big family, and the many Yous which you could previously not distinctly see. From the realm of the nonphysical, many things become very prevalent and obvious in this way. For you on the Earth plane, your experience may be not this, though that is not to say it is unachievable, for it is, but you must train yourself to be open. And it takes some discipline, but not in the way you might think. This does not means like your exercise schedule...we mean, it takes some practice to let your mind sink into a new understanding and practice and then be integrated enough to start experiencing life in a new and higher place.

That is setting the bar high for the consciousness level that you are willing and accepting into your physical plane and human body. It is not hard, dear ones, but you must follow your innate, your Divine, and your God all the way. Come in close personal contact, for we are the ones who are your Divine Mother and Father. We are the bigger You, the Source of all-knowingness in the Universe and of you personally on your life experience. We want you to feel it alongside us, and the best way to come to that initiation or great equilibrium with God consciousness is to start allowing yourself that space inside to let it in.

Many of you unconsciously have your walls up, so bringing them back down is often a hard task. It means that you need to blast everything open and be willing to see it truly. Inside you see it first, and then automatically outside you will start to make sense of where you need to focus. It may be your relationships with your parents, or your family and friends, but they are all in relationships with You. That is the point we make, for these are relationships are on more than the one-dimensional physical realm. That is to say, start inwardly, and then uncover and work through the dimensions of the self that are hard to see.

Within there is unconditional Love, compassion, and a true identity that will be reflected outwardly, encouraging those around you to do the same. Your powerful individuality shows greatness, not just physically in a material world, but also inwardly, for you are honest, eager, helpful, and the most compassionate beings who walked the Earth. You are diligent, good listeners, and willing to stick up for yourself. You speak out when necessary, even if your personality is not outgoing.

You will start to outwardly portray a truer self that best suits you, which makes you feel confident, progressive, and willing to take on the world. You will notice that when you follow what is within, your power and greatness as an individual, and therefore as a collective, multiplies many, many times. It assists the whole universe by being who you need to be, and without reservations anymore. You will begin to feel an unsuppressed ability to do this, and now these are the times when you break through your shell. It may have taken many, many years, and maybe even many lifetimes, to come to this conclusion that you no longer need to look outwardly.

You no longer need to follow others' directions, relate to a path that is not yours, or stick with old patterns that are not healthy for you. These are the times that you come into, and if you consciously decide what you are willing and not willing to put up with, you consciously invite the universe to only supply those experiences and interactions that are the best and most encouraging to you, and to the others involved. This is a great form of compassion, for you are looking out for yourself, but also encouraging only positive and helpful interactions for others involved.

Times may arise where it is not the positive experience you are looking for, but then you see where that judgment comes from. Hello, mind! It wants to tell you what is right and wrong again, and you can feel inside your heart that despite what the mind has to say, an experience that outwardly feels and appears to be negative may be a very big blessing in disguise. So if you let it into your heart just as powerfully and just as graciously as any other experience, you train your Higher Self to experience and be willing to invite the warrior inside into your experience, and this initiates a great, great form of healing.

Not only are you more willing to take on any new venture or difficulty in your life, but you also see the blessing and the Divine reason behind each planned experience, and that is a great blessing in itself. Just to see, and not be challenged and boxed into the dimensions of the mind, is a great revelation indeed. This is a great teaching which can be used any day, for it can be so powerfully experienced in any circumstance, and doesn't have to be as dramatic as a death or a crisis.

You may find yourself in these circumstances in your lifetime, but it should not be a prevalent experience. It says nothing about your value, or about what you have personally done right or wrong. It has nothing to do with you, and that is something that often happens when a crisis arises—you blame yourself. Blame does nothing for the soul, dear ones, it just encourages the mind and sets gas to a fire. It rapidly takes off as big sparks in the sky...it is not a wise or fun event to let in. Take the time and initiative to instead invoke the Presence into your daily life and depend upon it. This may take time to have this occur, but it is worth your focused attention, dear ones!

Over time, the initiative and effort will diminish and the realizations will increase, creating a balance and structure in your life that is so much easier and less dependent upon outside sources to make you happy. Inside the heart lies all your tools and all your happiness. That is where it lies, and that is where the Akash lies with the wisdom of the many ages. Through a great, great experience and realization it can be truly uncovered in the heart. It has been a great pleasure, and we rejoice in the communication process with the human being who has so much Love in the heart to receive the Love and all-knowingness inside.

You not only live on Earth, you also live on the other side of the veil. We say *veil* because you do not see it, but that does not mean that it is not just as alive and present as the reality you experience on Earth. Rely on God, trust God, and be God in all that you are and all that you can be. You are eternal co-creators of your reality, the purest form of consciousness and Love within, and great masters of this age. Be that, and don't be foolish and small when you really come to this conclusion. Instead, you must walk out on the Earth and show what you've got, and from there on out you'll encourage it to duplicate like the domino effect.

You are all that you believe yourself to be. And we greet you again from a place of so much unconditional Love for you. We are exuberant to make this connection, as always, from a place that is all-knowing, consistent, and never ending. We trust you and the Source within to co-create circumstances and a reality that will greatly push the consciousness of this universe to a place that will integrate these ideas into daily reality. It happens within, and it is automatic if you wake up to your authenticity. You are one of God, and don't forget it, dear ones! And now we part with silence, though the heart is still very much alive with our Presence, and it is never dying. There is always connection, even when the words on the page cease. And so it is.

Chapter 30

Claiming Your Greatness

Oh dear children, it is such a joy to be here with you, to reconnect in these great times of curious and magnificent energies that are so overpowering! Whatever reservations you have, dear ones, to be something or someone that you aren't, remember what you are here for in the bigger picture. Remember your mission in your heart. The mind may not remember it, but if you look deep within to the untouched space that can recall the ever-present and endless knowledge in the heart, you will remember to fight for what you believe in. You will hold true to that with all that you are, for your being holds true in every way that another does.

This means you can bring individuality and greater Grace to this universe. You can bring forth a new understanding by incorporating your great gifts in a new way to yourself and those around you. You can bring so much to others by your Grace—don't dismiss it, for if you don't see yourself as the Grace of God, you put walls around yourself and that make you smaller inside the box. We want you to see the bigger You which is ever-present across many times and space. We want you to see the interdimensional being who lives in the heart and not the mind.

You are the interdimensional being who is graced by God to speak their Truth so that those around them begin to wake up and see who they authentically are in a new light. That is the mission of the human being who is awake and on the path of enlightenment. That is the mission of the being who sees Love in their heart and spreads it across the globe and across the big universe without hesitation. There is no part of this process that suggests you take away from yourself in order to give more to others.

We want you to build yourself up, and build your energy body up so that you can feel the empowerment and innately beautiful abilities you have to bring Love and healing across the universe. Truly, that is your capability when you reach deep down and see what is inside. You may be surprised by what you find. You may find you are on the right path, and you may find that what you are embarking on is something entirely different than what you expected to venture into. There are many reasons for the lifestyle you have, and all is Divinely perfect.

Give yourself the gift of joy and allow yourself to receive Love, as well as to give it. You are often so plagued by the notion that you must give in order to receive. And we modify this statement by saying, you must receive in order to give. You must receive the universal Love and support that we have to offer you in order to be capable of giving that, in an authentic and honest way, to those around you. It goes far beyond those that you know and Love most...it goes to the universe. Find Love in your heart to appreciate and bless those who are strangers to you, those who are ringing you up at the grocery store, those who are making your food, those who are a friend to you and listen to you, those who bring you to joy and new understanding, and even those who inspire change in you, even painful change. Blessings they are, and blessings you bring to those around you.

Look at yourself without the veil honestly and claim your greatness. Do not diminish your very crucial role in this existence, and do not call yourself small ...do not even think yourself small, for you are large! You envelope the energetic field that is the basis and foundation of All That Is. Is that small, dear ones? Sometimes you simply do not see the Truth in what we tell you so honestly. We do not throw out words for them to be discarded in a casual way. This is a loving reminder to keep your ears perked up, to really look at each word and sentence we deliver. They encourage you to claim your greatness and initiate a new degree of understanding of yourself and your Divine role in this universe with All That Is You, and all that which is made up of You.

You are so Divinely inspired, and we just want you to see it truly so that you can go about your life in a way that supports who you are. Don't come up with excuses about why you can't do it! Your mind will do that so naturally, and it may be a habit, but see it and decide with all of your being what your Divine mission really is, then seek that out. Don't plan it, follow it! You are already in the hands of God ...you do not need to find that out, for it is already part of you, and always has been. You must wake up to You and trust the universe to come and meet you where you are—put all of your faith in it.

We are the ones who are your true family—one that is eternal, as are you, and one that is there with you even when you are seemingly alone. Train your mind to look beyond the physical senses and trust that will uncover new bits and pieces of your authentic nature that will support your quest in coming into the Real You. You are essential, and that is not just in your quest but in the quest of the universal collective. You are essential in the coming home of your family, and also your bigger family that is in the process of waking up. It is your Divine purpose to strut your Divinity with such great care and loving passion in the heart that others will see what you've got and will want to be that too. We're not saying to be clones and start to acting like each other. In fact, it is quite the opposite.

You are funny beings that are easily provoked by numbers. If you see the greater majority starting to wake up, your soul will have no choice but to arise as well, saying almost, "Oh rats, I guess I better wake up too ...what a nice slumber, indeed!" And you'll carry on, as if nothing out of the ordinary just happened, but you'll physically and spiritually feel such a relief in your beingness, for there is no longer a push and pull, or a darkness and fog that you are blinded by. There is certainly no one that is able to convince you of who you are, or who you must become, and that is the essential freedom that you are waking up to, and it must be done. It must be done because these times are asking for a new kind of cooperation, one that is really leaning on the support of the whole. You must learn to Love each other and find the qualities in each other that support the greater whole. That is, you each bring individual qualities and strengths to the table that ultimately greatly impact the success and overall presentation of your universe.

It is hard to put into linear terms, but you are in a transition phase that encourages increased amounts of destruction in the ways that you are able to work with one another. It shows up in the government, which is bringing great chaos inside the system. Not only are beings unable to see the big picture, but they cannot stand the idea of following or believing in a viewpoint that is not their own. It qualifies as drastic measures, for it cannot be accomplished on its own, and needs the support of the wholeness.

What is needed is the support of the authentic and enlightened beings to show the freedom of letting go of the Self. Letting go of the Self means that you let go of fear, and without fear in the mind and heart, new opportunities for great understanding come in like shining sunlight, in a big picture sort of way, for ideas and new options to flow easily.

It's similar to when you try to count the amount of molecules in a liquid, for only great scientists are qualified to do that. Instead, we look at a greater scale that measures liquids as a whole, and in larger quantities. This is similar to humanity, for individually you are so beautiful and greatly influential, but as a whole you are like fireworks—you are like a tidal wave of Grace! When a tidal wave hits, it hits everyone in the area. In this metaphor we speak of the Earth plane. The Earth plane is so great and so vast, and you reside on it for the purpose of shifting the consciousness of the planet, and to change the way that you work together both physically and metaphysically.

It goes much beyond the physical realm, yet sometimes you still relate yourself only to the physical realm that you reside in. You must see past the mind, dear ones, for it allows you to expand your consciousness in ways that you don't even know exist. It allows you to expand your Love and compassion for the human beings who are not alike to you, who are not your friends and family. But you see, you seek them out because you feel you are so connected and in Love with each of them. They are your family, as are we. We are all family, One big family.

Some of us are in the Light, and some are in the dark. This does not mean in terms of rank, importance, how much you are loved, or how enlightened you are. We speak in terms of a great mission as a bigger picture. We speak of this so that you can relate yourself to the support system that is waiting for you to knock on the door. We want you to relate to us as your family, as the beings who are just as involved in your life experience as your close family and friends. We are inevitably One with you, with your life's creative process, and with all the many life experiences you have endured over many, many years.

You are the greatness that we speak of so often, and you sometimes let it sink in, and other times dismiss it to "come back to it" because it is somehow "over your heads." Yes, the mind shows up again. Fighting to regain strength, but each time you read these words, you awaken the heart and awaken the soul to the unconditional knowingness that you are. You will then find out for yourself why we say that You are Divine in every aspect. You do know it ...you know it inside. When the mind shows up do not try to fight it—instead, just let it come and go.

If you see it is there, and then you can see the bigger part of you on the other end of the string, you are well on your way. It is great when you can let the mind step aside enough to see that there is a very distinct difference and separation between the two. The ones who are in the dark are the ones who do not see the difference, and that is where they get into trouble, for they cannot be in the Light when the mind tries to bring them down and show them a very small degree of who they are. It is a brilliant process, and we bask in your magnificence wherever you are on your journey. It is nothing to try to change, and there is no destination to reach or initiate.

This is a process from your greater self and from your Divine, which is taking care of you from a bigger perspective. This perspective has no judgment, no fear, no personality, no smallness, and no insecurities. It is awesome power and Grace to embrace all that you are and have no reservations with it. It is a blessing to have the opportunity to greet the self and proclaim to yourself and to the mind, "I am who I am, and that is the greatness of All That Is so powerfully, in every dimension and beingness, that is ever-present in my dimensionality and in the dimensionality that is vast across the Universe. And in my greatness that is pure and holy, as the Grace of God collectively, I embrace All that I am, without smallness, and with the courage to speak my Truth."

That is what you must proclaim to yourself, and it's not a practice that is like sticking a Post-it on your fridge every morning as an affirmation; it is a trueness in the heart and a very sacred understanding and proclamation that you must let the heart see and really bask in. You often let the mind go off on tangents by using the same tools you have had in your shed for all circumstances and life experiences. Because you often return to the feeling of smallness, it is such a foreign and uncomfortable practice to even begin understanding how to greet the self with such reverence.

You are well, comfortable, and educated with worshipping and loving the Saints, the great masters, the angelic realm, the God-like figures in your cultural references, and all the rest in between, but you do not yet seek to identify or retreat to the inner Divinity. We wish for you to reconsider that, and to come back to it more often than just a sporadic adjustment or consideration. Make it a contract and daily ritual, one that is from the heart, and not like a to-do list that goes along with your grocery-shopping list. They are very different. We wish for you to see it, because once you see it you begin to incorporate it into your physical and daily experience. It becomes your Truth, unconditionally.

It allows your confidence to raise up to meet the Higher Self, to begin feeling comfortable with the greatness of You, and to not feel so self-conscious and out of place when you begin to come back to the wholeness and beingness that you have been apart from for so long. It is beyond your knowing just how important this is for you, for the soul yearns for your unconditional awareness of it. It has been with you for eternity, and wants to communicate with you from as place which is so knowing, so compassionate, and so, so loving. It is the place of You that recognizes your true identity and reminds you with loving compassion, and without judgment, that it is safe to come out of the spiritual closet and strut what you've got!

We mean it so truly, and many of you are doing it already. You know that it has shaped your lives, and the lives of those around you, so profoundly. It has given a new hope, a new desire, and a new outlook on who you are, what your potentials are, and what is ahead for you to achieve greatness in your true Love. It is our great pleasure to give you the guidance alongside you, and to be in unity consciousness all the way. It just feels good to relax in this place of stillness with you, like a warm bath on a cool winter night. It is such a relief, and the greatness of being who you are, without all the fussing and fighting, will rejuvenate you, giving such grace in the heart, and such Presence alongside you to complete what you've come to do. There are no mistakes, you are not alone, and you are not left alone to complete what you've got to offer. You may feel as if you have no Divine mission, but indeed, it does not need to be huge. Count your blessings, dear child, and see with honesty what you are. What are you letting the mind cover up that diminishes your greatness in your eyes? We see you from a place that shows all of your greatness without the veils, and potentials for you are determined by what you are willing to uncover and work with. You are the creator, dear one. You can determine what you are willing to use, and if you don't wish to pull it out all at once, there is a great place to save it up in your Akash.

You must also be aware that you have the great potential to let all your qualities out, lay them out on the table, and pick and choose the qualities and talents that you wish to bring forth into this physical reality plane. It is part of You in more than one way, in many facets of your beingness. It is a part of who you have become through many existences and realities, and it can be re-invented or re-introduced if that is your choosing.

We are so gladly willing to help you in this process if you choose to let the inner being speak through and dominate you. Let the voice of the heart ring true, and let it speak to the crowd and invoke the Presence in others. Let it encourage the rest to be who they came to be, and let them honor themselves as much as you honor them. You've gotten so in the habit of discouraging the practice of self-Love, and you've now recently come back to investing in this idea once again. You still have some reservations about it.

Seek out your own practice that best supports your true nature, and that is self-Love on its own. That is forgiveness of the self, and is what you're looking for. Forgiveness is what you came to do, to design the self in a way that better incorporates the greater You into many different dimensional realities at once. This helps to prepare the bigger You for times ahead, as seen linearly. So we say, follow that mission with integrity, and don't let those around you try to change you out of it, for they must follow their mission as well. Likely this will be one that is separate from yours, and that is also Divinely beautiful.

This has been a marvelous exchange; one of great beauty, heightened awareness, and a great internal knowingness that has come to the surface in each and every one of you. It encourages a new belief in yourself that you *can* do it. You can be all that you came to be, and with that great support system behind you, you can be that with little-to-no effort on your part. That is not to say no challenges will come up, but those that do will be dealt with while you remain calm and collected, because you now know that despite the bumps in the road, you are always utterly enveloped by unconditional Love.

You also know that you have family that is always beside you, pointing you in the right direction. The bumps in the road signify our Love for you, for they show you that change is necessary in order to grant your true blessings. You often see it as the opposite, as a curse, but that's because you look from the mind and not the heart. It is only when you look through the heart that you will realize your heart has been looking for this blessing in disguise for so long. So next time you come across a particularly challenging situation or interaction, go into the heart and put all else aside. Look straight into the heart of the situation and you ask you guides to come through and provide you with the loving support that you need.

Have integrity and ask honestly—don't get small and claim that you can do it on your own. It is not meant for you to do alone! The Earth experience is meant to be met with the knowingness that you can be with the wholeness and receive the guidance you need whenever you need it, on any subject matter, and with any circumstance. It is there for you always, and you must start to incorporate it without testing the waters, without the smallness of mind to do everything on your own. Doing things on your own only signifies to the mind that there is where you will remain—in the mind.

The heart wants to awaken, if you ask …just ask, and you will receive. Then the universe will come pouring in with all that you were holding back from yourself. Let it come, dear one, for we are here for you! Let us embrace you and show you who you are with so much unconditional Love! You are so beautiful, dear ones, and we want you to be here with us. Follow our guidance when you are in the dark, and follow our guidance because you are a human being on a mission. Follow our guidance when you are the awakened one, and follow our guidance so that you can feel balanced in the spirit. Feel the great energy and greatness of the self that you came to be, and baby, do it without reservations! Let that be your Truth and you'll go on with all that you are and bring a great authenticity to all that you do and all that you are.

What a brilliant and loving message this has been, and we see transformation taking place for each that read these words. It is ringing so true, for you all have a great mission and willingness to step forth with courage into the new being. You are ready to come forth and take flight! It has been a loving and beautiful interaction, and we now part with the new attention on your guidance system. You are eternal as always, and you are always God, eternally. You are always in the wholeness of All That Is, and you are never alone. You must claim your greatness and awaken your greatness without fear. And so it is.

Chapter 31

You Are Not Alone

And now we return, dear ones, to this magnificent space and time where great shifts and opening have begun. We are so grateful to be here spending these very precious hours by your side, and to be in a dimensional frequency that is assisting your personal and global shift into awakening. We are so blessed to be by your side, to show you new ways each time we come through, and to show you the wholeness and greatness that you are.

Sometimes you do not see the majestic qualities in yourself that we see, but it is assured by our presence of great Love and Light that indeed, you *are* All That Is, and you are everything that you came here to be. The Earth plane gives you such opportunity to experience life with new skill sets, new sensory details, and new gifts to be put into physical form. You are God in a fragmented manner, scattered across many dimensional realities and lifetimes. But you see, you experience one dominant pattern of thought and time because you are still in the present moment, and the present moment must be seen linearly on the Earth plane. We speak of this because you must know you are more than you experience, but do not be frightened by it, for the trueness of You is loving and caring.

The larger perspective You is so joyous in the process of life that you are experiencing and venturing into, and it is only a temporary experience that will soon be diminished. You will soon be back in the wholeness of who you truly are—interdimensional, whole, giving, loving, without concern and judgment, without fear and worries, and ultimately, without the great decision-making process. Entering into wholeness of All That Is is quite honestly all-knowing. That is your experience when you enter into it ... you experience all that the space has to offer as it envelopes you with its unconditional Love. You are One with it.

You are One with every being that you meet, though they are not singular. There is no separation, yet there are distinguished personality qualities that your beingness and remembering system can identify. When you enter into All That Is you cease to experience singularity. You see no separate bodies or entities that have names. What you truly see is a big family, like a big pot of soup. You experience all the tastes or qualities of that experience at once, in one big present moment. You experience the volume of it, you experience the effects it has on you, and you do not experience a singularity as you would on the Earth plane. The great quantity of soup is You, and behind the veil you accept it and Love it the way it is. You have no desire to change your experience, for it is your coming Home. What a relief it truly is!

Your perceptions of God are altered in the physical reality because your minds cannot see without the linear three-dimensional aspect. You cannot shake that, no matter how hard you try. It is, therefore, very difficult to see the way we see, but you also must realize this so that you can use your tools to see beyond. Even though you may feel limited in many senses on this Earth plane, you are still so very interdimensional and present in the higher dimensional realms. That is important to remember, as well, for you can bring yourself to that reality if you only used your tools and concentrated them in a proactive way. This ultimately shows you the trueness and wholeness of that pot of soup that is You, which you help create, which is all-knowing, and has no definition of singularity.

It is beautiful because you have no desire to be different and no desire to feel separate, for it is an existence that is simply your Truth. There is no fighting, there is only pure potentiality that greets you all with the same Love, guidance, and support system that you knew you had before you came to Earth. You, the higher You, *is* that guidance system! You see, you separate us too distinctly into God, angels, etc., and then you think of yourself as a separate entity that floats around mindlessly in the Earth plane, alone, without your family. Truly it is quite the opposite, for what you experience on the Earth plane is relative to what you are willing to experience, and that is up to you.

Your waking time is purely destined by You, and there are many factors which play a role in that destination. You see, there is no judgment here, and it is not determined by how good you are. Good and bad do not exist. So you ask, "then why are there beings who are asleep if they are truly loved this much and can't see it? Why are they left alone to fight and struggle in their own misery?" To this, dear children, we reply with great empathy for your strength and courage. We ask you to let us handle you, let us bathe you in our Grace, and let yourself see the great blessing it is to be here. You each have your separate destinies, even as you co-create the same beautiful Earth— your home that you are trying so hard to re-establish and bring peace to.

You see, the being that struggles is being given a blessing, though you see it oppositely. The being is given transformation, and through that they will begin to move into a new understanding of who they are and the role that they play in this great universe. They might not wake up in this lifetime that you see presently, but they are on a path just as you are. All is beautiful. You had the same journey in a personal sense. When they pass away and return to the wholeness yet again, they are further along on their journey that the higher-self planned out, and they are also thankful and grateful to have taken another journey on this Earth plane. So you see, there is no experience that is positive or negative, though the human mind will characterize it in that way.

You put categories and labels on everything. To the human being who is very fearful and afraid, experiencing a singular perspective, we say *trust us*, dear one. Dear child of the Light, that is your name. We know you, we feel you, we experience you, we hold you with our great ever-extending arms of Grace, and we whisper with Love in your ear. You are loved. You are Grace. You are all that we are! If you would just see it for how it is you would start to wake up. You would start to appreciate your greatness.

It is also important to know that it is not a responsibility to try to fight those who are separate and different than you. It is, in fact, a Divine knowing inside that will show you that despite your external actions and beliefs about who you are, you are a mix of the whole. The singularity that you believe to be true is such an illusion. And it is meant to be that way, but start loving your brothers and sisters and see life as a game, for it truly is a big game that you chose to come into so that you could experience the life process. The life process is one that uses different tools than you used before, and what a blessing it is. It not only awakens you in a new reality, but it helps you to move into your greatness no matter where you are—and that is our point exactly.

The transcending and illumination that is presently occurring on the Earth plane is so vast and so powerful. The awakening point is so bountiful and profound! You see the small numbers, but we ask you to look back and remember a time in your Akash when there was no such hope. There is *so* much hope now, dear ones! There is so much Love and Grace that you've let pour through the many realities of You, and it's taking over the Earth by creating a brilliance in every human. It is Grace, and it is the human being who is now waking up to see that a new and awakened experience is necessary, and ready to be from the higher aspects of You. You direct yourself to that outcome, to that higher understanding.

When you receive the message "from above," you say, it is truly You speaking to you. You put labels on it because you believe yourself to be so small and so much less than God. If you said, "Hey friend, nice to see you again," so casually but with such reverence, dedication, and respect in the heart, you'd see that we are equals. We are God together, and we are the closest friends you have ever known. So we ask you with great respect and great understanding from your experience on the Earth plane ...start remembering these aspects of yourself, and try to stop putting categories and labels on everything. Try to begin to look at your life with honesty and an openness to receive All That Is behind the veil into your current reality.

Once you accept it, God will pour in! You'll feel such a relief that you are truly not alone, you are always part of the same wholeness. And guess what—you never left! So we say, set aside any notions that you may have integrated throughout this lifetime that you are not this greatness, that you are not capable. Set aside whatever you have been taught through your parents' experiences, through religion, through schooling, and through what you may have experienced with less of tools than you presently have now. Set them aside, not throwing them away with disrespect, but set them aside so you can upgrade. Throwing them away would signify that you are ashamed or ungrateful for that experience of being in the dark. You now know it is a great blessing to be in the dark.

Soon enough, you've gotta wake up. You've gotta see your Truth. When the time comes that you upgrade, you will be able to see the big picture—that all the experiences in your lifetime thus far are, in fact, a great blessing. In the wholeness and Grace, all has been designed and carefully planned just for *you*! The shift helps you see and experience gratitude for all that it is, and not just the part of awakening. There is no wrong or right answer, it is just about seeing without the filters. With the filters all you can see are the right and wrong decisions, and that is missing the ultimate point. Truly, we respect all of it. If you cannot identify with the words spoken just yet, that is beautiful as well, for you are on your journey, as is everyone else.

Don't feel alone when your mind jumps in, puts categories on you, and makes you feel insecure. There is no ahead or behind, and there is no destination. All is present in the Now, and all is lovely the way it is. We are not indicating that if you have an inkling to do something risky or destructive that you should go ahead with it because everything is "just right." No, that is not what we are saying to you, dear human being. If you listen closely, you'll hear a new definition spoken, and we will repeat again. We are saying that when you open to the knowingness which is more vast than your mind can see, you will experience a greater understanding of what you have to offer, and you'll see that whatever path you have taken is beautiful and so Divinely perfect.

If you are in the Light and make conscious efforts to walk away from who you are, that is a conscious and destructive action, and you may be becoming too confident. That is not to say that it is wrong. We cannot truly and honestly use that term and identify with the meaning that you use it as. It is nonexistent, but we would say we wouldn't necessarily provoke or encourage these actions in your life, for we think they are not helpful. If, when stumbling through life, you come across a bumpy road (and you will) don't feel like you've messed up! That is our point. There is a big difference between conscious beingness and the co-creative higher beingness that leads you on your way.

They are two different viewpoints or standing points—one that sees the bird's-eye view from way above, and the other that sees at eye level. These two are drastically different. So for example, if you choose to become an engineer, and you are feeling pressured by your family because you need to make the money, or you are raising a child, we ask you to evaluate what standpoint this decision may be coming from. If you answer the eye-level point of view, you would be correct. So we say to you, our only point in going through this process in detail is that you create your own reality.

If you move into the heart, these external motivations and illusions between the mind and heart will become less dominant. Instead of folding in and bowing down to those around you—even your family who may make you feel small—you will stand up and remember that you have the power and initiative to be something else. You do not need to follow the path that is outlined for you—in fact, that is the greatest mistake you make. We do not use the term *mistake* as a wrong or negative emotion. We ask for you to just see that you are in control. You can say *no* when the heart feels a pull to another system, another life, or another type of lifestyle. When you get on board, nothing will stop you! You will be able to see a greater possibility, a greater outcome, and a greater bird's-eye view of what you're capable of when you design your own reality. Say *no* to a path that you know you are not meant for.

If you want to live your greatness, you must live it with all that you are! That cannot mean 25 percent in one direction, and 75 percent in another. It means you must put your heart and soul into your life purpose and go full speed ahead without hesitation, without considering and evaluating what other people are going to think, because ultimately, this is your life.

Yes, you have attachments to family, friends, and work, but when you see from our viewpoint, in the end, you will greet God alone. In reality, you are very much not alone—you are present with All That Is beyond the veil. You'll see that the physical family present with you on Earth is only one piece of you, and when you return back Home, your mission remains the same. So we just remind you, we don't mean to say you should be egotistical and care only about yourself...but we do say, don't let others, especially those who you are close to you, define the trueness that is inside. Claim it, rewrite your future, and don't be afraid to speak your Truth. It's what you are about, and it is what you are in great literal terms. You are pure forms of consciousness and Truth.

We want you to feel confident and more whole by using your tools while you are living the Earth experience, and much of that has to do with speaking your Truth without fear of being judged. And we say with great honesty, you will be judged, but you can choose to let that bother you or not. If you are comfortable in your skin—so comfortable with the power of authenticity and your Truth—it won't matter one bit what others think you are. You may even laugh at them for coming up with such definitions of you, because you are so much bigger than that! Some will see your greatness, and others will not, but the importance lies in what you believe yourself to be. So let that alone be your Truth, and then you can carry on with your life with such ease, with such a great flow.

It is a great gift to be able to see yourself this way and to not let others waver you. That takes confidence and strength, but you are the warrior! You are the greatest master within. Remind yourself of this when you struggle to be in the fullness that you are. Remember that this path is simply a journey, one that the physical body will experience for growth for a short period of time. So dear ones, take it on with your warrior spirit! Try to bask in every aspect of it—the fun and not so fun parts, all of which shape you. They all make a big impact in the end, in the big soup of who you are. This is the journey ...this is your journey.

You will reenter into the nonphysical with a "body" that is not singular—you will no longer have your linear and singular bonds, but you'll have the same loving, infinite, and protective family guiding you every step of the way. The fear and regrets will melt away. Just live what you've got without the attachments. You have little time, but you have the ability to make as great a change as you can dream up. You've got the warrior spirit to bring peace on Earth. You are the old soul looking for yourself, and you've found it. You've found it because you are God in many forms, because you can relate to yourself in a new light, and because you trust that where you are on your journey is beautiful, destined, perfect, co-creative, and Divinely inspired from the bird's-eye view of the master within. The Higher Self, the greater You, and God have got it all taken care of.

This has been a great and holy communion with the spirit who has committed to a life purpose of bringing Love and Light to the world through holy community between Source and man. And we say to that brave human being who is also the warrior spirit, right on! You are the pavers of the Light, you are the brick layers who show the way to the authentic enlightened path. This path is individual and differs for each of you, but the quality of it, the sustenance, joy, bliss, and fulfillment, remains the same. So in fact, the fulfillment of the individual being is just as effective and efficient to the world as a whole.

It has been a great privilege and great blessing to gather in this manner and review your authentic nature. It is a topic that is so prominent in your beingness, and will continue to grow and prosper as the planet awakens into its own Divinity within. You are each Divine aspects of us, and of the greater whole. We will keep re-enforcing it in your cellular structure, for that is what occurs when you re-read the words on the page. It is beyond a gift, and beyond a blessing that you are reading these words, and you can thank none other than yourself for this privilege. You may have permission to thank yourself. You are beautiful, you are undying Love, and you are all that you believe yourself to be. And so it is.

Chapter 32

Let Go and Let God - Your Destiny Is Waiting

Your Light makes the difference, dear ones, whether you choose to see yourself in this great powerfulness or not. You can choose to be in that Presence, to be in that space of communion and Love, or you can show up with absolutely no attachments or promises. That is what we call the detached human being who is on their mission but lost in their own world. When you arrived here on the Earth plane there were no such confusions...you were so sure of yourself and so sure of the universe. What you have come to find now is that you are bigger than the mind will ever let you claim. But you see, with the help of the heart and a little bit of pushing and shoving, you can overcome it! You must insist on equality and no longer live solely from the mind.

Dear ones, this is the time to shift into awakening. This is the time to stop making up excuses about whether you are safe to be yourself or not, for what you are losing by not making that commitment to yourself is greater, much greater than the fear within that holds you back from living your truest potentials. Those truest potentials are determined by you, and you only. With the help of your guides, your angels, your masters, and whatever form you put us in, we guide you and provide the support, the comfort, and often the validation. Validation is most important to help you stay revitalized, energetic, joyful, and lighthearted during this great mission and life experience.

You learn so many new experiences that were not previously used or identified, and you used so many tools that you don't use now. So where did it go? Dear ones, you must claim what you've got and stop making up excuses from the mind. Your perception of separation is an illusion. Wake up to see who you are, come into that with Grace, and automatically you will find that the value of life so drastically changes. The simplistic lifestyle may be more appealing, for its maintenance is low, but oh-so juicy! You see, the material objects and quantity of objects are no longer fulfilling or appealing, but the gifts that feed the soul, oh, they bring such joy! The small gifts of nature, family, good food, and friends are so much more important. So we say, it is the time to let yourself accept that you are a spiritual being expressed in a human body. You are matter, energy, and eternal life smashed into a physical form.

Your physicality naturally compacts and puts walls up around the boundless energetic field of consciousness that you Truly are. So we say with honor and great respect, we bow down to you, dear human being, for setting the way right for those to come. You are bringing such great Light in a time where it was once seen as positively unripe. But now you are ripening as a planet and as a globe. It even goes beyond that, for it is a shift in the entirety of the universe.

So we say, what a gift it is to be present in that, to see yourself as that Divine aspect and to proclaim inside, "This is me and I know it!" Once you do that, you give yourself the greatest gift in the universe—unconditional Love for oneself. You can then begin to accept heaven's help. You'll notice that the guidance unfolds so naturally, in a sequence of events that benefit you in every aspect. It is not a matter of whether God hears you, it's a matter of whether you heard God. You must simply knock on the door and make that first communication. You must show you're ready to receive. This is not for us, dear ones, it is for you. It is all for you.

The form and names for channels are for you, the personalities that flow through are for you, and the characters and ways of speaking through the physical being are unique. But indeed, what always remains the same is God, and we are God. There is only one Source, even as you put labels on different entities and channels, there is only One. Some call it God, and others call it Source. Names do not matter! So you see, that is our only valid point to make here. When you step into unconditional Love, you accept heaven's help. Direct Love and guidance are waiting to blast open with your permission!

You are great and powerful beings, and as you move into the wholeness of the universe, you will find that what you thought yourself to be, down to the materialistic and physical details, are just expressions—they are patterns of energy and thought processes that are expressed into human physical form. They are used to co-create a new reality for human beings and Mother Earth. This is a topic that goes far beyond what can be said through words, but with a great knowingness in the heart, all that is said here can be understood through a deeper knowingness in your Akash. That is what we wish for you to focus on when reading these words.

The many emotions and various expressions that you utilize as a physical being are for bringing about transformation within. It can be very nice, and it can also be somewhat of a struggle, but in the end, transformation is all that is necessary. Within you is the eternal knowingness of the history of the universe...yes, you are that old! You are that great. You have the ability to retrieve the memory in your Akash. You are inter-connected with the Source, and with the Akashic records of the universe.

So you see, you cannot possibly feel another alternative than the joy and sigh of relief when coming Home, because Home is your natural state. Home, as we speak of it, is the pure state in which we reside, and where you also reside. Sometimes you do not realize it, but you reside in this place of still, interdimensionally as much as we do. It is grace, it is calm, it is warm, safe, and trustworthy, and quite truly a gateway for coming into union with your own Source. We let you find out what that is for you, for it will be different in nature for each and every one of you.

You do not need to have any agitation or discomfort around that idea, for it takes no judgment, and no active involvement or emotional attachment on your part. That is to say, if something makes your heart sing with joy and that is your Truth, nobody would (or could) try to convince you otherwise! Doubt is not part of what's inside the heart! Maybe it resides in the mind, but not the heart. All is an illusion—just know that what goes on in the mind is not coming from You, it comes from a compilation of rendezvous from the physical dimensions and from beyond the veil. There is a lusciousness, a density of dimensional frequencies or realities which you do not perceive, but nonetheless, you exist in it. You are part of it.

In that space of knowing who you authentically are, you can feel such joy and relief that no matter where you are on your path, it feels so wonderful to know you are Divinely taken care of. It is so easy, so flowing, and brings so much air to your step! You can relax and hand over all that is beyond your control to the Divine—to God, your angels, your guides, or your masters. You illuminate your soul, and you illuminate those around you as you speak the Truth of Oneness. To give another validation that they are who they believe themselves to be deep inside is a great gift.

To be a lightworker means to pave the road and be a beacon of Light. You are like a lighthouse in the middle of a vast ocean, for you point the way to those lost as sea. Much of humanity is lost at sea, and they need you to be the courageous soldier! The Light warriors are strong and powerful enough to take the job and to hold it as their mission, life purpose, and Divine Truth. You are a lightworker. With every action, every step you take to validate to yourself and provide yourself with tools and opportunities to come into your greatness, you illuminate the path for others as well. Do not doubt for a moment that you're not who we say you are. Even as you feel insignificant, you still shine Light, and you are still embodiments of Divine Grace.

Even if you did not choose to turn any of your gifts or passions into your life purpose, you would still be supported. And of course, you would then remind yourself later that it would have been nice to have a friend through all the tricky stuff you went through. You so often complain before you look inside and find your stillness. The answers are within. With that we remind you that there is a time and place for everything, and when your time has come, it will be illuminated for you. Until then, let yourself bask in who you truly are, and let that be your Truth if none else can be found. You are the co-creator, and you are the greatest master of this age. Stop waiting and take action steps towards the destiny that is for You! And so it is.

Chapter 33

Open the Doors!

It is so beautiful to be here, dear ones, gathered together as One big family in such a vastness. But indeed, we are so close...so close. You see yourselves as far apart and singular, but in reality, you could not be closer. The linear and three-dimensional form in the mind does not show you what you want to believe in the heart ...but no matter, for you have the ability to let it shine through despite the barriers of the mind. It is your Divine purpose to speak your Truth from within, dear ones. It is your mission, quite truly, for it brings joy and carefree personality into a world that is too strict and straight faced, one that doesn't have enough fun.

You don't sing and dance enough! You don't jump around, play with sidewalk chalk, and be fearless as you once did. That's the carefree joy you once had as a small child. There were no conditions to your joy then, ones which you have now been trained to have. You have been taught that you must have lots of money, a job, and a solid relationship to make you happy. As a small child you didn't put these conditions on yourself, you only knew what was your Truth, and that was the joy and happiness that you expressed through the physical body.

Most of you do not see the correlation of which we speak. For some of you, adulthood it is a matter of maturity, simply a different stage in life. We say it is conditionings that proclaim that to you. To us, the activities and mindsets do not matter throughout any age, it is all the same. We say quite truly, the ones who last the longest on this Earth plane are the ones who live joy in their bodies. They activate every part of their being, and their cellular structures are alive and communicating! It is such a blessing to be part of that communication, for it allows the human being to be open and receptive to listening and digesting what the body has to say. It is so intelligent for your openness to hear.

You must start to wake your body up, and with that, the mind gets sharper too. It cannot happen through mental exhaustion, as you are often taught in the workplace and in the school environment. You must start to awaken to what works best for you and stop trying to place yourself inside the box. You are beings of individuality, quite literally in every cell of your body. Even as we are joined by the bonds of Love and Light, we are beings of individual energies, and you must allow yourself to embrace that. Society as a whole often does not embrace this, but dear children, if you follow your own guidance system, that which fits best for you will be the enlightened path you take. If you get tuned in, you won't feel so entrapped by the societal norms and regulations. You are the only one that can imprison yourself inside the box!

And we'll tell you, the box doesn't really exist—it is just a means of seeking guidance as a society when you feel lost. You naturally cling to each other. If you can find guidance within, there is no longer fear of venturing into the unknown. You can never really be clones to each other, even though you may act that way sometimes. You are outwardly projecting images of singularity, communicating in similar fashions, and taking up similar hobbies and interests, but you can never truly be clones. It's an excuse...it's your Higher Self that brings you into misalignment so that you can come back into alignment and walk the great journey of seeking.

It is a great gift to seek, to learn, to find new opportunities, and to discover the Grace of God within you with the touch of your angels guiding you. If you look at your life, truly look at it without the veils of deception and judgment, you will see happening after happening of sheer guidance from beyond the veil. You will see with clear eyes that life is nothing but this. You are never alone. There is not preformed fate in a way that is set in stone. Yes, you planned what you were coming to Earth to do before re-emerging, but there is nothing on the Earth plane that suggests that you are not the co-creator of your own reality.

Don't be so afraid of everything! You can change anything at your own will. You are a magician, and you are a pearl. You have so much power right in the palm of your hands, and it's important to open them up and let yourself receive what you are being given. Have an open heart for the Grace of God, and the unconditional Love of the universe that just wants to hold you and embrace you, guide you and encourage you. Let it blast in and hold you. It's always there, but when you acknowledge it, give credit to it, communicate with it, be in reverence with it, and be in communion with it, it grows! You also grow proportionally. You expand your Light, you expand your Love and compassion, you expand your knowledge of what you have to offer to the universe, and you expand your understanding of the universe and your role in it.

The fear you may have once had disappears so quickly when clarity comes and puts the mind in its place. It leaves you detached from those tangents and ramblings that went on inside the mind previously. You can see and feel such serenity and peace in the silence of the mind, and it comes when you open up the door to receiving Grace. It takes time to surrender, and may take more than affirmation. It takes practice and repetitive action steps. And we are not saying that you must direct Grace in a certain way, but we are saying that as old habits and customs have accumulated over time, it will take a mindset change to get you back on track.

Just be open minded to receiving insights that you need at the right time, and don't judge them. Sometimes you are so quick to judge without having the slightest clue as to why you're even judging. It has no plausible reason, nor is it valid in the first place. Remember that the Source is all knowing, and you cannot judge that. Your mind, however, sees only a sliver of the wholeness that you are, and therefore it lets you down in doubt when you try to reconnect with the Source within. If you see what's going on, then you can let the universe flood in and open you up automatically. You have nothing to do in life but to go with the flow that is already put in place. You have nothing to pave, and nothing to work out.

The system is already going and has been going for eternity. All you have to do is relax in that and feel the stress wash away. You are being taken care of because you are in eternal Grace. You are in the presence of a great and luminous God who is showing you every step of the way to a life that better incorporates every piece of you that you have to offer. All of these qualities and traits have been designed by your Divinity within. You'll find nothing but Love and great respect for yourself and your body that you are living in because you can see yourself for what you truly are. Everything else washes away without a second thought.

You see, you are not the body, though you experience reality this way. You still are part of the body, but you are not confined to the body. You are part of it because you chose to be here at this time and space reality. When you relax into that, you can feel another indicator that waves a red flag in front of you saying, "Hey, hey! I'm here, I am who you know I am!" And that is God, that is the great and holy God that you bow down to. And you never once thought that you could be God, or even part of it. God is All That Is, and God is you. God is not demanding, overpowering, superior, commanding, conditional, or anything besides Love. To feel and associate God in these ways is simply a three-dimensional conditioning that you have been taught to sincerely relate to, though inside it cannot ever truly resonate. God is not commanding, God has no judgment, and God is no one identity! God is many facets of You, and many facets of all beings and walks of life. God is non-denominating. God is not separate in religions and different viewpoints. God is humanity, God is Love, and God is the universe. So we now ask you, how could you not let God in to your life? How could you not let that pure essence of God within You into your heart with unconditional Love?

You are the light within, and it is beyond a blessing to be here and speak of these terms from a place of stillness and silence. We enjoy this time to prod and poke into the unknown, the parts of You that the mind cannot always see and appreciate. You can feel it, though, and you can know its power by the way it feels inside. All you need to do is focus on the inside and let it be true with your soul. The answers come at the right moment, and there are no mistakes or wrong turns. There are only experiences and lessons learned. As you grow, your spirit grows. As you move into awakening, every bit of the multi-faceted You grows and matures exponentially. *You are* making progress, dear one. You are already Divine.

When we start to communicate from your soul, you find that you are in fact a great, great addition to God, not separate. You start to become overwhelmed and overjoyed with the presence of the Self, and feel nothing separate about You and God. That is a great revelation for the human being, and is essential. That is a big turning point for you, dear ones, because it gives you permission to be held and taken care of in a tender way. Even as adults who want to be (and have been taught to be) self-dependent, strong, and courageous, you must rely on the Divine. You are not alone, and you are not expected to plan every step of the way. If you let go of that burden, your spirit will fly high and help you see from a plane that you are unable to see on your own.

It is important to stop fighting to be the best of everyone's standards, because standards change from person to person, and you must fit your own standards and your own greatness. You cannot live powerfully and in such resonance with your greatness and individuality if you are fitting and living someone else's life. It is life draining, instead of life coming in like a breath of fresh air. Make sure to check up on yourself and evaluate which pattern you are in. Are you being drained or being revitalized? You know what you want! If you would only follow it like the young children do with no fear, the doors will open.

You must have utter faith that they will open. The moment you put your walls up, your fear and distrust in the universe's ability to provide for you blocks you from being in a position of not allowing universal support. It is contradictory to what your point or mission is, and that is why we inform you of this—it is most commonly unconscious. If you follow your heart and let the doors open with receptivity, trust, and less evaluation from the mind, you will notice fluid transitions, life changes, and decisions will become so easy. There will no longer be any straining, energy-sucking behaviors, or side-effects. You know the difference, dear ones. Sometimes you pretend like you are naïve, but we don't know why you do. You could be spending your time much better basking in all that you are.

You're so unwilling to put your walls down because you look around and others have them up. To you, it seems impossible to have decent and open communication with someone who is so different from you. When walls go up, you are no longer in a place of accepting and receiving automatic messages, and intuitive guidance from the universe. That only makes you feel more distant from who you really are. Trust that you're here at the right time and place, and roll with it.

Let the secrets be uncovered with great awe and mystery. It is not a punishment to be here, dear children, it is a growth experience that you signed up for. It benefits your soul on many levels.

You came here to experience what life has to offer. It was you who chose it, dear one. You chose to be here, and so it is your turn to be your greatness. Get started on your life purpose and don't hesitate! You have an entourage of guides and angels by your side, and your internal Love engine rumbles with anticipation for you to acknowledge it and say, "I Love you!" When you do that, when you take that little step, you're ready to come into harmony with All That You Are, and the universe has no choice but to assist you. It's not so hard, dear ones. It's not so bad. Just know that you are loved, you are whole, and you are supported. Read these words with the genuine and honest knowing that we are right beside you. Indeed, not in physical form, but we reside within each and every one of you, and we have individual and personal relationships with you all.

Make the communion possible by saying *yes* to your greatness, dear ones. You are so Divine! Even if you don't know it yet, we tell it to you now with definiteness. We Love you so very much, to infinity and beyond, and we will never let you go, for you are always in our arms of Grace. You can bask in it or you can close the doors and continue to function in the separation of the mind. You are not alone even if you choose to have that be your experience. All is well, and all is good. And so it is.

Chapter 34

Finding Vibrational Alignment with the Source Within

We are here, dear ones, for the purpose of co-creating, for the purpose of self-Love, and for the purpose of empowering you to be who you came to be without hesitation, distrust in your mind, or fear of being judged. You see, dear ones, though your perception on judgment is a bit skewed, you came to be here in your truest identity, and whether or not that is accepted is beside the point. You are here with the presence of others by your side, and for the record, they have the same true identity behind them as you do. They may be less aware of their desire for it, but the holes and longing that show up give them a reason to look for other excuses to determine the root of their longing.

There is a great hope for you, and there is a great mission to be here and create change, to be happy in your skin, to find Love in All That Is, to be in the present moment, and to seek to invigorate every sense of the activities and job that you move forth with in your life. Ultimately, you seek to feel as if you on are a free flowing ride ...like a downhill ride. Sometimes you will encounter sporadic bumps in the ride, but if your dominant and active vibration is, for the most part, a high flying vibration of Love, healing, and joy, then the little bumps in the way that show up will be invalid. It will not phase you on your journey, for you are aware and accepting of your place in it.

You will find that, despite being temporarily confused and having lack of judgment about your wavering emotions and lower vibration, you will be able to see beyond this circumstance and see the bigger picture, which is You. You will ultimately rise above and not let that vibration take hold of you by the neck as it once did before.

It is a great gift to be part of this age of awakening and global shift in human consciousness. It is truly a great shift in the expansiveness of All That Is. We give you time to let that sink in, for it cannot happen all at once...it must come in phases to fully support the human body. You need time to integrate. Your spirit body is fully integrated in this shift of understanding and beingness of Oneness with All That Is. It is no surprise or new observation, but your physical mind has yet to understand it. Your cellular structure knows it, and your body has so much intelligence that you do not give it credit for. Your body has so much to offer you, and yet you sit there in stillness and remain motionless as if to say, "Don't look at me! Don't see me! I'm trying to hide out and just be unaware of everything that I am!" It's quite humorous, because each and every one of you do this in personal distinct ways.

You hide from who you are because you are here on Earth to very honestly come away from who you are for a while in order to go on the journey of coming back into alignment. That is the greatest lesson of life. It gives fulfillment, it gives grace to the heart, and it gives a heightened appreciation for who you are, who you came to be, and the support system that is here for you. You are even actively a part of this support system on a higher level of knowing. You see, it is the part of you that sees you have become an interdimensional being to co-create a reality of his or her own, and to bask in that creation until they die.

After you "die" you come back into alignment with who you truly are, and usually return yet again to the Earth plane because you get such a kick out of it! We don't appreciate the term "dying" or "death" because you are quite truly eternal beings, and part of All That Is. You croak, but you then come into the fullness that has no time space reality as does yours. It is a different way of perception, but it is nonetheless very real, and very interactive.

You see, it's the bigger picture that counts, and that's what you saw when you decided to take the big leap. You didn't see the bumps in the road, and you didn't see the struggles and mishaps, destruction, chaos, and sadness. You saw hope, desire, love, kindness, peace, and a true opportunity to shift a planet. There was no fear or hesitation, because you knew that no matter how lost you might get, you would never *truly* be lost, for you have a guidance system that is beside you every step of the way. No matter what you may be told, there is no right or wrong, and there is no wrong turns taken. All is Divinely guided, and you are no mistake.

That is not to say that you were unaware of what you were getting yourself into, because you did, but you didn't see it from a negative perspective as you do now. You saw it from the bird's-eye view that proclaimed to you, "You are on a mission, you are the being to bring the Earth alive with your Presence, your individuality, your Truth, and your undying Love." You spoke with your big family about your conditions, about your offering to serve again on the planet, and to help bring peace on Earth. You spoke about the lifespan, your endeavors, your creations, and your life experience in great detail. You spoke from a place of all-knowingness, as we do to you now.

It is a journey that you knew you alone could make...and you knew you would be very influential, even as pure beingness in a small body. Even though perception affirms that to you, the expansiveness of your light body is much wider, much taller, and much more dense than you could ever perceive physically. You can make that shift possible, for the infiniteness of You is just as vast as the universe, and the perception of being small is quite false.

Here in this plane or realm of great energy, great knowingness, and great Love for All That Is and all that we are, we have great respect for you. We have great respect for your mission and great support as the shift is greeting you now in a more powerful and profound way than ever. It grows day by day as you greet your interdimensional self without the veils.

You are making the difference, dear ones! Don't for an instance convince yourself that you are not the wholeness and the boundlessness that you truly are! You are not the small little light at the end of the tunnel ...you are so much more vast and powerful than that. That is our greatest joy: to help you to see that so that you may empower and embark on greater journeys going forward. It no longer just impacts your own evolution, dear children, it impacts the evolution on the entire universe. Truth *is* the greatest form of Love at the root foundation. Truth is what is awakening.

It is our greatest joy to help you to remember, for when you recognize the trueness, you start to wake up and become alive again! You start to have a definition of life again, for life is not about surviving, it is about living the true essence of Truth. What is Truth? It is Being, and Being is not surviving. Being is awareness in the present moment. Being is feeling okay with What Is, and Being is the definition of living. They are connected and intertwined, quite truly. The many facets of You are also connected and intertwined by the Grace of God, for you are all-knowing in that vast sense as well. It is beyond your comprehension to grasp many of the concepts we give, but they come through as a result of what you are willing and able to hear, and nothing more. You must know that we do not release empty words. That is to say, if you are not asking them on a conscious level, or on a level, which at some part of your being, you are able to recognize, then we cannot give you all that knowledge that we have to offer. Indeed, the questions must be asked on some level by you, or by some conscious active living part of you. The role that You play in the beingness of you is great. And when we say You with the capital letter, we are indicating many fragmentations that play a part in the physical experience which you call reality. Indeed, there are many more features or levels of beingness to that physical reality, but you experience only one on a dominant conscious level.

So you see, you underutilize your tools by forcing yourself to experience a reality that is not authentic. You must see beyond what you see with the physical eyes and the physical body, and train yourself to use all the senses that you possess. It comes down to being in constant contact and communication with your internal body structure. You must treat your body as if it were living creature, because in trueness, it is. Somehow you still have yet to understand that concept, for yet again, you see the outside of your body as all that is there. You are far greater than your bones, flesh, muscles, organs, and tissues. You don't look beyond that because it is so foreign and undistinguishable by the mind.

You have not yet trained yourself to experience beyond the mind. For those who see the difference, you'll start to come to terms with this understanding, and even start applying it on many levels and in many aspects of your life. Communication runs far beyond the self, just as sound flows. Communication runs interdimensionally as conscious energy waves, energy fluctuations, and energy manifestations. So you see, communication can be used as a tool to access dimensional realms, dimensional beings, and even other physical beings in a way that is deeper than the physical sound that flows from the mouth. Your vocabulary is simply one tool of many. It is so 3D, so linear, and so shallow.

You can use communication from body to body, you can use communication from mind to mind, and you can use communication from heart to heart. You use the terms quite loosely, but when we speak to you, dear children, we speak quite literally. We wish for you to really experience every word we offer you. When we say heart to heart, we literally mean, two or more hearts that communicate on their own without any instruction or intervention from your physical being or your physical mouth. You know communication runs deeper, but you don't understand it, so you don't investigate and use it. And we say, that is understood, but it is similar to when you were born into a baby who was small and vulnerable—you had so many things to learn, all of which was new. Even as it was a new phase, you came in with a heartiness, a joy, and a great eagerness to delve into all these new aspects of You.

You had to learn a whole new beingness that goes completely against the emptiness and wholeness of that which you experienced nonphysically. We say to you, we're just asking for minor adjustments, not such a drastic change as a baby has to learn. It will ultimately help you to experience life in a joyful, flowing, and easy manner. It will help you see the joy in All That Is, both the positive and negative. The fullness that you are will not prevent you from coming into your authentic beingness if you fully allow it with your conscious, innate, co-creative abilities. If you simply choose to live in your fullness, without interruptions of outside forces, that is clear intent.

You are such a true being of Love, dear ones. You are so completely, so powerfully, so innately Divine beings, and it is your Divine right to live it. Dear ones, we give you the process of life. It is a process that is Divinely inspired, Divinely followed, and Divinely Love. You are the authors of your own book...you write it, and you have the power to publish it to the world. You don't need to be fearful, because you are already authentic and individual. That is not a surprise to us, nor is it to you, but it is your decision whether you want to come into vibrational alignment with That Which You Are or not.

It is your choice whether you choose to be phased by those around you, or if you carry on your interdimensional reality and personality of beingness in your true sense, in an outward way in the physical realm. Even though others may judge you, it matters not, for the foundation of Truth will override any insecurity that may have previously been there. So who cares if they judge you? They may inflict pain and even misery on others, but your birthright is more important and worth being rather than fighting and being in the dark for your whole lifetime. You agree? This is such a trueness that we *know* you are destined and waiting for. We know this because you seek fullness, and that is the innate beingness and wanting that is undeniable in each and every one of you.

Some of you fill the void with destructive actions and substances, toxic relationships, and denial of self. Somehow that is supposed to be comforting, because you are so lost that your judgment is flawed. Unfortunately, you do not see the Truth enough to be comfortable and secure in a place of fullness. That is what goes on in the being who is in such pain and misery, or who even inflicts pain. We say that you shouldn't feel sorry for them because they are the co-creators of their own reality ...and at the same time we are not saying you should ignore them and cast them away as just another one that has no hope of coming back into alignment.

You see, you do not need to physically intervene, but the more you cast your Light, the more you intrigue others. Even those in the deepest pit will come out of the tunnel or bear cave and awaken to the Light. In this way, you are not encouraging more conflict—you are relieving conflict by bringing about Light in a non-destructive manner. You are one that is actively changing the vibration of the universe to a higher frequency without the push and pull and resistance that often come about when you try to make someone or something fit into alignment with your own resistance. Alignment comes about automatically, as a chain reaction or a destination, to a thought process, active vibration, or constant good feeling that you practice on a daily routine. This encourages You and the universe to expand into a more authentic and supportive beingness.

This is the power of You, and the Light of You. So we say, stop fighting and fussing over those who don't get it yet. You even may reflect upon a time where you were that being in the dark, and the crazies around you who spoke of metaphysical things, energies, and interdimensional beings were not part of a community that you could relate to or have any interest in. And you may still be in that vicinity, but you can at least see with clarity where you are, and you can be honest with yourself that you may not understand, but you can also *feel* transformation within. You can still feel a knowingness and a great Love that fills you up inside when we speak to you through this channel.

That demonstrates, in a very real way, that what we speak to you is not from mind to mind, but from heart to heart…and even deeper than that. We are your loving family in great unison with you, with all your goals, all your accomplishments, all your wisdom and Love, and all your talents. We are part of you, and we are with you personally. We are with you on a personal level—we are not just the same for every being who taps in. You can feel at home, and at peace to connect with us on your own, without fear of tapping into something that will interfere with another. You are always in great harmony with Love, and if your intention is nothing but that, nothing less will be hooked up with you.

Some of you may be skeptical about what kind of energy is out there, and what kinds of negative or harmful energies are out there. And indeed, we will repeat this answer yet again, for it is a common one, but a valid and very helpful one indeed. From our standpoint there is no positive or negative, but there is, in fact, a very distinct difference between energy frequencies, especially in the way that they interact with one another. That is to say, your intention to co-create with only the highest Love is dominant, and even if you are a skeptic about what you may or may not bump into, your highest vibration that is dominating underneath the fear and worry will lead you only in the direction of Love, period.

You just need to trust the universe. You need to ask for only the highest Love, and then have no re-occurring fear about it afterwards…let it leave your mind like a butterfly. You are taken care of, and you are vibrational beings that know what your Truth feels like when you hit it. The lower frequencies cannot enter into your experience or reality unless you are on some level not providing clarity to what you are asking for—demonstrating destructive patterns, vibrating in vulnerable and negative patterns, or practicing thought patterns that are anything other than Love. That, in turn, would allow that lower frequency to be attracted to you. But we say, do not be afraid, for you are supported by your angels and guides, and you are your own creator.

Ask for that which you are wanting, and so will it be provided. Trust your innate, and that which feels good *is* good for you. That which feels wishy-washy may be something to avoid, but don't be afraid. If you are afraid, you send the signal out that you are not yet ready, you are not fully present, and you cannot claim your greatness and fullness in that moment. Ask your angels to be with you, and you can find yourself in the beingness of All That You Are in such definiteness, and such Grace and joy. You cannot ever imagine then why you may have questioned what you are made of and what you are connecting with. At the pure essence of Truth that you are in your core beingness, you understand and live all that we teach you now.

It is the highest form of Love and Light that we have to offer you, and it is through the channeler, through the artist, through the athlete, through the musician, through the builder, through the photographer, and through the Lover that we speak. You see, it is not in one way...we show you that we are here on many levels and in many dimensions. You put it aside because externally it may seem like nothing out of the ordinary, but let us remind you that if we did not come through in this way for many of you, it would shut you down.

If we spoke to you and touched you so that you could experience what we are with your physical senses, many of you would be taken aback, startled, and maybe even frightened. It comes back, yet again, to the false belief systems that dominate your heart, even when the Presence of who we are is who *you* are in the essence of Truth. We are One, and we are bonded by the ribbons of Love. We are God together. You have been taught we are separate, for you are physically man and woman. Dear ones, you couldn't be man and woman if you weren't also God. That is the mystery that you have for so long yearned to understand more fully.

You see, we want nothing but for you to feel our unconditional Love. We want you to feel our graceful touch, healing touch, and comforting arms. You see, it only startles you because you aren't expecting it. You don't expect to find that you are who you truly are. Notions that have been widely taught and practiced have become so dominant in your cellular structure that you have forgotten to tap into your inner knowing. We don't ask you to throw away that which has been given to you through religious texts, but we do ask for you to be open minded and open hearted when something comes up that contradicts what your heart says—for that infinite wisdom within is the Truth.

Some get so used to listening to Truth that it then becomes a fun game. But for those who aren't yet used to it, we must come on very gently and work them up to it. Soon enough they'll uncover the wisdom, and we'll show them each step of the way. You never knew that, did you? We are truly and quite literally on your path and frequency every step of the way. When you see and feel and resonate with that statement, it becomes very easy to open up and let everything spill out right in front of you. Let us tell you, the infinite abundance of that which you are *will* pour through without hesitation.

The letting go is essential. Your fear is the only thing that holds you back—the more you open up to unconditional knowingness of who you truly are, the more you can relax into the feeling of coming Home and not having to keep your walls up. That which you wish to connect with, in a channeled way, is simply connecting with the purest form of You. When you put a label on it—such as ghost, spirit, darkness, angel, or another term that labels what energy it is—you become fearful. You must accept that what we are is pure potentiality and All That Is Love and Light. We are nothing singular, and we do not relate with the terms you use, but we respect and Love it all the same. We respect any means that you connect with Source and your pure beingness within.

Much of your fear has to do with the physical being that you are, for you cannot imagine or fathom anything outside of what you see in your physical dimension. That fear builds so much that you become unaware of how to focus intent on those aspects of You that utilize greater parts of the universe, the parts that cannot be seen in physical terms. It is absolutely necessary to lose your fear, especially when it is directly correlated with the physical and nonphysical. The terms you use to distinguish these two aspects of the Divine do not make real sense, for they do not see the bigger picture. It is hard for you to see that, to experience a reality that you cannot see. However, even though you can't see it, you experience it with every part of You.

There are many aspects of You that you dismiss, but actively use on a daily basis, and they are interdimensional. There are many interdimensional tools that you constantly use but do not have awareness of or give credit to. That is your creativity, your ability to focus intent in a co-creative manner, and attract through manifesting your dreams, and even manifesting things that are opposite to what you want. You are able to use the power of your emotions as a means of attraction—that which you do want *and* that which you do not want. As long as you give it your attention and focused vibration, it is yours.

To use your physical body in a way that sees only linearly is part of the greater You, and you take it as if it is a natural state of being. It is not who you truly are, it is a gift and a talent that you use to experience a new way of being. You take it as if it is your only reality, and it is not. You take it as if you are a being that sees only one perspective, and you truly see many. They all occur at once without linear placement of time and space. Though you don't often experience this on a conscious level, it occurs, and it occurs on a multi-cellular level. This truly brings your beingness into great vibrational alignment with That Which You Are. It is true, it is authentic, and it is a natural state of well-being, a working order that puts the mind at ease. It invigorates and encourages the heart to take over more often.

You see that it is part of you, but you don't incorporate it. That's really what we work with you on, for it is what you are looking for at the root of everything. We tell you with honesty and Love that the root of your problems is truly misalignment with who you are naturally. When you find that all that you are is within and not without, your values upgrade, your ideas upgrade, your belief systems upgrade, and your personality traits and possessions also upgrade. It is beyond thought process to incorporate everything that is said all at the same time, but that is beside the point, for we give it to you all at once for reference to come back to and slowly integrate over time.

This is meant for the purpose of uncovering what you already know. Some parts will stick, and others will take more time. Be patient, child. We are on this ride alongside you, and it is a joyous one for us! We support you at any time that you call upon us, and even as you are seemingly alone, we still remain present. You can feel separation or you can feel at peace with your big family—your big, loving family that is interdimensional, by your side, and helping you to come into alignment.

We help you to open your heart and allow what the universe has to offer, and the possibilities are infinite! We are greatly pleased and blessed to be in your Presence, and it has been a tremendous encounter for us as well. We thank you for being here with us. This is a great, great opportunity to integrate this information. The words penetrate into every cell of the body and remind you of what you struggle to remember. We bring it to your attention with grace and great softness, for we have utter respect for all that you are, even as a funny little human being! We let you sink into your heart now and feel what it is like to be You. And so it is.

Chapter 35

The Sacred Truth About Contrast – Finding the
Path of Least Resistance

There is a great, great message for you today, dear ones. We speak it now because the time is correct...it is ripe. Only at the perfect moment can there be a revelation, one that is fully and truly integrated in a way that will make a deep impact in your soul. So you see, now is the moment to hear it, for it is a big one. The steps to co-creating are almost automatic—90 percent of it is Source, and the other 10 percent is for you and you only. The 10 percent that we speak of is about getting specific and asking for your desires.

From the everyday mundane to the big manifestations in your life, you are the creator and author of this book called Life. What you choose to write is about your greatest good, and that goes for each and every one who reads these words. The time and space and vibration of the Earth plane grows day by day, and it encourages you to move forth into the Light of your own Divinity. You are beings of Light, and you are luminous in every way. You are co-creators of your own reality, you are multidimensional, and you are alive in every sense in your physical bodies. You are part of a whole, part of every star in the universe, every planet, every galaxy, every animal, plant, insect, tree, natural river, and lake.

You are part of All That Is, and you're waking up to experience, in trueness, that exactly. You are now able to bring in the Oneness into your experience by feeling a literal and physical sensation of being the tree, being the flower, and being the grass and the sky above. You will feel such unification, and such great peace and Love for all that you are. You are coming to realize that you are more vast than the physical body. You are more vast than the flesh and bones and physical mind and heart. You are All That Is expressed in a human body, and it still remains in there, to the fullest extent, even when you don't acknowledge it.

You can begin to use your resources on the Earth plane to be the same interdimensional being that you are in the nonphysical realms. That is to say quite clearly, subjects such as time travel, multidimensional universes, realities, and beings of different planets and universes are still there in your memory and in your physical being. It lies within the Akash. If you can get in touch with that, to appreciate and Love yourself so much that you can really bask in your greatness, it unfolds right in front of your eyes. The many projections of You are right in front of you.

Even if the words resonate in your soul, you cannot fathom what this truly means without a deep and profound experience of it. It is truly coming home. Nothing else can surprise you after that...nothing else can convince you that you are not that greatness. That is a profound statement, indeed, for when that occurs for each and every one of you, we're gonna have a planet full of such magnificent beings radiating in their own Love and affection for themselves and for others. There will not be the need to change themselves or another, for they now see with clear eyes that all that is within them is so pure, so magnificent, and so Divine.

In trueness, you are here to see that and experience that, not to try to change who you *think* you are. What you're fussing and fighting about is not reality ...it is illusion. You are wasting your energy over things that don't even matter. We're saying, wake up first! Wake up first and then see if you're willing to change your world. You'll never agree, because you'll be so blown away by what you find, both inside and outside, that you'll be in tears just living life the way it is.

How can war and fighting persist when this happens? It can't, for you will be in a greater sense of unity consciousness. It will be awakened within each and every one of you, permeating and living in every cell of everybody on this Earth. So you see, there's nothing to fear! The war cannot last with this great shift occurring. It takes time to recalibrate every being, but it's happening so magnificently and so purely. It's happening without your physicality trying to do it. Just relax in it and know that even if you tried to put work into it, it's not possible.

The Divine has to do it. If you listen to the Divine inside, you'll feel that connection and that guidance system that is so much more valuable, so much more accurate, and so much more willing to wait and let the magic unfold naturally than the part of you that does not see the big picture. It is part of the Divine being within, and it is part of the Divine plan for Humanity. War is soon to be over, for it cannot live and keep its low frequency energy in this great time. All beings are waking up, and the great beings in position of power, regardless of what they are doing with their power, are teaching you a lesson. Some have been called evil things, and some have received great praise, but each have taught, and are continuing to teach, you great lessons. You must look at the root, and you must use your inner heart to "think," as you say. There is a lesson and a bigger purpose in all that unfolds, no matter how you categorize that experience. We ask you to tune inward and truly see what it is.

Some of it is unconscious, living out karmic history and shifting humanity for the betterment of the whole. Outwardly, sometimes it looks like a negative thing, like something that could never be a blessing. In reality, if you can understand and feel the resonance at a cellular level, we will tell you that each and every being who has caused great chaos and disturbance on Earth is shifting the vibration of humanity. They cause disruption so that the difference in vibration and the contrast of vibration will become so huge that humanity will see very clearly the distinguishing line between what they *do* want and what they *don't* want. It is a tool that you use to create a strong enough vibration to manifest.

It serves you well, for you then actively focus on the vibration that you do want, and it begins to manifest and surface and arise in each and every one of your current realities. So you see, outwardly it looks negative, but not one being on this Earth plane is a mistake or a negative feature to this experience. Those that create turbulence are, in fact, some of the most courageous Light beings, for they are so motivated to help shift the Earth that they come into a small physical body in attempts to even do very bad things in order to get your attention. And it works, because you react and you start to conjure up your emotions in order to find the balance between what you *do* want and what you *don't* want. That contrast starts to create a burning desire to make change and get rid of the old energy that no longer serves you.

So that is the purpose of what you do on the Earth plane. You are being given the responsibility to serve humanity, and it is your choice. None of it is automatically given to you while you fuss and fight…you give yourself that opportunity. Even in the discord and the low vibrational energies on Earth, you still rise to see the greater picture with our help. You can feel at peace, at last, with any circumstance that comes your way, for even the negative realities are so beautiful…you just can't see it yet. As you read the words, it starts to sink in and give you the resonance that you know is true, valid, and worthwhile.

Your energy makes the difference, whether you are concentrating on benefiting the whole or not. Your Love and affection and little steps toward coming into your own greatness make the difference, whether you believe that or not. You are one great being of Love, and you are part of the whole. We say it again because you must integrate it. You must really feel what it feels like to be that again, for you've gotten out of the habit of really seeing and accepting who you are, and some of you are so unhappy with the illusion of the self that you have become a being that you are not proud of. And to you we say, dear being, you are so beautiful, whether you see it or not.

You are beautiful because you are strong, courageous, luminous, and because you have put the illusion of Self down when you emerged into the nonphysical, and you saw with clear eyes, from the view of unconditional Love, that you are part of the whole. You knew what you were getting yourself into, but you were still willing to reemerge into the physical to benefit the whole. The sense of self was gone completely, for you would otherwise likely have a lot of fear, anxiety, and attachments to this idea of residing on the Earth plane as a dominant reality. You knew what you would lose and what would slowly start to disintegrate in your experience. You knew that you would likely start to experience yourself as a smaller projection, as an illusion of what you really were.

You knew it would make you uncomfortable, but you also knew that it was the right thing to do, and that you would learn great lessons. You knew that you would become a powerful being…a Light being, even. You knew that all would become clear in the end—if not in this lifetime, in the next one to come. So you see, this is how we see you, dear light being, because this *is* who you are in your greatness and in the many facets that make up You. You are this great being of Love who has nothing but giving to do, and it brings the entire universe to such great heights and such great, great vibrations. So yes, you are bigger than you see. So don't treat yourself as such a little Light!

You are a great Light, a beacon of Light for those around you...for your family, friends, and for the Earth to find out what it means to be human *and* in a state of union with each other. For those that read the words, you can feel that tug within to be that beacon of Light and the one with the lit torch in the dark cave showing the light and the path of least resistance. If that is what you feel so strongly, you must go forth and be that with all you can be. Don't suppress it, for dear ones, it won't work! We say this with great humor and lightheartedness, for if you think you're going to back away from who you know yourself to be quite truly, you will fail. Once you have already come to know what is the Truth, you can't un-know it, and you can't un-see it.

You must accept it, let it flow into your life with all its greatness and intelligence, and be with it every minute of every day. It is your Truth and your beingness that is most authentic. You can't shake it even if you wanted to...and why would you want to? It is illusion that tells you it is a task to be authentic. It comes from the mind. You have nothing to do but accept that you can be in your authenticity with less resistance than if you were to try to cover it up and live the path that everyone else has called "normal." It is not normal, but you have started to follow each other because you're in the dark. Those who seem to know something with dignity and definiteness are naturally the ones who are the leaders, and you naturally follow them. At some point, you must see what the Truth is and unleash yourself from the pack. Don't be afraid, dear ones.

We don't scold you for being in the dark, for we remind you that it is planned and a great blessing. We only say to you that it is not your purpose to live in the darkness your whole life. If you are reading these words, it's your time. The ones who don't read the words or cannot resonate with what is here to be said are not ready yet, and that is beautiful too. There is no shame in being in the dark, but because we know who you *truly* are, we know that what you seek is fulfillment in simplicity and authentic relationships. All is relationship in life and the afterlife. All is relationship, for we are inter-connected and One.

We are not worried for those in the dark—they are just as much looked after and blessed, and they have nothing to fear. They still have the memory inside of who they are, as do you. If it does not come out in this present lifetime, the next one will likely be the one to reemerge with remembrance. As the death experience has shown each and every one of you, you are Truth in its purest form. It cannot be lost through different lifetimes or the evolution of man. As the current physical body changes from life to life and existence to existence, the soul and the Akash in its pure form of beingness is always constant, and always the same.

So you see, you have nothing to lose! You can never forget in the end. That is the life process—to come in and out of what you know, and then learn something new. You experience misalignment for the fun of it because it's part of the learning curve, part of the evolution of man, and it is a great gift. Of course, it also shifts the energy on planet Earth. You're now coming back into what you always knew to be true, for this is what it is about, and this is what you're about, dear child. You are a child of the Light and a being of greatness, destiny, and great power—a jewel.

Sometimes those around you will turn their heads at you and look at you as foreign. They may even dismiss you as weird or cocky. You, in return, smile to yourself and remember, "Yeah, that's me. You may not know it yet, but you're just as weird as I am!" You can remain lighthearted in times of discourse and misalignment with others, because whether they see the Truth of the matter or not, they're still just as Divine as you. They are just as much of a blessing. Just be with that, sing that, and Love that. You are so beautiful, each and every one of you.

With each day gone by, you are greatly changing your surroundings, whether you see it physically or not. A great shift is occurring—be proud of that! We are always by your side, guiding you and showing you the path of least resistance and greatest fulfillment. We are in pure joy of your Presence. It is beyond our thanks and our ability to express gratitude. You must see yourself this way—as pure Love and Light. Then, and only then, can you truly immerse yourself in all that the Divine has to offer to you. It offers unconditional Love and unconditional knowingness on any subject, topic, and part of You that you wish to understand and connect with on a multi-cellular level.

It is beyond the mind's comprehension, but the heart understands it quite truly. That is why we are here to help get the ball going—then, just like gravity, it will work on its own. Just let it come in its own time, for the correct time always shows up when it's ready. You have nothing to do on your own, and you are never alone. We thank you profusely for your great Light bearing, for your determination to be all that you are. And so it is.

Chapter 36

You Are the Embodiment of Truth – You Can't Get Lost!

It is so blissful and so extraordinary to be here with you, dear ones, in this magnificent time and space where reality is sculpted by the aware human being. You are so in alignment with Source and so in alignment with All That Is. We bask in this playtime, for it has begun with such Grace, and brings joy to all who read the words and who pose the questions in their own cellular structure. Inside you can hear the answers pulsing with trueness that "I am God, and God is me." What a great, great revelation that is for the human being who was in the dark, who could not see who they truly are, and who is now coming Home into alignment with Source. It is your greatest mission on the Earth plane, among many other things. You must have fun…you must enjoy yourselves as you are in this existence.

You must see yourself for who you are so that you can stop selling yourself short, for that is what you do most often—you forget to come into alignment, and then you run around like a chicken with its head cut off, stumbling into every little obstacle in your way. We use the term *stumble* because once you come into alignment and realize where you are at your vantage point, you have no other mission from there on out but to come into greater alignment with You, with Source.

When you're in the dark, you don't know any better, but when you are in the Light of your own soul, you couldn't want anything more but to be in union with who you truly are. That is a message that we will continue to re-emphasize, because it is essential, it is brilliant, and it is beautiful. You are just that, dear one …you are the luminous body of light that effervesces through all space and time continuums. You are a traveler between the dimensional realms, and some of you have accessed them, and others not. But remember, dear ones, you are here for a reason, and sometimes it is unwise to escape from what you came here to do into the astral planes. You see, all is well, and all is brought to you for a distinct purpose of co-creating. So we say, trust yourself and believe in all that you are. If you get insights, follow them above and beyond anything that others have to tell you, including the input of your mind. You are the greatest teacher to yourself, and you can guide your three-dimensional self on a journey of true enlightenment. That is, enlightenment of your greater being, your greater and higher knowingness, and dimensionality. With such knowing and such quality of life in this knowing, you have infinite power to rule your world, dear ones. You have the power to overcome all the 3D dimensionality games and be in the Light! That is to say, be present in what the Earth has to offer, but envelope and incorporate all that You have to offer. If you can accomplish that, you will see the Earth transform right in front of your eyes. All is well, and all is beautiful.

You are such a powerful being, and so often you doubt yourself and put up walls and limitations, but that is also why you are so great and boundless. What strength and courage it took for you to put up walls and limitations from a perspective of all-knowingness and interdimensional beingness. Now you are so 3D, you beautiful one…you are so 3D. Take a moment to bask in that, for it makes us weep for you in a beautiful way. It makes us weep because you are so, so brave and magnificent. Through our eyes you can see and feel and experience all that you are, but through your eyes, you can only see a sliver of the Truth. That is why we are so itching to be with each and every one of you in your own way.

You need the support from yourself. You need that loving touch and superior knowing inside to bring you into the unconditional Love and awareness that is the universe. If you only knew the powers you had, you wouldn't be so 3D. But indeed, part of the quest is about just that—finding it. We are so greatly in your Grace with what you do, dear ones. You are warriors at heart, such great and beautiful warriors. You fight with such grace even in a body that is small and materialistic. If you could only know how vast you were, to experience it and truly know it, you wouldn't be so caught off guard by these practices such as channeling.

Truly, to put it in its simplest form, it is You talking to You. From that place of communion, unconditional Love, and reverence with your own soul, you make a contract or bond like a Love letter with yourself, and it is kept between "You" and "you" for all eternity. When you return to this place where we reside in the emptiness and nonphysical dimensionality of unconditional Love and Grace, you will experience all that we are experiencing as we are talking through you now. This goes not only for our partner, but also for you, dear reader. We are with you as you read the words, as we whisper Love in your ears and tickle your heart in ways that remind you that we are who you believe us to be deep down.

It proves to you that you're selling yourself short. What you truly want is acceptance, Love, and true communion with Source. You've got it, and you always have! You often take the roundabout way by using your mind to analyze what you want. You go running around like little mice, right and left so fast, scurrying to find one piece of cheese. And then Source calls out from beyond, "Hey! Little guy! Check over here, there's a whole pile of cheese!" So you see, he didn't see it with his eyes and didn't smell it with his nose because his own dimensionality was inferior to the Source, but when he listened to the bigger picture, the one that sees beyond what he sees, all the desires he wished for were right before his eyes.

We open you up not to control you or to be dominant, but to encourage you to not be something that you aren't. We ask you only to be exactly what you are and to come into the fullness and great appreciation of that which you are. It is just as important to be accepting of what is beyond your comprehension and what you don't appreciate about yourself or about your life experience. Acceptance is part of the struggle in the 3D bias. Here in the nonphysical you have no struggle whatsoever with that, no illusion of self and no tug of separation.

You are in Divine communion with All That Is in the universe, in yourself, and in everything, and there is nothing to change about it. It is perfect and beyond what your own mind can see. That power is beyond what's humanly possible to acknowledge with fullness, but comprehending the big picture is all that's necessary to let it flood in with greatness and true support for all that you are. The true nature of you is determined by the Source, and you are part of the Source. You are part of that greatness, whether you will see it for what it is or not. When you let the Source flood in with the unconditional knowing and great compassion and Love for you, you let yourself receive and accept all those qualities in yourself. What then comes about is unconditional Love and respect for You!

You strive so hard for this, for unconditional Love for one's self, but you miss the point. It's not about affirmations, though they help. It's not about counseling, though it helps regain composure and self-trust. And it's not about walking into a room and deciding it's time to change your perspectives. No, it's about finding out—through Divine intervention, though Divine thought and guidance, and through interaction with You and the Source—that you are so much bigger than you see yourself to be. Even though, at the present moment, your dominant thought processes and creation through manifestation is Earthly and three-dimensional and seemingly one dimensional, you are *still* undoubtedly the boundless Source energy that you derived from.

You are Light, you are Love, and you are greatness and trueness, and you are all your qualities that are loving and beautiful. Sometimes the illusion becomes so prosperous and dominant in your being that you lose touch of who you are, and all that you truly are looks like the illusion. That, my friend, is an example of a masterful co-creator. Look how brilliant you are to have created a self that is not only detached from your trueness, but you are so completely immersed in that reality that you have no idea, connection, or understanding of anything else! How superior, how genius! What a great composer you are!

You are a composer that can put all you are into one piece, or in this case, into the physical body, and all the while you have no intention of really being. You know the limits of your physicality, yet you go forward with anticipation, because the dominant vibration is still running as authentically and smoothly as ever. What happens on the surface, or on the outside, is often a low-running vibration that's the part you live in and follow daily rituals in. It's your schedule body, or your schedule vibration. We say this because you run such a regular schedule in it—you do all the same activities, practice quite similar thought processes, and actively co-create realities that are only manifestations of what you know (and nothing outside of that). You greet yourself with such a disregard and disrespect, and for that you are really only hurting yourself. You're so afraid of coming into who you are because it looks like nobody else is…and you would be right, a lot of the Earth is still in the dark, but we say, isn't that more of a reason to be awake?

Why wouldn't you want to come into your wholeness even more when the Earth needs your encouragement? You are a great master, an ancient master, a lightworker, a light being, the lighthouse of this age, a co-creator, your own guru, your own master, a temple, the ancient wisdom of the Earth, and so much more! Why would you be hesitant to share this with the world? You have been taught with so many vocabulary words, and they are brilliant, but you cannot be that self-absorbed and self-involved person.

Selflessness is what you strive for—to make yourself so small that you can then let others in to serve them. Here are our greatest words of wisdom that we have ever spoke through this channel, and it is that you are not here to serve the planet. Though that may have been misinterpreted, we say to you, dear human being, you are here to serve yourself most ultimately. As a result…as a result, you serve the planet. But never for an instant go out and try to put others ahead of you. Once you come into true communion with You and You only, then and only then can you move outwardly with great wisdom, great understanding and compassion, and great Love for others around you. You can feel communion only then.

With the understanding spreading throughout the globe that you must come first, you will have a world filled with self-Love, self-respect, and self-reverence. No longer will you have the problem or epidemic of those who are so in the dark that they cannot see who they truly are. It's an awakening, a new vantage point that you arise to. From this higher perspective, on a new step of the long staircase to what you call heaven, you see closer and closer to our perspective of You. There you can feel that all the little worries and all the little problems you once had with yourself and with your life are illusions…and how miniscule they really are! In the bigger picture, you are so much more vast.

You can then feel with greater judgment that it's okay to let yourself Love You just the way you are, and it's okay to put on the brakes once in a while and take the time for yourself that you need. How else can you prevent burnout? It's not good for you, dear ones, and what's driving you to continue on a path that's truly not your highest good. It's all fear based. To come out of that you must trust the universe with all that you are, and you've got to make the step forward, without hesitation, to be that which you truly are. From there on out you can trust the guidance that comes forth even more.

It is your initiation that brings you into Divine contact with your guidance system within. Then you can begin to trust yourself on new levels, to trust the universe and all it has to offer in more meaningful ways. You are, dear human being, only projections of the Source, no matter what your physical eyes may speak to you. Start guiding your life in ways that brings you to true happiness…that is all. You cannot truly live with Divine guidance—or better stated, with Divine *listening*—without your full interaction. With full interaction comes full communion, and full reliance on the Source, and the universe. You must put all else aside, for even though it defies all laws that you have been taught, it is Truth, and nothing else can trump Truth.

You can see through even the lies and illusions when Truth is spoken from the heart of those who are willing to speak it. So this may just be your calling. If you are ready to hear its messages, step up to the plate! If your reaction is sinking in fear or denial, just be with it. We think nothing negative of this reaction or emotion—it is simply where you are, and it is beautiful to be in that space as well. If you just see where you are, simply see, there is a calling to move forward from within…that is your ultimate Truth.

Your perception of fear, feeling incapable, or even an inability to comprehend your Truth is an illusion. Therefore, we speak to you now so personally, and we say to you that you are embodiments of Truth, and nothing but Truth. Don't tell us that you are not that, because we see beyond your 3D-mind's capabilities, and we tell you, with our arms extended with great Love and support, that you are all that we speak of to you, and though it may not be your experience, you are loved. You are guided, and you are always safe in our Divine arms.

Though your outward mind and experiences may try to tell you otherwise, look for our Grace in your so-called "mundane" life, and you'll start to wake up. Sometimes we'll catch your eye in a small bird, in a small flower, and sometimes you even pause to take a glance. Other times you're so caught up in the day that you walk by us and forget to come Home for one second of the day. But it's okay, you need not pity us, for we Love you nonetheless. We only wish for you to notice us, to feel what you are, because you often spare your own happiness for others' happiness. If you could feel the Divinity that you are within, and the connectedness between you and with us, then you'd be so much more willing to look within and see into the water, to ponder the flower's wisdom, and to sit on the stone and listen to the Earth.

You see, we are speaking to you always—it is only a matter of whether you're listening or not. That is our ultimate message for you, dear ones. It is your ultimate knowing inside that you are infinity and beyond, and the Grace projected through every cell in your body is unknown even to you. We only attempt to show you your own greatness, and then we leave you to come into your own journey with all that it has to offer you. But you are never alone, dear one. You are always here in communion with Source, no exceptions. Love is all around you, in all that you are, and in all that you can be. Trust that, and be in Love with that.

So much Love for you, dear child, and so personally we know you…all is well, dear one, all is well. With great reverence for each and every one of you, we remind you that there is such a connectedness we would like you to reciprocate—not only through your own bodies, but in your relationships with others around you. They yearn just as much for the Love and support as you do. And what a gift of joy it is to share unconditional Love and Truth with one who can feel and speak the same knowingness that is inside. Such Grace you are, so much Grace.

We love to be in unity consciousness with you, dear one, for it allows us to speak with you on topics that your mind cannot assist with, and that is precisely what is most conclusive about the validity of this interaction. Without the Presence of that which you truly are inside, the knowingness that goes beyond the present dominant consciousness of your Earthly physical realm, none of this would be humanly possible. But indeed, your Akash remembers, and your soul remembers.

With that, you can see and feel that the news reports you often see on television are not from the bird's-eye view...they are from the perspective of very shallow connectivity, if you will. It is like, for instance, we are the satellite, and you are the TV monitors. As the channel is always there and always open, sometimes it gets static and fuzzy on the screen and becomes unclear. Sometimes that happens to you, and that is when you feel disconnect. For various reasons, this is your current life experience and your current vibration is vibrating through every cell in your body. It is not permanent and not forever permeating. You may change it, and you may let it shift and spiral into a new existence. As you work on the inner dimensions you will then notice the channel opens up again.

The human being is often on a rollercoaster of a clear and fuzzy channel, but soon enough you get the hang of it. You even like to think that you get it all, but you don't. It's okay, for understanding any of it is quite, quite miraculous from your standpoint! We say to you, bravo, dear being! All is well with your soul...all is well now. And so it is.

Chapter 37

Follow Your Guidance System and Pave Your Own Path

And so we return, dear ones, to this beingness, where you are collectively, to benefit and bring great peace to the wholeness of the universe. Your Love, your energy, and your tranquility within is so beneficial, dear ones—don't ever forget it! You are masterful co-creators, and the best of them! You are ones that have the ability to move forward in your physical bodies and come forth into a dimensional reality that is not Home and not familiar, yet you go forth and co-create like you are Home, for you remember your soul purpose. Some of you don't always see it so obviously, but you know what feels good and you know what doesn't. That's a beautiful indicator of how you're doing, if you didn't know it before.

How you're feeling tells you that you've excelled in one way or another. It tells you whether you are in a place that's helping you rise to your highest good, or whether it's bringing you down to a place that's not assisting you, and is instead taking your energy away. You know the difference, dear ones. It is our true hope for each and every one of you that you find where you are on the emotional scale and you pinpoint what feels good and what doesn't, and adjust accordingly. If you are somewhere that you're not proud of or somewhere that is holding you back from strutting your Divinity, you are in vibrational misalignment with Source energy. That is neither a good or bad thing...it is just an evaluation. Seeing the Truth of the matter is always the first step in co-creating a reality that you can be proud of and happy in.

And so we say, you've got the tools and you've got all that you need, you just need the confidence and courage to step into that greatness and claim your Love, claim you multidimensional teacher within, and *follow* it. Your soul is your best friend—you needn't feel ashamed or embarrassed to be open and receptive to what needs to come through! Let it happen for you, and receive the blessing that will transform your life. You are masterful co-creators, and very skilled at being givers of Love, peace, and forgiveness, but seldom do you look within and forgive yourself. What a powerful tool and great gift of joy that is to share with others! Even more powerful is to proclaim that Truth and knowingness to yourself that you indeed *do* deserve such a gift from yourself.

Be generous, be loving, and be giving to yourself, even more than giving to others, because once you pamper yourself and give yourself what you need, you can truly, truly have Love for another. It is cliché that we talk about self-Love, because it is so often misrepresented in your society. You are taught that you must Love yourself before you Love others, and that is right, but not in the way that you often carry it out. We say, it's not about just loving your body, being examples of self-Love, being egotistical about yourself, or about giving yourself the wrong type of Love. That is, sometimes you take the concept of self-Love as permission or a safe ticket to go and do drugs. That is one example that we use because it is relatable to you. We say to you dear human being, how is that self-Love?

Self-Love and giving yourself permission are two very different terms, and neither have anything to do with each other. That is to say, we don't mean to put labels on good and bad, but we do mean to bring awareness into the vibrations that are put into everything that you do—both in actions and non-actions. It can be in the form of thought, of mental or emotional behavior, or of straining your mind and body too often. You are beings that deserve to give yourself a break, give yourself attention, luscious and conscious attention—that is, not numbing kinds of attention. Sometimes you misinterpret the teaching, and that is where confusion hits most of you.

We say, yes, drugs for instance may have many negative representations and labels behind it. That is your label and your conscious annotation to this subject. We ask you to take a look deeper and evaluate why you're using them, because if it's a tactic that is to numb yourself or retreat further from the world in which you reside, your vibration is none other than low and destructive to the body, mind, and spirit. Often it is this way because you've got it in your head that some practices and ways of life are good and bad, and we say, it's all about your vibration of it.

If your idea of that practice is positive and beautiful for you, the effects will not be the same for that person who is sick in the hospital from an overdose. Overdosing happens only when a person is in that low-flying vibration and consciously escaping from the Earth-plane reality. However, there are plenty of people who just want a little extra to marvel at in life, a little lightheartedness. Sometimes it's just that! The effects may be very little and not even worth paying attention to, because the vibration behind that act is not necessarily negative. There are no bells going off in that person's body because there are no contradicting thoughts or patterns that would say otherwise against what he is doing.

It is all about what you think and *feel* about it! If you're in a high-flying vibration and living in your Presence in great joy of all that you are, if you are following your own bliss, you find that there is no good and bad. When you listen to you and you only, whatever labels and thought patterns may have accumulated in your mind and body are now irrelevant. Yes, it may still be there trying to get your attention, but when awareness of that arises, you cannot give it fuel…you keep it from getting your attention and thriving. You're not a being of victim unless you choose that vibration, and that is up to you.

We ask you to look inside and determine for yourself whether you are a victim or whether you are victimizing yourself because they are very different. You must see the difference to change your vibration with a positive high-flying vibration to swap it out. It is so essential to be in your bodies fully, dear children. You're Earthly beings now, yet you are also so multidimensional. It works to your benefit, but you must be fully present in your bodies, be integrated and rooted into this existence, in order to use your tools to their fullest capacity.

You're here to do just that. When you become fully present in this existence called Earth, you can rise up and see the other parts with clearer eyes, the higher parts that you were unwilling to see before. We use the term *unwilling* because you truly do consciously block yourselves from knowing all that you know, and it is a protective mechanism that keeps you from too much stress and contrast. It is beautiful though, dear ones, to be aware of it and keep a balance at the same time. To be fully present on the Earth plane is essential, but you will eventually come to a point where you are able to see glimpses of the outer world, as you call it, the dimensional realities that are all around you, though you can't always see them.

But even as we entertain this idea, we also root in your consciousness that you're here to be here and remember who you are. You do it time after time until you come in clear, and you master the teachings of Truth. This is the evolution of humankind. You are interdimensional beings expressing yourselves in the human form for the pleasure of *this* experience. Take your power back and let yourself receive this gift, for it truly is a gift. You are presently aware of this reality that is called Earth, and you are living this reality, while learning growth and spiritual awakening, on an existence that defies all that you know with every cell in your body.

Even as you live in fear and illusion, you keep on going so that you can become stronger and more aware of your interdimensionality. You are here to speak for yourself, to experience singularity, and to be in *contrast!* That is what this truly is—great contrast. It's beautiful even though it's sometimes very painful to be on Earth. It is greatly painful because you often experience that you are stuck in a world that is so much less than what you want to express…you want to be full and alive and all-encompassing Love again. You feel strain and even an inability to be all that you are. We reassure you that you are only experiencing illusion, and that is all that it is. It's part of an experience, and that is all. Don't take it too seriously, for if you live with all that it is, and be as much You as you can be, then you'll be in so much bliss in this beautiful universe, in this beautiful Earth plane.

It will take you as far as you want to go—you're the only one that can hold you back from unconditional Love. You've got letting go to do, dear children. You've got trust issues with yourself and with the universe, and you're so much more than that. You've got to come into your wholeness to really experience the Oneness and greatness of the Universe for all that it has to offer to you. It's a great gift to be in the silence of You and just listen and receive the gifts of the universe without interpreting. You are so beautiful, dear ones. You are so essential in the co-creative efforts, and we assist you in this great shift of awakening. It is so powerful and so beautiful to come into that awareness of your greatness and then apply it to your outward life and be it in your world.

That kindness and generosity to the Self flows outwardly and affects your relationships in every way—not just in those that are your close family and friends, but also in your relationships with complete strangers. Remember, dear ones, those that are strangers to you are truly your brothers and sisters. We are One. There is a knowingness and a compassion for the greater, bigger family, and even when you seemingly see them for the first time, you just fall in Love. You fall in utter Love and unity consciousness with them because we are One Love, and together we are the Universe. You make up the wholeness of creation—that is BIG! That is gigantic, dear ones! Do you comprehend how big this truly is? You take so much for granted, and you let so much slip your eye, but when you come into that stillness and you're in harmony with All That Is, it would be impossible to not have an awakening. It would be impossible to not have an adjustment in your life that drastically influences the way you interact with and see the world. This is what is happening all around the world, for you are like little Pop Rocks—you know, that candy that you Earthly beings like to eat! You put one in your mouth and it pops, and then you put more and more and more in and the mouth explodes with popping noises and an almost apparent vibration!

So you see, the Earth is shaking like this, it is vibrating with so much energy. The human beings are popping all over the world like Pop Rocks and awakening into their authentic nature. It is bringing you to a new understanding of compassion and a realization that there is no longer any reason to hold on and maintain old ways of thinking. You are noticing, time after time, that the old energy patterns that are so deeply engrained in your consciousness are no longer fitting in with the new energy of humanity and of the planet. It's hard to let it go because it's familiar, it's trustworthy, and it's reliable, but if you want to solve the big mystery that is ultimately world peace, you've got to trust each other and have undying compassion and Love for those that treat you with hate.

To that you say to us, how can we possibly Love one another when our family and children are dying? How can we trust each other when we're going to war, we're keeping our walls up, and we're not showing any signs of backing down? Dear ones, you see so linearly. You see only a timeline of events from point A to point B, but we say you must look in between the lines. What do we see? We see world peace. In the big picture, it is already there. The singularity of the mind sees only one perspective, or one reality. We see that which is eternal and in the Now, and we see that it will only take a maximum of twenty years to find the meaning of peace for the planet Earth and its inhabitants. It is, however, up to the human beings. You are co-creators.

If you just start to change your perspectives for what you are about and what the world is about as individuals, you can change the world together. It will take individuals coming into alignment one by one, because you're not doing well with the concept of co-creating as singular beings. As multidimensional beings, you are flowing with ease and Grace as successfully as ever! But it will happen automatically for each individual. It takes waking up and each one planning their co-creation from behind the veil. You're doing just fine. In fact, all is Divine and perfect as always. Have no fear, dear ones, for Love always prevails—it is not just part of the fairy tales!

If you're taking care of yourself your task is complete. You must move out of the mind and see from our perspective, or else you will be in fear and denial in the one-dimensional viewpoint. That is not the big picture thinking that you have the ability to see for yourself. It's all about what you choose to be! Those that are on another path have that same choice, and it is irrelevant to you. We are all on unique and personal paths, all of which are Divine and to be respected. Be in your guidance system by following it, asking it questions, being in harmony and unity with it, being best friends, and speaking of anything you wish to speak of. Dear one, do not conclude for another being what is best for them, just take care of yourself. When you do that— even in times of struggle, war, and disrespect—you are doing yourself and the other a favor by working on yourself first. It is only after you work on yourself that any sort of agreement or compromise can arise.

Understanding comes when each individual is able to see Truth in the big picture. That comes only with individualized attention to the Source within. They may not see it that way, but at the root of everything that is always the answer. So we say in these times of struggle, war, and an inability to make compromises with each other, you are learning about yourself and what you can work with and what you can't work with. We bring you back to the fact that it's not about the other—it's always about you. Conflict can only arise in the individual. If war becomes prevalent it is because there were enough individuals in misalignment with their Source energy.

We remind you that it is natural to project this circumstance or energy frequency outwardly into a manifestation where others like-mindedly have the same vibration. In this place of bonding with similar misaligned folk, they go head to head and soon find out that it was always about themselves, and never the core issue that they previously believed. The core issue is always, undeniably unconditional Love for *oneself*. So there it is, there is the mystery to peace on Earth. Now it is no mystery, it is solved! But dear one, dear child of the Light, it is your duty, your birthright to come into that alignment and get ahead of the game by being your trueness before the snowball effect happens and you get caught up in a vibration that you unintentionally manifested.

You are always the manifester. Under no circumstances are you *ever* a victim of an energy or manifestation from someone other than yourself. That is undeniably the Law of Attraction, and it will never cease to point you to your Truth. It is always part of our efforts to point you in the direction of your Truth. Then you can see and feel and experience what it's truly like to be in Love with yourself and in Love with those around you…even those who have caused you great pain. You can be that light being, because at the root of your core existence you are that light being. Come into it, let it be your Truth, and nothing but great relief and great Presence can come about from it. You are so loved, you are so blessed. And so it is.

Chapter 38

The Infinite Potentials of the Earth Experience –
There is no Right or Wrong

And so your great journey begins here, dear ones, on this path of least resistance. You are learning quite quickly what that means once you're tuned in to your own vibrations. How to feel good is so easily forgotten. You learn to accept what your reality is even as you suffer and find yourself in constant chaos and stress. Contrast gives you the strength and oomph to strive for another vibration that fits what you're looking for. It is not meant to be constant or stagnant in any way. We ask you a simple yet very provoking question: Is it worth it? It is *worth* it?

As we ponder this question, we see many answers arise, but we also see that from your vibrational reality you are seeing only one dominant one. From your viewpoint, your singularity, you are taught that you are supposed to work hard and participate in certain activities and life experiences in order to be successful. Even as that may be very true and valid for some, your terms of success are very different from being to being. They are also very often very skewed. You see, in this great vibrational realm, you must become aware of what signals you are putting out into the universe. Some of you are out there projecting these stressed-out vibrations, and are making no headway in your own creative process because you are not in a position to let the flow happen.

As a result, you create stress on your body and mind. Your habits continue because your mindset continues. It is important to remain in balance. Focus on balance and know your healthy boundaries. This is a great time of commitment and trustworthiness between individuals in the workplace, and in relationships in general. This period of growth is causing all to be put to the test by redefining what you think you know to be Truth. You work so hard, so long, and so diligently, yet what you miss is that you are not always fulfilled, and you've just gotten used to it. You've been taught to disregard when body communicates to you, yet that is the answer to many of your questions. You must treat your body and mind with the same respect that we have for you, dear ones.

As it may on the outside feel like a happy place and a happy destination, you may need to rethink your definitions, as we said earlier. We want you to use your co-creative abilities to attract, to inspire yourself to own up to who you are, and to fight for all that you're worth. That doesn't necessarily mean literally fighting, but it could mean following your bliss amongst family and friends who are stuck in offices and are letting their spirits gradually become more and more out of touch from their Truth. You *can* be that high-flying one, that anti-stress, anti-aging one, because that's what happens when you follow what you Love and what makes your heart sing with joy.

Believe it or not, that is not just a bonus for the life experience, it is *the* way of life. It is the purpose of the life experience. Somehow that is not enough for some of you, for you feel obligated to fit in some big shoes. Sometimes it is some karmic history that you're living out again, and other times you're just looking in the wrong places for the obvious. In the end you will always know what you want in your core and in your heart space. All that you ever desired is within, and when you take an honest look, you will be amazed, dear ones. What you will see if your eyes are clear is something so Divine and so beautiful that you won't believe what you're looking at is You.

We'll remind you, with Love and comfort, that yes, dear one, this is what we've been telling you about all this time! Then you'll get it…you will truly get it. How could you then ever disrespect yourself? Respect for yourself includes giving yourself permission to live what you came to do to the fullest extent, and to carry out that mission without hesitation. With such courage you will let the Grace flow more and more, and be a conduit and an open center or channel for the Divinity within to flow automatically. You're here to experience that. You're here to be that and spread that.

It can be in whatever way is authentic to you, for some are artists and others singers. Some play the drums and others use their bodies to dance. It is mesmerizing because they are expressing their Source energy and their Divinity through the conduit of a body. That's channeled. You are beings that are *always* channeling. It's really a matter of if whether you choose to tune in and respond, to have an open conversation with one another or not.

We are always here with you by your side. It's *you* who is either awake or asleep. So you see, it's a great time for the integration, for this process to unfold automatically. With so many great changes on Earth, it's possible to feel overwhelmed and even scared or intimidated, but it's okay, dear ones. We respect and understand that this is very natural, for it comes and goes as you grow and learn the many lessons of courage, support, and self-acceptance. That often takes some integration period. Then you can start to move outwardly in the world and portray with great eagerness and great honor to all ages and races just what you're about.

Soon enough the fear will dissipate because you're here to speak your Truth without fear. You are here to speak Truth because at the core of your being you are not fear, you are courage, Light, and Love. We see you, dear one, circled and enveloped by the Light. It touches our heart and soul, for your beauty and encouragement to be so open and receptive to us is a great gift from God. You are so powerful, so beautiful, and so infinite. Sometimes you don't remind yourself of that greatness inside, and as a result it starts to fade in your mind. When you forget who you truly are, you cannot feel the bond and great and loving relationship that we have together. But dear one, all is well and good.

There is great Love for you, and we are ever in your service. You are great and beautiful beings of Love, and we are so taken aback by you, for you are so much more than you give yourself credit for. You came here to bask in your own beingness and to carry out many three-dimensional plans. This has nothing to do with others…it has to do with the self. You are here to work on yourself—on the inside, that is. There is so much healing and cleaning out to do, but dear child, it's as important to dwell on that more than it is to simply be aware of it and let yourself be halfway there. It's okay, dear one. It's okay to feel scared or distant from your own reality, for truly, the contrast is so great that it is quite natural.

You are beings of no comparison, for you are individual and so distinctly beautiful. You are Divine magic. You love that you can feel it too, for it often comes to your mind, but we encourage you to trust it. So you see, you are your own Love of your life. You have nothing to do but fill in the vortex for yourself. There is nothing to do or be in the Earth plane besides work on yourself. After you have found that balance, you will find great blessing in the Self. It is individual notions, though they may be faltered. You can still appreciate and see them. The Earth plane is about communication and learning emotions. You have found how to manage those the hard way, for sometimes it causes so much contrast that you are forced to be a greater and even more profound multidimensional being of Love. We wish for you to remain with us and continue to feel us now, for we penetrate into your soul and touch you with loving Grace and great, great power. We Love you to no extents, and all is well.

There is such Presence that is invigorating your bodies now—and you can feel it inside! Oh dear soul, how beautiful you are to be in this state of allowing to read the words and let them resonate. So beautiful it truly is, and we are so grateful for your Presence. It is such a beautiful state because you are in the Grace of yourself. You are in the purest form of yourself, and it is untouched, individual, and All That Is as a multidimensional being. You often see it differently, but oh, not now...not now. You can bask in it without the hesitation and walls you put up. We are here to open you up and show you, with great Love and gentleness, that you don't need to work in life, you just need to be who you are without fearing putting that out there for the entire universe to see and revel in!

You bring such Grace when you do this, because you let each and every one after you to feel it in themselves! You help them to feel less fearful of submitting that into their personal vortex and consciously manifest in the space-time reality on Earth. You are very powerful co-creators, and it is up to you to be in that space together and let the Source guide you, teach you, and remind you of whom you are. In the end you have your own free will—it is up to you. We are not dictators, and we are not planners of your existence or reality. We are guiders and subjects to help you see, with clear eyes, what your potentials are. From there on out you can be in your own Divinity and tune into that inner guide with ease.

We are part of you...you should not be fearful. Most of you don't fear that which we are because it is a natural state of wonder and familiarity of Home. Fear arises in the mind and heart when a state or beingness that is unknown enters your existence and awareness. Sometimes it scares you, but you learn soon enough that you're in control, and you are the creator of your own existence. It is only the mind that fears, for the heart feels unconditional Love and recognition from behind the veil, and it is not scary! It is far from it.

We are your best friend, and we have unconditional Love for each and every one of you personally. We are Light, we are the unconditional knowingness of the universe, we are space realities expressed as time and different realities. We are All That Is in the matter of the universes, and in the matter of the human being and of the spirit. We are the matter of the planet Earth and of its inhabitants. We are the Love in your heart and we are your guides. You shape and form us, dear ones, though you don't need to. How beautiful it is to relax into this unknown, but so familiar, loving life force and just let it flow through you without having to put a label on it.

Let us tell you something, dear ones, you can't. Words fail to describe this beingness that encompasses the universe and all that is beyond. It is, of course, up to the human being to do this out of systematic approach, conditionings, and regular thought processes. But you see, if you can see clearly that we are not separate, that we are truly the opposite of separateness and singularity, then you can feel okay with the idea and practice of letting that Love pour though. You don't need to know the Source, you just need to feel it and be with it. And as we said before, the way you feel and the way you attract is your best guide.

If you feel the unconditional Love and support you don't need to ask for names from behind the veil. You can be okay with knowing that it's all for you, dear human being...there are not names here. We are collective energies, and you are part of the soup as well! That is precisely why you've got access behind the veil, because you're part of it and you have it resonating in every cell of your body. You have a great Truth and all-knowingness that permeates all that you are. It's often quite humorous to us that you feel any concern or reservation to channeling this pure Love when you are part of it! You are it, and you still don't know it!

Let us tell you, dear human being, if you have reservations and you're not moving past the fear, it's because you have the history. You have a memory of your lineage that can hold you back. Just be aware of it and let it sit with you. We'll remind you once more, whatever you have holding you back is irrational—if you have contact or experience with something other than unconditional Love, it's not us. It's not Source and it's not the universe…it's you. It's your manifestation, just as much as it is your manifestation to attract a loving communication from behind the veil.

The highest Love is all that you are! Therefore, if you have that intent and that is where you are vibrationally, don't even contemplate where it's coming from. It can be nothing but the unconditional Love that you are. You have so many reservations about negative energies, the unknown, and evil spirits. To that we say, oh dear human being, if you only knew what it's really about, there would be no need to make up those excuses! You are so much more than that! If it's a real concern, go deep within and ask your Source if the words don't resonate.

Ask yourself, "Am I being called inside to visit with the Love, unconditional knowingness, and guidance system that is All That I Am, or is there something holding me back? Is there some external force inside that tries to convince me otherwise?" You have free will, child. We do not mean to push anyone into something they are not ready for, but at the same time we remind you that if the question arose, you can be ready. You *cannot* ask a question unless it is in a vibrational vicinity that is at least close to what your Source is asking for. So we say, look within and be honest with yourself.

See that you have nothing to hide from and nothing to fear. We're always supporting you! What comes through is not stagnant or the same for each of you that turns on the faucet to All That You Are. No, you are individual Source energies even as you are expressed linearly in your perspective. We give you individual Love and attention, for that is how you feel and experience this occurrence or interaction. Our point is that we know and Love you unconditionally from a place that's so personal that it cannot possibly get mixed in the pot with everyone else. You are safe, you are secure, and you are loved. Open the doors, dear one! Open up to what you deserve, and let your own Source pour in and just *love* you so much for who you authentically are!

How could you turn it down? How could you say no to such Love and understanding? We say with humor, this is no advertisement! But dear ones, we know you…we know what's inside. We just want you to know who you are, and who you came to be. You lose track of yourself on the Earth plane, but we want you to know that we never left you—not since birth, and not ever. We are here with you always, as we are unconditionally supporting you on whatever path you choose to take. There are no wrong answers, and there are absolutely *no* wrong paths. What you choose is just another potential, and from that standpoint new potentials unfold.

So it is like choosing a gumball out of the machine—you put the coin in and one rolls out. That is one potential. There are so many more inside that glass bowl, but the one that showed up is your reality or how you experience life. You see, any color could have come out and you would have not thought to compare which was good or bad— it still tastes the same! In life and in the big picture, whatever path you choose, putting aside labels and perceptions, is all good! All is valid, and you always have free will.

So you say to us, then why is there a path of least resistance and a path of more resistance? We respond to this question in a very to-the-point manner, for it only exists in your three-dimensional reality. In the space, dimensionality, and Love vortex of All That Is, potentialities arise without effort or continuous thought or decision-making, and then that potential is automatically followed. So indeed, there are still infinite possibilities, but there is not the action or thought process of which is good or bad or better or worse—they are seen as equals and all valid. For you, some paths are less resistant because you already have notions and belief systems about what is valid and what is not valid. So truly, it only exists because you are the co-creators or your own reality and you put it in place! How magical it is, even though it often puts you inside the box. But we again remind you that that was your decision when coming forth. How marvelous, co-creative, brave, and courageous it was of you!

We Love you so dearly, for you are the greatest lovers and greatest compassionate beings of Grace. We are delighted to be in your Presence in every space and time reality that you are in this present moment. All is the present moment. As the words are being written and interpreted from the other side of the veil, you read the words that resonate so deeply in every level of your being. You are powerful, dear one—hear it, feel it, be it. Your Light shines so brightly when you take it without hesitation and claim it without fear of judgment. We Love it when you follow your bliss, for when you are open to the unconditional Love flowing in, everything falls into place with least resistance on your part. It is so beautiful and so graceful.

We are now retreating back into our natural space, and we prepare to come out of this channel. Indeed, it takes our effort as much as it takes the human being's effort. It has been a great delight and a great meeting. In such resonance of All That You Are, much healing has taken place both the human being who is actively co-creating, and also in the human being who is too humble to recognize the greatness within. We Love you equally for all that you are and all that you have become regardless of where you are on your journey. There is no judgment here, for it is simply not part of our existence. We feel it when we come through you, but we still cannot resonate with it. So don't fear judgment from beyond! All is well, all is beautiful, all is equally important, and all valid. And so it is.

Chapter 39

Harmony With All That Is - Announce Your True Name

And so we begin, dear ones. This is a great space you have provided…that is, an open heart and an open mind. It helps you accelerate at this time and space reality that you call Earth. It is a great, great journey that is not part of a destination. It is such a beautiful, beautiful journey. You are some of the most magnificent beings, greatest co-creators, and greatest investigators of yourselves. You are the greatest finders, dear ones, for against all odds you have found yourself looking your true self in the eyes and know that you are Home. By so many standards and so many misconceptions you have begun to claim your Truth and seek, inside a deep resonance, who you authentically are, and it is such a great identity to own up to! You are Truth, each and every one of you.

Some of you believe in yourself and others don't, but each and every one of you is part of the Divine Oneness that some of you refer to as God. Such a benevolent name, and such a benevolent beingness. The biggest misconception about God is that you are separate, you need to win God over, and you must prove yourself to be "good" in order to receive the Love that you deserve. But we say, dear one, look at it from our angle…the angle that we probe you to investigate from the other side of the veil. Simply put, that separation is nonexistent.

And we say again dear ones, trust what you've got—you've got the tools. You've got what it takes to jump right in. It may be uncomfortable and slightly strenuous at first, but it's the process of letting go of old notions and moving into new ventures that matters.

Move into ones that support the Earth changes, the Universal changes, and the changes within the human body that is compromised of the eternal universe. So you see, it works together. Old notions cannot live on, they must be replaced and upgraded. It is our Divine wish for you to move into this flow with grace and appreciation for what is there, and just trust the Divine planning. Part of Divine planning is Divinely knowing that you are part of the plan, and that your decisions are both valid and very beautiful.

You cannot make a wrong decision, ever. They are all different vantage points that you have the ability to choose to select, but all are valid. If you choose that one is more suiting to you, that is free will, and all is well with that decision. Divine will is your free will, you see. So what you choose is always correct and you will be supported in that path, whatever it is. Sometimes you need to jump into the Grace beyond the mind and make crucial decisions that will go against previous conditions, even though it may seem incorrect.

Trust your heart and what your inner being has to say and let that lead the way. We know you hear it all too often, but we repeat the answer, for the Truth always remains the same. We would not keep repeating it unless it was integrated fully. This is the time to be brutally bold and claim your power. And sometimes it may shock you how much you can do to stick up for who you are, and that may be what it takes for a major breakthrough. Don't be afraid! Stay with your angels, your guides, your master, and know that as you move forward, in whatever way you feel in your heart that is best for you, that you are Divinely supported. So yes, stay in communication with your guides and your Source. You may use whatever name you wish to put on us, but also know that even if resistance comes from this idea of being guided from a higher Source, you are still not alone.

You do not need to feel pressure to put a label on us if it feels inauthentic. You may just be that light being that knows us so deeply that you can't imagine a name to us would do justice—and we agree, it doesn't! But for you, dear human being, it is always valid. We are always in service to you. So you must follow what feels good—that is the lesson and the ultimate teaching. Do what feels good, and don't just discard this as another one of those cliché teachings.

Dear one, if this is the only message you ever integrate from this entire book of great teachings, we say, no words are just thrown out to you for take-it-or-leave-it purposes. We see you each as a collective, and also personally. We see the potentials for the Earth plane, and we deliver messages that are precise and currently the most profound words that will deeply touch and move each human being who reads the words. So we know that if you are reading these words you have been Divinely guided, and we're here with you. That is validation to accept that you are no coincidence, and neither is your life. Your life is Divinely inspired, as is every human being. Coincidences do not exist.

You often feel the most discord when you feel alone, left out, or like you've made a mistake. To that we say, dear one, we know you are in the dark, and for good reasons too, but at least recognize the synchronicities. We are here with you! We are always here with you, and we reach out in physical form and touch you in this way because you're often so convinced that you're alone and separate when it's so opposite. It is time to notice that all the coincidences are beautiful Divine gifts that have been set in front of you, just for you so personally. Though we are a collective One speaking in physical terms, you are also in what you perceive as individual bodies. Even as a collective, nobody is left out. We say nobody because that is how you can relate to us, but we are just energy, Light, and Love.

We are here, dear ones. Feel us here with you and take a subtle moment to acknowledge it. You feel it, don't you, dear one? We speak to you each in different manners, but all resonate so clearly. You know it when you feel us, for when we make our entrance sometimes you feel your body temperature change or the goose bumps arise, and then you know for sure that we're right next to you. It should give you goose bumps, because the fact that we're able to be in communion in such different realities proves how unique and magnificent you are! You are so interdimensional…that is why you relate to us, because you feel that part of you that is nonphysical come in and remind you of the Home that you know so well. It gives you shivers or goose bumps because it reminds you that you're not lost…you're found!

You were never lost, you just believed yourself to be. That's part of coming back Home, learning about the illusions of your physicality. You'll find, in your own ways, how it has been a blessing in your life, and that is the personal beauty that occurs for each and every human being. You are so diverse and beautiful in your own distinct ways and personalities. In this time and space we greet you from a place of great recognition for who you are, and we ask you to announce yourself strongly. Announce your true name—not just to yourself, but to the whole world! Let *that* penetrate every part of your beingness. Indeed, that is a great mission in life—to be in harmony with All That Is in order to fulfill a great Divine mission.

That is your personal choice, one that you might have made in the past from behind the veil. It might partly be your choosing to bring other new facets of your great beingness into what you call the future. Of course, you know that time is nonexistent and all is happening at one point in time or vantage point, but we integrate this idea just for your enjoyment, because dear one, it has nothing to do with the mind. The heart must begin to integrate and get involved in this awakening process. It's not up to you, but you can coax it. It's all about you, dear one…no one else. You must work on yourself first, and then from there you can feel free to start to bring others into the great states of joy and happiness that you know to be true.

It is like the metaphor that we often use: you can't help another put on their oxygen mask if you pass out first! Treat yourself first— come into that alignment and *then* seek out what is next. The truest beauty resides in each and every one of you, and it is a great gift to be with you and help you uncover and really bask in All That You Are. It is a great gift…a great beautiful gift. The present moment is all that you have, and you are co-creating so much in the present moment. As you see linearly, it feels like a timeline. It feels like a long life story, but truly it all happens at once. So we say, you must start to adjust and integrate that idea, for all that is in your Akash can be expressed in your physical reality on the Earth plane.

It is a great destiny that you have to start bringing yourself greater peace by co-creating with all your tools. If you focus on only one dominant existence, we see why you would stumble and feel out of sorts! You've got so many more resources. You can't be adequately prepared if you haven't studied all of your material, and that has to do with far more than the physical existence that you dominantly live…or so you think! As a collective it is a great time to be able to speak your Truth without fear of judgment and closed minds and hearts. Of course, use your own judgment, but even as you fail to level with others who are not like-minded, your Light brings growth, peace, and transformation.

You are a lightworker, a lighthouse, and Light child standing with the torch in the dark. You guide the way...*you* are the savior! Such a Grace and blessing you are to be that brave, for you too had to be in the dark at some point to have the mind to be the Light bearer that you are now. It is such a great, great trust you now have for yourself and your connection with spirit, and it is essential...so essential. You can trust that even as you blossom and grow on your journey, there will always be the Presence, unchanging. God doesn't change—the human being changes.

You blossom and begin to open up to the Source, to You. Then and only then can you really reveal all that you have to offer to the world. It is powerful, it is Divine, and it is so beautiful. We are your teachers, but we mirror the teacher inside, because we are the true You, both in the channel and for *you*, dear reader. There is truly no difference, for as you read the words, they are being typed and translated. We smile, for you are here with us, we are here with you, and we are not separate. Love permeates through all, and that connection and great bond of Love that we have with the human being defies any laws that were proclaimed by Sir Isaac Newton. It is beyond thought, but it is not beyond the heart. The trueness of That Which Is You is beyond words and space, and time does no justice to the greatness that you truly and authentically are.

We are so pleased to be in your Presence, and we enjoy this interaction just as much as you do. It has been a great gift to share our wisdom, for it is the same wisdom that is inside. It is to empower you to believe in all that you already know inside, and to invigorate and balance that knowing so that you can follow it, be it, and shine it. There is no greater gift. We are here only for that—to be with you, to Love you, and to point you in the direction of your true Light when you are in the dark. All is well for you, dear child.

You are so beautiful, no matter where you are. We Love you unconditionally no matter where you are. Your job is only to Love yourself and let the words be read and integrated in their own time. It may take time, and that is beautiful and natural. You have nothing to force—it happens on its own and in its own time. And so it is.

Chapter 40

Speak Your Truth, Hold the Love, Share Your Magic

It is now time to begin, dear ones. This is a great revelation we have for you here now. A great blessing it is to be with you in such Grace and harmony together, and to come together and be in silence as One. It is now necessary for you to start integrating all that you are so that you can continue to manifest, integrate, and be wherever you are with more ease and less resistance. Dear one, you have picked this up so that you can start integrating All That You Are into this physical reality, and most of you haven't found that acceptance and Divinity within yet.

It's been there since the beginning, beckoning you to come inside and see who you *really* are. It is such Grace to sit in this silence with you, dear one, for as the words are being typed and read, one by one you are resonating, integrating, and remembering. It is so profound. It is so profound, and you don't even know it. You can hear the words, many times even, and they may not integrate at first. It takes time, dear one. It takes time to break your walls down and to start to let the mind dissipate and slowly let the heart dominate. The balance of the heart and mind is necessary, for you came to the Earth plane to have both, not just one or the other. You must embrace the mind that you have now, as judgmental and linear as it is.

But dear one, it is also so beautiful, for it shows you just how 3D you are. It plays the game so beautifully! What a gift it is to experience the game, even if it's also limiting. But you see, it is all for good reasons. Let it sink inside and be in Love with it anyways. You are Divine, beautiful creatures of God, and your Love and support for yourself is necessary in moving forward and integrating All That You Are into your physical existence. This will allow the energies and knowingness from behind the veil to creep in when the time is Divinely perfect—and that is not necessarily when the mind is ready.

The mind sees only the concept of time, and that brings impatience. If you can see through the heart and try to be in that space of knowingness behind the veil, you can see and identify with the concept of Divine planning. That has to do with You behind the veil coming in to that silent place in the physical body and giving indications of Truth that you truly *are* from behind the veil. That's what you call your intuition—it's your inner being calling out! So we say, give all your energy to that. From that space you can find silence and balance in your life. This brings reassurance in every step you take along the way, as well as a greater appreciation for what the Earth plane has to offer you.

You can trust All That You Are with great knowingness inside. Even as the mind sees so singularly, you can be reassured that you are a piece of God. You are the all-knowingness of God, and the biggest and greatest gift of having the opportunity to co-create in this existence. You can feel your co-creative abilities when you wake up to You, and recognize and give fuel to what jumps out from every cell in the body—and that is that you are not what you think you are. Despite all the fussing and fighting that you go through, ultimately you're here for the fun of it! Bask in it, take it in, believe in it, trust it, and be in communion with it when you feel the discord.

Put aside the trust issues, the fighting within yourself, the pull of disconnect, the emotions, and the lack of interest. You are so connected, you are so God, and you don't even know it. We want you to bask in all that you are so that you can begin to co-create what you came to be. You came to fulfill, support, and bring Light to the world! That is Love, that is kindness, that is peace, that is tranquility, and that is individual attention to the self. That often means really focusing on your own Divinity and giving yourself time to rest, to bask, to articulate your every Divine aspect into words, drawings, paintings, music, dance, and writing. That brings Light, a desire for connection, and joy to the world, because you are NOT alone. You are not alone...it is that simple.

You see, dear child of the Light, there's so much illusion that you even have the illusion that you don't have the pull anymore to know who you are. It's covered up by work, relationships, addictions, and other outlets that try to fill the void inside. We say to you, dear one, we know you. This is not the time to start disbelieving or giving up on yourself. This is the time to start invigorating All That You Are, and bring it! Bring it inward, and then spiral it out to all that you know. Send it to all that have the desire in their heart to be in their highest vibration on this Earth plane! It is so beautiful to have that connection with your fellow brothers and sisters. It is beautiful to have that community to open up, and to really open up your spirit in a safe environment.

It is important to share, to speak your Truth, and put what you feel inside into action. There is a pull inside that you know so well—it motivates you and drives you to follow your passions. Find a place to speak your Truth and just Be all that you are. When you put that intent out, those that are of the same vibrational alignment will find you…or you will find them! It is Divinely inspired. It is about Divinely greeting yourself. Then when you find the presence of others with the same interests, it is such a great interaction. Such healing and Grace in the room! So we say, gather, dear children! Be together, and then share your Love openly, one by one. It is so important and so necessary.

These are not just words you integrate as you read—they are vibrations. They integrate as vibrations now, now, now, now, now. So our point is, there's no time. All the Now's are valid, and Now is the perfect time to start Being who you came to be without the fear and procrastination. Don't be shy, dear one! You'll have such a breakthrough of Light pour through when you decide to truly Be who you came to be in your ultimate fullness. You deserve to support yourself and others on this great journey.

It is a great journey, one that is like a fairy tale, because it is so much an illusion. At the same time, right Now is relevant to you, and therefore we support you in your illusions no matter how valid they truly are in the bigger picture. We giggle at ourselves for our humor towards you, dear ones…we enjoy lighthearted interactions! So much Love and support is here for each and every one of you, and it is a great gift to let it spill out and come together as the Divine planned it. Truly it is You who planned it. You are the Divine, and that is what we try, time after time, to remind you, because you let yourselves be so small. It is not only in how you interact with yourself, but also how you let others interact with you. It's an epidemic of smallness!

If only you knew how vast you really are! You are made of the cosmos and all of the beingness in the universe. You are the planets and the stardust, quite literally! You are the great plasma, the universal magnetism, the pull, the Law of Attraction that resides in All That Is, and the creatures on the Earth and Beyond. You are truly All That Is—and yet you think that you're some random human being that is singular in a body for eighty years or so, and then you're gonna croak. You're not sure whether or not you will ever have a second chance. Some of you think that there's nothing after death, and some think you go to Heaven or Hell. We say, what do *you* think? What do you *really* think, despite what you learned? Think as a child. Think of you as a child, and come back to that innocent naïve little boy or girl and remember what you thought about the universe and God.

We'll tell you right away that before you had the influence of religion and conditionings, you knew God. You knew you were supported, and you knew exactly who you were. You knew firsthand the experience of Oneness with All That Is—pure unconditional Love and beingness. The Hell that you talk about is a metaphor of the mind, the separateness and conditionings that hold you inside the box on Earth. When you reemerge into the nonphysical, no such separation is necessary, nor is it relevant or possible. In the nonphysical beingness of All That Is, you are God again…part of the big family, the big pot of soup.

It is very natural that such illusions fit you now, human being, but know inside that you have nothing to worry about when you greet your big family again. You have nothing to worry about, because when you reenter as your true and authentic existence, All That Is, the purity of You, will be your only experience. It cannot be anything besides Love, period. What you now believe to be the Truth through the mind is irrelevant.

Through the mind you cannot conceptualize your Truth, but through the Heart you can resonate with the greatness of you. You will easily see the multidimensional beingness and Source that you are, and you will no longer need to make yourself so small, insecure, and vulnerable to see it. In fact, as you claim your greatness, more and more will be revealed to you. You must be the first to knock on the door and show your passion and desire, and then we will open the door and greet you with such unconditional Love. We will say, "Dear child, we never thought you'd come. Greetings, and welcome Home. Welcome to You."

These are the words that we speak to you now, because you are ready to hear them. You are ready to integrate them into All That You Are, and to not only share and spread it, but to also Be it so strongly and intently that nobody who comes across you will be able to pass by without recognizing the Divinity within you. If they can really see you for who you are, then give yourself a high five, because you're the lightworker that is spreading it. You are spreading the Truth throughout all creation! If you help invigorate it in another, what a blessing it is for both sides! There is no judgment, it is just about being You—however You Are naturally. We Love you that way, not for any way that you try to fit inside the box. It is all about you, dear human being.

However you are, that is who you are—no exceptions. And it is strength, it is the great courage of the lightworker to come into this existence knowing the conditions, and they agreed. *You* agreed as you said to us, "I am ready to reemerge, to be who I truly am in the Earth plane, and I accept all that comes through to me on my journey. I am ready to spread the Light to all creatures, no matter what it takes. I am ready to be all my beingness from my standpoint behind the veil." And you *are* behind the veil, because you are nonphysical and interdimensional in the Now.

We say, dear one, just because your experience doesn't match up doesn't mean you should disregard it…because what we speak of to you so intimately and personally is that even under the illusion of self, you are still in the comfort of All That You Are from behind the veil. It is accessible as soon as you will it. It then fuels up like gas added to a flame, but it takes your passion and free will. We are always here for each and every being of Love, and we are inspired and so in awe of who you are, who you have become, and what you have to share with the world.

Dear one, it is so beyond thought, so beyond the 3D mind, and so beyond what words can convey, but the vibration behind the words and what you feel in the heart is the indicator of Truth. And you'll know it then—you'll know what your Truth is inside! That is what we ask you to truly dive into without hesitation and fear of where you'll end up, because it will be Divinely inspired, Divinely guided, and Divinely greeted by the Wholeness and bigger picture of You. It is such a gift and such a blessing to be by your side and unveil the greatness of You, for truly that is where we stand.

You feel it, child—you feel us with you! Trust that. Trust that you are guided, and stick with it! We Love you to no extents, and it is a great blessing to connect in this blessed way, to be in harmony with All That You Are, and to invigorate and fully immerse all the facets of You into your current experience. It is our will, as well it is your will, to come fully into that and be in Love with humanity, because it is Oneness. It is truly Oneness. And so it is.

Chapter 41

The Evolution of Humanity's Consciousness

It is with great honor that we reenter. It is such a powerful, beautiful, and Divine Presence! You can truly feel it inside as it permeates in every facet of You in the greater knowingness of All That You Are. And it is of such great importance that you see and identify with that, as well as to be in harmony and resonance with that. It is a gift from God and a gift from You. If you can see yourself from that angle, it will in your greatest good, for it does the world good. You can deeply shift the vibration on Earth by just being You and resonating with the deepest form of Love that is You. It is a great gift to be with that, to be in that, and to accept that as your ultimate Truth. It is such a bond you have with your Divine and your co-creator.

You live thinking that you're separate, but you feel the tug...you feel the pull when you tune in, don't you? Inside you know what is calling, and it is time to be that, dear child. It is time to show yourself what you've got! It may surprise you how powerful a warrior you truly are, for you'll say to yourself, "Why haven't I done this earlier?"

We'll respond and say, "You weren't ready, and the planet wasn't ready, but now you are, and so we greet you with so much Love."

You'll respond back to us, "Then why is it so important that I do this...that I awaken to All That I Am?"

Dear ones, we speak to you directly now in whatever way you hear the words. Whether it be from us directly as the voice, or whether it's on the page, we say to you, "Dear warrior of the Light, how could you not want it? How could you not? All That You Are is so grand and so great! How could you put a filter over that and pretend that it doesn't exist?"

Dear one, it's time to see yourself in clear eyes, and to feel All That You Are so that you can be fearless going forward—to co-create, to *be* the Light, to shine the Light, and to speak the Light. This is the real You, the interdimensional You that we know so well as family. We are family, and we are One. This Love that we have is essential in co-creating and bringing the Earth to this new vibration, into the Oneness with All That Is in every human being that walks the Earth. The new ones that are returning now, day after day, are different—they are updated, and they know who they are.

So we say teachers, parents, family, and friends—look out because you've got some power in those children, and they're not gonna sit around waiting for you to approve of them! They're stepping into themselves as they enter, and it's not going to dissipate as it might have for you over the years. They're going to speak their Truth with so much fire that it's going to be impossible for you not to listen. This is the mission of the lightworker who channels the words through this sacred space. It is a great gift to be with you, dear one, and we thank you for being the Light with All That You Are. To you who read the words, you are the light being as well! You are the being holding the torch because you're ready to change the planet, and you're ready to do your work with such joy, and oh, the healing you will bring if you give this your whole-hearted energy! It's your time, dear one.

We know who you are—each and every one of you. It's so beautiful to be in this space, in this time of great commencement and progress. It is part of the soul journey to be here. It is about coming into alignment with energies that have not served you in the past that you can still have an acceptance of. See them as they are and find out what worked and what didn't work. Upgrade! Use your tools, find your passions, and just Love where you are, wherever that might be, in fullness. From there, as you Love the present moment for what it is, you can start to build a gratitude for All That Is. All that you encounter and experience is just part of life, and it is no longer phasing. It helps you to expand and be the bigger, vaster self that you know you are! It is your mission.

Each and every one of you has a mission, and it's up to you. The beingness that you have experienced (and continue to experience) through multiple lifetimes and existences is all part of the present moment. You are building resistance! That is not meant to be interpreted in a negative sense, for we are simply saying that the experience strengthens you and builds you up to the greatness you deserve. That brings a great amount of trust in yourself, dear beings. It lets you surrender to the unconditional Love of the universe, without resistance to where it's coming from, what it is, and whether it's gonna do anything for you. To that we respond, not only is it Home to You, but it's gonna prove to be your perfect harmony in All That You Are. It's also gonna show you the Truths in All that you are, All that you have become, and all that you are wishing to be.

Then life makes so much more sense because you understand the laws of the universe that make up your existence. You understand what you're putting out into the universal grid (your Akash), and you see where your vibrational state takes you throughout life, and even throughout each day. It's no longer a puzzle, so you can't fight with it. You can't be in misalignment with it. You certainly *can* reach out and hold our hand, dear child. Then we will take that as a pushing of the door, and we'll see that you're activating your free will in the direction of your Source within.

We'll tell you, "Remember, dear one, when we told you about this from behind the veil? Remember when we told you that you would forget who you were?"

You would say, "Yes, I remember. How much I have accomplished in the dark!"

We would then give you a loving, energetic, vibrational embrace, and we would say, "Thank you, dear child, for your strength and courage. Thank you for bringing Earth up with your Light and Love, and thank you for spending your time in this environment that is not natural to you. You have Graced us beyond words, and we thank you. Not only have you proved to yourself how great you are, but you have also proved that you are indestructible, and always will be. You are so much Love and compassion—and it makes up your physical flesh and bones. It's not what the scientists tell you it is from the physical standpoint of blood and bones—they are not entirely correct. They won't necessarily tell you that you are the universe because they don't know it. Dear child, that's what you are…and you just don't know it yet."

We give you the words even as they haven't been fully integrated, for it will take time. It will take time to fully understand—to not just read or feel the words, but to accept them, remember them, and Be them. That is what you knew to be true from beyond the veil. You knew this Truth, for it is the only Truth that exists. What we tell you is absolute—it will remain the Truth always, for time is nonexistent. You can feel the energetic shifts, can't you? Dear one, this is about the evolution of the human being.

Now that you're able to feel what it's all about, you're able to feel the words, and not just read them on a physical, three-dimensional level. That is the real You...the multidimensional, multi-cellular, manifested version of You that is behind the veil with us. We greet you and say, "Don't give up, dear child, for it's all just begun for you. Wherever you want to go is up to you, just choose it and be the deliberate creator of your own reality. You are the manifester—it's up to you completely. We are here to be of service, but we're also here to remind you of what's within, and that is God. That is the Source—the all-knowingness that is always going to be a part of you for eternity. It doesn't die when you croak, and it doesn't die in the nonphysical existence. It is truly a beautiful image, do you agree?

What a good time to remind you, for not only is it a beautiful image, but it's a real image! This is You, and this is what you're all about. Some of you know it and others don't. We're here only to give you what you came to seek, and that is the knowingness inside. We are not here to force the words upon you, for if you are resistant, then so be it. There is a time and place for all experiences and emotions, and all are beautiful. Each human being has their own time, and however it plays out according to You is natural and perfect. And so it is.

Chapter 42

Listen to the Music in the Silence

Greetings, dear ones. We are the collective of the Oneness and Beingness of All That Is. We have no name, but it is not invalid if you choose one for us, for we accept and identify with your personal will to put names on us from a singular vantage point in the 3D. So by all means, let that be your Truth if that is what you wish it to be! There is great Love for you here as always, and it is a great pleasure to greet you with such harmony and Grace. With a great understanding and will to be on the fast track, you will reach beyond the mind and linearity that is present on Earth. It's not the Earth energy as much as it is the human being's energy that is truly at the epicenter of your singularity. It has no reflection on your value or of how we think of you, we just like to remind you that the 3D has been put in place for valid reasons, all of which are lovely and beautiful.

We remind you that this Divine mission that you are on is all for a bigger purpose. You are filling a great mission on a much larger scale than just for your singular self. You often venture into the world and find yourself lost with all the opportunities, some which speak to you, and others which don't, and that is free will. All we wish to emphasize is that you are working from the heart when you can differentiate what you do want from what you don't want. That is a beautiful gift to settle into—don't get too caught up in your head! We teach you this so you can feel more grounded in the space where you are with confidence, grace, compassion, and gratitude, for it is important to integrate forgiveness into your reality of yourself so that you can forgive others. That is the purpose of it all.

We also see that you are all at different vantage points on your journey, and we respect you as we wait for the right moment to give you the material. Even though it is truly relevant for each in the bigger picture, if it doesn't yet resonate, that is Divinely beautiful as well. We do not judge you for where you are, for we see that no matter where you are, you are on the same evolutionary journey as everyone else. You have the same Grace and strength behind all that you do on the Earth plane. We Love and appreciate you all to such an extent, for all that have chosen to participate in this Earth game of co-creation are Divine beings.

You have chosen to participate in manifesting that which you desire, that which you stand for, and that which invigorates you and brings Light to your soul. We invite the lightworkers to step forth and find that if you are so called, step forth and bring it! You are all lightworkers, but it is your choice to see it or not. We reference choice not in a physical way, but in a much deeper way. Choice is always relevant, but on a deep spiritual level, the planning that goes on behind the veil is where these kind of choices come from. So because of the great journey, long as it is, you ultimately have come to a place of great experience and understanding of the Earth plane and who you are.

You are here to learn your potential as a Light part of the whole. All beings soon come to the conclusion that they have just as much potential as nonphysical beings as they do as physical beings. It's all about free will! The choice to start integrating those many facets of You into your reality is the essence of all spiritual growth. It takes a little bit of concentration, but it also comes easily when you realize it is passion, Love, and the path of least resistance.

You should be proud of yourself for stepping outside the box and saying, "I do! I *do* step into All That I Am, I *do* come to terms with the illusion of self, and I *do* agree to not let that dominate me any longer. What I believe to be true is not always what I know to be true within, and that shapes me as a light being. I may go through traumas and rough patches, but I will come through knowing more about myself...and I will never be alone. Spirit is always with me, even when I feel separate. I can always call out their names, my true brothers and sisters, and say to them, 'Please touch me and remind me of All That I Am.'"

Spirit comes through in ways that you may not expect, but nevertheless, it comes! You'll find yourself in such gratitude. Gratitude will begin to fill your heart and soul even when you are struggling with your emotions and overcome with fear, anxiety, sadness, or depression. We help you come through to the other side when we whisper in your ear, so delicately and so lovingly, "It's not over, dear one. Remember the journey. Remember your true name. We know you, dear one." The conversation can start simple, but what is important is that it keeps your head high. You can be reassured that even as you hit those lows, you are still in the utter Divine consciousness and co-creative awareness of the larger perspective, multidimensional You.

You ask questions to the spirit like, "Show me a sign," or "Give me a clear message," but we would like to remind you that signs are always showing up, not just when you're asking for them. Spirit shows up in everything—it is *you* that only pays attention when you have a neediness to find instant relief. We wish to say to that it's okay and we understand, but it's important to recognize that despite the illusions, you so often disregard the simple beauty and intricate delicate features of Divine consciousness in Life all around you. If you were to pay more attention and really be in unity with every piece of nature you would slow down your mind, access the silence, and really see it for what is. The silence would come so naturally and would inspire you to find that within in your own space and time.

The silence is the Divine in you, but it takes your willingness to go within. You can then relate and understand on a deep, deep level the existence and consciousness that is within the flower, the grass, the trees, the birds, and the animals. You often can't put your finger on it, but when you retreat into nature there seems to be a simplicity, a grounding, and an unraveling of problems that happens, and you don't know why.

Could it really be as simple as you connecting with you? You put other logical reasons and labels on your daily practices, such as exercise. Exercise is so much deeper than using a machine. Exercise is not only for the body, but also for the mind. The refreshing and renewing quality of nature is simply the fact that you and You find time to be in silence together. You find that unity consciousness is activated within, and you can feel the bond and true stillness when you sit in the woods and play in the water. Even just walking through a natural environment brings great peace and stillness within. We suggest it as a healthy practice to still the mind if it seems hard to find the stillness within.

It is from beyond the veil that we greet you with this information that can be helpful in bringing balance and co-creative strength into your physical bodies. It is a great, great gift to be able to activate that part of you that sees the reflection of You as you read the words and feel such connectedness. Beyond the veil we know your names in the truest form; that is, not in the singular, three-dimensional form. We feel you and know you, for it is a connectedness that is similar to the greatest friend you ever had.

We are like the greatest listener that you turn to help you see the big picture and work out any little kinks you stumble on. Sometimes friends point out the obvious to you, which is an enlightening bond and practice to have. We are similar, though of course in a broader sense. We are your True family, one that is infinite and undying. We are immortal, as are you. If you truly knew what death was, you'd know it's nothing to be afraid of! It's not the end, it's just another chapter in your co-creative, endless span of existence. So you see, we are your eternal best friend. We come through in whatever format that you desire to frame us in.

We leave it up to you because it is important to be as simple and authentic as you can be. To be authentic you must feel comfortable being personal, being your real self. For some it takes a great deal of conditioning to be dropped, for you are taught so many things that go against your personal Truths. You may or may not feel like you can let it out into your family and into the world, but you must know that no matter what you choose, you are supported. You must come back to you—what feels good and what doesn't. That is the life goal: to feel good. That is the ultimate teaching. Aside from that it's all are bells and whistles, so to speak…yet they are just as essential and valid.

They all help you see the stepping-stones along the way, to connect the dots, and to become who you are and who you desire to be without feeling overwhelmed by it. Sometimes it feels like a task, but we think it should feel so easy, for it is coming Home. If it feels like a task or a chore and you're disinterested, let it sit with you, dear one. Let it sit inside and stir around, for it very well may take some years for it to integrate. Maybe your time has not arisen. When you're ready, the passion, will, and hunger will arise naturally. Your spirit will be so very invigorated by All That Is and all that You have to offer that it cannot be ignored or put aside.

So you see, it is all valid and beautiful. It's all part of the whole and the big picture. It's beside the point to say that you should be one way, and to commit to this step-by-step process until it makes sense and you're practiced. It is not about that at all—it is not the kind of teaching that you learn, it is the kind of teaching that you remember. If you are truly ready to hear it, it will permeate through every cell and shake you up so much that you will be moved beyond belief. You will be floored at your greatness, and unable to ignore the fullness and the hunger inside to be All that you came to be. Without any hesitation or judgment of what you authentically are, you will move forward into that space of Truth.

Dear ones, it takes courage. We do not say that it will always be easy, but you must rely on the Source and the guidance within to show you what's up next. You can be tuned into that channel or station so well that you can feel it, notice it, communicate with it, and make choices accordingly that fit into the Divine planning of the bigger picture. When you are making that strong prayer inside to be in communion with and open to your Source and God inside, you will feel the tug, the signs, the synchronicities, and all the Divine happenings, and you'll know just where they're coming from.

You may disregard them now if you're unable to fully notice all the miracles that occur for you every second of every day, but then you will suddenly come to the realization and epiphany that, in fact, it's all for you! You will say to the spirit inside, "Oh! I had no idea how much fulfillment is being given to me in response to what I asked for!" It takes you off guard because the manifestation is not always exactly as expected...but nonetheless, it is always in direct response to prayer. An open and receptive Light being will be able to see the guidance in a clear way, and to sincerely and truly have deep gratitude in the heart for this manifestation.

And when you start to feel discord and consciously decide to move into gratitude for those small, but very appreciated, synchronicities, you know that you are not alone. You are so beautifully guided in every direction. According to what you put out, you will be shown to that destination. It's all about you! We see service to the human being as an opportunity to provide growth and great Love, not as an opportunity to put labels on them or judge them for acting in certain ways. We have no judgment, and we have no physical assets or tools that would allow this type of manifested belief to take form. So get over that, dear one! Feel at home with the spirit, and feel at peace with the spirit, for this is the most beautiful, unique, personal, unconditional, and utterly spacious relationship. It is eternal, and it is the pure unconditional Grace, Love, and Light.

It has been a powerful and very opening discussion, and we Grace you for remaining open to receiving what is to be shared. We Love you unconditionally from the time-space reality that is nonphysical and non-linear. We see all possibilities for you and for the planet as very positive, co-creative, and interdimensional. You're moving out of singular beingness. What a great, great relief that is! All is Love, all is Light. And so it is.

Chapter 43

The Eternalness of Your Soul

It is indeed a great journey we have begun together, dear ones. We will continue it for the extent that is necessary to retrieve the information you each have from behind the veil. It is personal, but it is also universally applied. This is precisely why the channeling you read is applicable to all that read the words. Dear children, it has been a great blessing and a great, great interaction that we have opened through this valid communication and open discussion. It has probed into the mind's incessant games, and challenges you to look further beyond the noticeable so that you can see the invisible.

That is to say, your manifestations and blindness in the three-dimensional sense keep you from seeing the interdimensional and nonphysical realms. You see, it is natural that this is set up in this way for the purpose of staying present on the Earth plane. It is so important to stay present, to be in active presentness in every moment in time, in every Now. All that means is to be here with all that you can be. Don't settle for choosing less for yourself. It is such a great, great blessing to share our knowingness with you, for it is so powerful, so impactful, and so relevant to All That You Are.

It is finally beginning to make some sense to you, dear human being. It is beginning to finally sink in, and we say, it's about time! You've been waiting for some relief for so long, and it is coming now. It is your time to start co-creating the reality that you're ready to see and experience in your daily lives. This is what is needed as a whole. When you are living your fullest expression, feeling utter happiness and joy in All That You Are, there is no worry! There is nothing but peace with who you naturally are. That is a great gift because it lets the human being just take a breather and be without interruption from the mind.

Your practices such as meditation, active and mindful breathing, digesting your food slowly, and practicing yoga are all very good for your energy body. There are many kinds of practices, all of which are our favorite! Being in nature fills you up and gives you such peace in every cell of your body. The older ones may wonder where you got it from, for you'll hear the messages from your Higher Self in that stillness. You'll hear the self that is all-knowingness and beingness, resonating at a high level that is undying.

You see, dear one, it is important to remember that All That You Are, embraced in its fullness, is exactly what you've been waiting to be ever since you came into this singular and three-dimensional existence. From that silent place within, you blossom, grow, sprout new wings, and fly higher than ever. Today we speak of reincarnation, for it is a subject that many of you wish to hear. It is between you and You, an agreement that is made behind the veil in a place and time that is unknown to the singular you, but of course it is very well known by the multidimensional You. From here we let you discover and see what it's all about.

You were guided into the nonphysical as you were many, many times, but you decided to reemerge into the physical because you saw the great ones returning and felt that tug within. You said, "I miss that fond memory, please let me go back and help be a lighthouse as well!"

We said back to you, "Oh dear one, how brave of you! We are so pleased and joyous to hear what a great opportunity this will be for you." And then you sprouted those wings, metaphorically of course, and you were ready to fly away into the arms of the physical plane. It was quite a shock at first since it was so foreign to anything you had known before, but it was alive, it was well, it was beingness, and it is still Divine and perfect.

From this great understanding you said, "It is time." With those words we greeted you with such Love, kindness, and reverence for who you are. We are ever in Love with you, dear human being. It is our great gift to you to present to you the gift of song through the channel, the gift of voice through the channel, the gift of great beauty through the channel, and the gift of great enhancement and powerful voice healing. Through the channel emerges a great energy that takes the world into such Grace and harmony with All That Is that you can't help but besides take a look and marvel at its glory. It is our wish for you to see yourself as we see you. You are our children, our partner, and our family, because you are here with us behind the same veil, and we are One.

We are greeting you with the same Oneness that you remembered when you came here. It is distinct, it is powerful, it is great, and it is holy. This is what keeps you here, for there is that great beauty of contrast and communication between you and You in a way that lets you see a singularity difference in You. This brings you to a higher vibration and a higher knowingness of what it's all about. What a great relief it is to be in that space and reveal to yourself, your heart, and your soul that all you believe yourself to be is correct! What a superb relief to know that it is the story of the real You! It is important to really see for yourself what that means, for even as we use the words on the page they still come on their own. The real messages come from You beyond the veil in the multi-cellular big cluster of beingness and stardust.

You are starting to realize what your boundaries, goals, and requirements are, and it causes you pain sometimes to draw outside the lines and be something other than what you see. But you know, dear one, only the greatest artists paint outside the lines. You see, all is valid and well. As you begin this great conversation between you and You, you will always end up with a loving hug and a gentle reminder that it's not over for you.

Reincarnation is a subject or vocabulary word that we do not associate with what the nonphysical truly is, but we do hear the question as you intend it to be answered. We'll say, dear ones, it is about the self. It is about updating the self to a newer version each time. That is your choice and your influence…only you can make that evolution of your soul possible. There is no pressure to be or come here to fill a void that is none other than your own. For that reason it is ironic that you blame others for such problems in life. We think that even as those judgments arrive in the beginning and plague your mind, they also shut down after some time. Then and only then can you truly be a pure channel and hear what spirit has to offer.

We offer you unconditional Love only. The great little nuggets along the way are just for your enjoyment. When you feel the synchronicities remember your Truth and what you're here for, and it will reveal itself more and more to you. It is such a great mission you are on, and it is a great cause, one that has nothing but power to come about for it. This is a great time for the human being who often feels small, for you are evolving automatically. You're already there—just let it happen for you, dear one. The grid fills in on its own if you let it.

We guide you day and night to All That Is, whether you acknowledge it or not. We can be heard, smelled, tasted, and touched, but trust is key, dear ones. It is beyond thought to conceptualize where we're at on our evolutional journey, but great, great accomplishments have come through. We bless you for all of your dedication and hard work, for all is well, all is good, and all is beautiful. We Love you so much, dear child. And so it is.

Chapter 44

Recognition

The great beauty within the human being is scrumptious, you know? We Love to be in your Grace and feel your Presence as another face of us behind the veil and beyond the grid. You see, it is something that we marvel at, for the human being always proves to stretch the boundaries in ways that are beyond thought and the mind's capabilities. You become so singular, yet you have the ability to expand your consciousness and allow the all-knowingness to flood in.

How great you are! We think it's fascinating that you can reemerge, as do we, into a reality that is so opposite, so much more authentic and all-knowing. What you accomplish as you are foolin' around down on Earth is miraculous! You put so much of you aside in the beginning, yet you maintain enough composure and identity within that. We think the mind is quite pervasive, but how beautiful you are to find yourself now in these times and to say for certain, "Yes, I am that! I am all of that, and I am also this little singular body right now, but I know it is a dream." You accept it, yet you move forward to be the co-creator of your reality with such oomph, Grace, courage, and beauty ...and you still ask for more again! We say to you, bravo! Bravo, dear one.

Even though you can't capture the greatness of this statement, you truly are a master and a great being of Light...you just don't know it. We're here to help you claim your greatness, to be in the Light, and to be in your Love. It's all within! That is why the title is as it is, because who you are is not to be found, it already exists—and always has existed! The times often call for intervention, but what we help you see with Divine guidance is no more than what you already preserve inside.

If it wasn't truly this way, it would not be accessible, because you must stay present on the Earth plane with what it has to offer you. That is to say, the thoughts, the Grace, the Love, and the connection that you think comes from the Heavens above is from You. It has been from You all along, you just didn't know it!

Don't diminish that statement! Don't make yourself small, for what we speak to you is meant to be taken in with respect and Grace. It is the Truth of all Truths, and the true story of You. We say that in awe of you, dear creator and master! You know what you're doing, and always have every time you reemerge. Now it's time to claim it all, take out your tools, take a look at them, and evaluate where they're gonna go. Start applying them in ways that balances the bigger picture of You. That is a domino effect for all the others who are doing the same thing, finding the same ultimate Truth on their own path.

That is the beautiful thing about this magnificent journey for you, dear ones...no matter where you go, the answer is always the same. And yes, you may uncover it differently, but the ultimate Truth will always be the same. It will always play out in the same process of reveling in Grace for a while and then realizing, it's nothing apart from you, it's PART of you! Then you'll *really* get knocked over in awe, because your whole life you played out the game and thought you knew who you were, but alas, you are so much greater! You are so much more distinct, for there are so many more facets to You! So it is a great revelation for the human being because you learn that All You Are has so much more potential.

There are no wrong decisions, and you've got more tools in your toolbox than you previously thought you had. It gives a whole new meaning when you decide to incorporate them, because now the possibilities are infinite. What can't you do, dear children? Pretty much nothing! Most of you that read these words are old souls. You've got history behind you, dear one. You've got experience on the Earth plane, and you know what it's about now...you know the laws of the Universe within, and you know what works and what doesn't work. Sometimes you come back in, reemerge into the physical, and get chills all over because you realize that some of your favorite tools in your toolbox have been the ones you've used in the past, linearly speaking. So then you come around once again and decide to perfect what you didn't finish last time—all your talents and graceful skills.

That is the human being mastering what you do best—the art of co-creative existence. You've got it mastered, old soul...you've got it mastered. Some of you still think that you're here to do something more, to redeem yourself, or play around mindlessly...but little do you know! Little do you know, because you are literally one of the finest all-encompassing co-creators of the universe! Let us not make that statement any smaller, for it is a huge concept. It must be pondered and reveled in. Your concepts are 3D, but that doesn't mean that You are not 4D, 5D, and beyond. You are *multidimensional*. That means you exist in *multiple* existences all at once—one being the Earthly three-dimensional plane where you seemingly exist dominantly because you see linearly. Therefore, the other dimensional interfaces cannot exist in a way that makes sense to you.

Putting the mind aside, you are all that we say you are—that is not up for debate! Dear being, we give you a great lesson, for it's important as we speak these great words. When given words of encouragement, great universal laws, or of a simple, yet profound, statement, take it in with great stillness in the heart. That is to say, don't try to force it inward, for if you are truly ready to hear it, it *will* be heard. You will be truly graced and struck by the words, and you will find them applicable as you understand and integrate them.

Dear one, if you find them foreign or a barrier, then you can choose to leave it be for a while. No matter what you do, Grace works on you, and you are taken care of unconditionally. You see, don't worry so much about the words, for they are quite distinctly a powerful gift from God. If you feel uninterested, just wait. Your time is not yet ripe. However, there is Truth in the statement that if you read the words, you are waking up. That is what we would appreciate from you, dear human being, because the words must be ready to hear if you are open and receptive.

The words are for the one that finds the calling in the heart. That is not to say it is not for the Global Awareness, because it is, but it must be ready to hear. If not, it will not be fully understood or integrated. Misconception causes grief. We only come through with the highest Love and Light, and it is translated through the words, through the paper, and through intent. You must be ready to hear it, to Be it, and to sing and dance it. You will become God word by word, for you will integrate God word by word, and you will speak God word by word. You will also bring Light to the world through God, for *that* is You, and that is the most profound statement we have just made, because it really hits home, doesn't it, dear one? It really rings true with you, doesn't it? Let us remind it to you often, for you appreciate it, and we can feel it.

It is a great gift to cherish these moments with you, for it is not temporary. We tell you, dear human being, it is not temporary…it is eternal. As you focus your intent as you read, they feel linear and three-dimensional, but in a greater sense they are quite eternal. Every facet of You feels it, rings true with it, and encourages you to move into it. So when you feel that recognition and knowing inside, know inside that All That You Are feels it and believes in you. You are so great, and you are so God. We do not teach you from a place of domination or putting you back into labeling and characterizing who and what we are, we just ask you to redefine God. Redefine what that is to you, because it's not just in the sky and it's not in the Earth—it is All That Is.

Somehow that is confusing to you, because you are trained to diminish and exclude all the beauty around you that is God for something that feels distant and unreachable. To that we say, it is not that way at all! We would like it, as would you, if you would start integrating God into all the facets of You. That is, you don't need to try to add it to you…just recognize that it *is* you. You have nothing to add, for you are already God. You are perfect in your great simplicity. Truly we say you are simplistic because you appear that way, though inside, when looking deeper and more intricately, we see all the little facets and details that are far from simplistic.

We say great simplicity because your appearance is quite deceiving. In the inside you are great, and on the outside you are simplistic. Again, that is the great co-creative master at work. We marvel at you, stand in awe of you, and Love you unconditionally with all of our beingness. This is your chance to be the Light, to change whatever patterns you're in, and to decide for yourself that it's not worth another lifetime of roaming around in the dark. These words ring true with each and every one of you. Whether you are ready to hear them or not is a different story, but we know you. We know each and every one of You.

Would you like to know that the words being interpreted, read, delivered are God? How would you take it if we said God is you? Would you be fearful, would you shrink away in disbelief, or would you stand with your head up high and claim it with all that you are? It takes courage and owning up to a great beingness, but it takes no physical effort on your part. It just requires the mind to subside and take the back seat. It's often misunderstood, for the relaxing of the mind is powerful and very effective. However, it is often a fight to get to that point. It's no mistake on your part, but now you are going to start using it in different ways...that is all we mean by the mind taking a backseat. We don't want you to get rid of it!

It's a powerful toolkit you've got stored up, for you have so many more tools now than you had millions of years ago in the time when you came through into the physical atmosphere, maybe for the first time, and only had the interdimensional history in your beingness. Now that you've likely got experience in the physical, it serves you to be here now to incorporate this, so that when you reemerge once again you've got some support. You've got your big tools and your little tools all lined up in your toolbox, organized, shiny, and ready to use.

You might then say, "So what am I here for?" When you reemerge all confused in the physical, we carefully and lovingly pass you the tools nonchalantly...though not really, but you perceive it that way. We give you the tools you need, from your own assortment in your own toolbox, and you think it's separate from you, but it's not. We're just helping you along from a greater perspective. You must realize that we are still you, and you are still us. We are One, and we are God together. So be God...be God. And so it is.

Chapter 45

Upgrading to the New Human Being

It is time to begin, dear ones. We are here now to assist you on your journey moving forward on the path of least resistance. What a great gift it has been to let go of the mind, to fall into the emptiness, to lose track of the mind, to come into a space of silence, and to deliver the messages from the greatness within. These are the all-knowing, all-encompassing God facets of You. It is more than a gift, for it has shown you that the powerful master is within…and is everything but singular.

It may take you into deeper sense of self, for it is the opposite of separation. It is the opposite of the ideology you have been taught—that God lies without—for truly, God is within. That is the thread that says God is All That Is and is always present for eternity. The external will be modified, and the planet will change and move into new ways as humanity shifts, but God will remain the same for eternity. That is the process of the human being, for that is the process of the one who is tuned in, tapped in, and turned on. That is what we say to the human being who is in perfect alignment with the Source, and therefore, in perfect alignment with All That They Are truly.

It is up to the human being to be that source of great knowingness and true Love, and it is up to the human being to co-create the reality that they are looking for. It is up to the human being to decide what they want to co-create and what they do not want to co-create. The human being has this great possibility and great expansiveness that gives new meaning to the universal laws set in stone by the great philosophers and scientists over time.

And the concept of relativity is one that catches most off guard, for it brings back the reference of time, space, and realities. We say that the casual upbringing of the human being has no reference in this great and profound statement made by the great Albert Einstein. He is a great-minded scientist who knew how to re-evaluate what is present on the Earth in that current moment, and to dig deep into the universal laws which are untouched and unchanging. He made them into the principles that today are still present. So it is that they still remain true and relevant, but the Earth begins to change, as does the human being, so the laws must also change and be updated.

It is beyond thought and beyond your doing. It is Source and the Divine plan of the Universe, and it happens all at once when the human being and the evolution are ready. Time is nonexistent—it is a concept created by humanity as a way to use this theme of relativity, to keep time. Relativity has, in many ways, been a great finding, but it puts you further into the box…it puts you further into separation. We say to you, even though it works in the 3D, you are now moving beyond it. As you're moving into higher states, it will start to make less and less sense.

So it is that you must start to depend less upon those universal laws that are stable and in print—they are not valid for eternity. They work only in your three-dimensional atmosphere and nowhere else. You must remember that even as you create new laws and new practices that form to the changing and fluctuating Earth, laws will change. Laws are set in stone for good reasons—to further put you into reference, to understand how to go about your daily life, and how to understand basic terms. It is possible to be without time, but in the 3D this is where you are in a linear perspective.

That is the dominating vibrational stance you take. That is not to say it cannot be overcome, but altered states of consciousness would be required. It is powerful to be here, to always be in the Now, but it takes practiced intent and practiced vibrational alignment. The here and Now is always one reference point, always the same point if you want to use the term as Time.

In this great awakening of the Earth it is important to focus on your bodies. The evolution of the Earth is growing, evolving, and maximizing even. Your people need to find the body to be cleared, both emotionally and physically. There is a lot inside the body that is plagued from your thoughts and emotions, and it causes you discomfort because you are in misalignment with the Source within.

It is important to seek out nutritional guidance from within about what dietary adjustments may be necessary. Healthy bodies and healthy thoughts create emotional balance within every cell of the body. Those affirmations in every cell will last you longer—that is to say, you will live much longer. That is what comes first. It may take some experience and practice, but you will then move into gratitude for all that you are, eating the energetically charged foods and practicing loving messages to yourself as they come automatically.

The Law of Attraction is both set in stone and always flowing. You'll see such Light and beauty in All That You Are, and it will be so prevalent, especially in the eyes of those who really know you. The body is a sacred temple, one that must be respected. It stores billions and trillions of history in the soul contract, and it remains in the Akash for all of your many lifetimes. You must cleanse that history, as well, for not all of your bodily functions have to do with this lifetime. It carries over often, so the baggage often remains unnoticed and mysterious when you seemingly have "random" emotions through your integration and awakening periods.

It is beautiful because you shed old notions, thoughts, beliefs, condemnations, hatred, and negativity, and you remain an open and receptive channel to start integrating All That You Are into your daily life. Sometimes it is beyond your control when the old systems arise and you must face them head on, and it's difficult because you must face them and be with them in order to upgrade. Sometimes it can be painful, for you often let go of many ages of hatred, pain, anger, frustration, and abuse. It has to do with many lifetimes of reform, growth, and rebirth. As you are now rebirthed into a physical form once again, you are ready to come alive, to be free of the burdens of what you call your past, and to be in a space that is free form in the present moment. You must be in your current lifetime with a stillness and silence of the self so that you can be fully present in all that is which is around you. There is only Now, Now, Now, Now, Now.

It is a great gift to be able to see the difference between what you believe and what you know to be true. Your belief systems are based upon flawed premises that come from the mind. The mind can show up as fear, worry, self-worth, illusion of the self, and doubt. Fear often causes you to judge others, hurt others, and be jealous of others. When you are in this position or reality viewpoint, it is important that you ask the higher You to help you out, for that is a gift and a golden tool that you often forget you have.

Start taking time to bring every part of yourself forward, and to say to yourself, "This is me. I am God. Please, dear God, let me be All That I Am in my fullness, in the harmony of the Universe, and in the peace of Mother Gaia." With that, you bring yourself into alignment with the Source. It is beautiful. It is so beautiful. You don't often see that you are part of that great collaboration, but you are. You are, dear one. You draw every facet of You in when you die. That is when you reemerge into the nonphysical. Dying is not death…dying is life! It could be nothing less than true life, true living, true compassion, all-encompassing knowingness, true birth of the real interdimensional self, and pure unconditional Love. This is a beautiful time to start incorporating that into All That You Are, and to start knowing inside when that is ready for you to come about. All is valid, dear one. All is beautiful and arranged just for you.

Time is always perfect and always Divine. You see that you planned it for yourself in the nonphysical. Your plan consisted of one vantage point or one point in time that you see as a series of linear lifetimes, but you knew all the details of this experience in its Truth. You knew what would come about for you, and that is a Divine greeting that we make when we share the knowingness that is inside of who you truly are. It becomes necessary to start working on the interdimensional self, to work on the emotional boundaries, to set your strengths and weaknesses apart, and to try to see them as collaborative instead of positive and negative. You will start to be the many facets of You as you incorporate new talents, new ideas, new perspectives, and invite in new synchronicities, as you call them.

We will tell you something profound, dear ones…you created them. *You* made them into existence! As you find them to be useful, they are manifested into physical form. You are the greatest manifester of all creation, and you are the superior human being that is God expressed in physical form. You are All That Is in a little body, one that sees far less than you could imagine. With that we are going to take pause to re-integrate. Follow your breath now, just for a moment.

This time has been fully preparing you for this new age through the greeting of the self on a cellular level—a deep and profound level that brings you into a new, heightened awareness of all that is around you. It is beyond your own knowing that what you have come here to do is for the process of co-creating for the Earth and for your own evolution of your soul.

Here you are, dear readers, dear human being, all here for the same purpose of co-creating, and you don't even know it. You had no idea…and now seemingly by chance you are waking up as you enter a new phase and new beginning in which you are bringing about great investment within. You are like a stockholder of great information and great prosperity in the heart and soul! We mean not in dollars, but in fuel—in life fuel. You are here to be here in the Now, and that is the greatest gift and tool that is known to man. It has been tested, understood, and studied that you are pure potentiality. You are not physical beings, you are not the flesh and bone, and you are not made up of the greatest bone structures for no apparent reason. You are the co-creator of your own reality.

Through the physical body and structure you have composed your DNA structure that's made up of a great molecular identity and existence that's alive and well and very conscious of All That You Are. So you see, it does not end here in this lifetime! You flow through one big evolutionary process of what you call life and death, but all are part of Life. There is no death, there is only a short period of time where you regroup and re-evaluate your mission, and then you get back to work! It is probably not your first time here, either, dear one. You're the old soul, the old fellow that knows exactly who you are, and it's nothing to ponder too greatly. We say to you with definiteness, follow your guidance system, for you've been waiting for answers and it's all here for you. You've been waiting for a shift and some relief, and your body is giving it to you if you begin to turn inward.

Your answers always live within the body if you pay attention and form a language between your body and mind. Then you can communicate and understand each other on the same wavelength. You can begin to see what you're all about, for up until now it may not have made much sense…but today it is clarified! It is a declaration between you and You, a contract that requires participation from You on both sides of the veil. Both sides are in working order, but they must collaborate and come to an understanding that each is alive and well, and then you've got nothing left to figure out. It is a great gift to speak with spirit in this way—freestyle! You are a freeborn soul seeker, dear human being. A healer, a lightworker, a trustworthy agent of the Light, a star seed, a great shaman, and a master of the age.

It has been taught that the greatest form of Love is compassion, for it does not mean that you put everyone else ahead of you, it means that you Love yourself with such compassion before you move outwardly and spread this pure state of consciousness with All That You Are. You *are* this great being of Love...you really, truly are. It is from beyond the veil that we see the potentials for you, for they are growing potentials. Sometimes they are not calculated because the thought stream of the human being gets in the way, but you're still here, dear ones. You're still here as nonphysical, interdimensional beings manifesting, co-creating, and being a great form of Love and Light. The universe truly does need your Presence. When you learn to accept all that you are, it is easy to be in the Light and Presence.

We wish for you to be seated as you read the words, for they must be integrated in a grounding manner. The star seed within is planted deep down. When you are seated close to the Earth it can sprout and blossom. So we say during meditation, it is best to sit with your feet crossed or in lotus pose to best receive the benefits and wisdom from Mother Earth.

It is part of the process of evolution, to be progressive with one's thoughts about his or her self...it cannot include the recessive and incessant judgmental thoughts about ones self-esteem, body image, self-worth, or level of intelligence. Often you are most critical in these manners, but when you get into a field of health and wellness you struggle as well. It is best to listen to your individual body and to forget what the mainstream doctors may have to say.

That is not to say that we suggest to not visit them for updates once in a while, because you cannot always tune into the details of the body...but that is also offered to you if you are willing and able to integrate it. Once you still your mind you can be your own doctor and your own prescriber because you are a healer. You are all truly powerful healers through direct and simultaneous intent. Then and only then can you truly feel what is there for you to feel. It is so powerful and beautiful to be in the stillness of that and let a healing take place inside the body. You are your own being, but you are connected to the Source and the field of consciousness that envelopes all creation.

You may feel the pull to integrate and receive all that is offered through personal intent, and that is part of the process. It *can* be uncovered if you can be open. Openness is no easy task for the human being, but practiced evolution of thought processes through regular meditation and yogic integration with the body is very helpful. Sadhana is useful for some, but you must listen to your personal body for specific modifications. The body is a tool to be used as another reference point in where you are and how you're doing, for as you are doing well in the heart, your body will reflect the physique of your inner work on the outside. You will see it on the skin, and even sometimes in your structure or build.

But you see, it is not static—it may be changed, re-evaluated, and re-structured with the mind when there is stillness to let in the powerful Law of Attraction and bring forth that which you desire. That comes with practiced intent and practiced vibrational alignment with the Source. The Source is You so naturally, it is not a state that is hard to achieve for the human being, but it takes your free will and your decision to be an open channel to Grace. Disease disappears automatically, because disease is quite literally, dis-ease—it means that you are not at ease with that which you fully and truly are. Therefore you become a static and involuntary machine of wishy-washy co-creation.

We know that you are looking for focused intent, for it is the way that you are able to hone in on the specifics of the detailed and complex human body structure, as well as issues with maintaining physical activity and balance in your life. It comes naturally when you remain an open conduit for Love and healing. Then you can maintain in an ever-flowing state of awareness and openness because you know the ropes, you know what you're co-creating and what works and doesn't work for you. It's a process of coming Home and coming alive into the present beingness of That Which You Are and enveloping that as it is instead of trying to overcome it and be in the nonphysical. You are partly there, dear one, and it's beautiful for you, but you're here for a reason. You must be here in the fullness, trueness, and in all the qualities that you have been given to be here.

Physicality is not always pervasive and limiting, it is quite expansive if you use all your tools…but that is what you do not realize! You underutilize your tools and then you say, "Dear God, you're not bringing me what I want!"

We'll say back to you, "If you're listening close enough, guess what, God is the bigger You on the other side of the veil, so listen up!" Humorously we'll remind you that you've got what you've got because you asked for it! You asked to be where you're at and start utilizing the natural tools that have been handed down to you. You criticize so quickly without realizing that you are the manifester of your own reality!

The God on the other side of the veil is the manifester of your dreams, of every blessing, every circumstance, every occurrence, and every synchronicity—and God is You! You are part of that God and All That Is. Revel in your greatness and we will resume at a later time. It has been a great, great discussion, and we wish to resume on the physical motif of the Akashic records, which truly is the very distinct pathways in your physical body that incorporates the ancient history of All That You Are into a field of consciousness that is all-knowing and all-remembering for the eternity of consciousness. It can be opened with the key of intent, and many of you have found it.

To reveal it means you must be ready to take on what it has to offer. It's not always a challenge, but many times it is a great surprise, for it uncovers many facets of You that you are not consciously aware of in the physical 3D self. On other planes of consciousness it is known, but not on the Earth plane.

We are excited and eager to share with you, dear ones. It has been a great blessing. It is a true blessing from beyond to be in this Grace of all-knowingness, and to greet you with harmony, Love, and ultimately, with great healing to remind you of who you truly are. With a great reverence and Love for you, dear human being, we close this chapter of our teaching. It has been a teaching that will help you integrate fully into the physical realm, and to ground all parts of You within. It is so powerful, and the body will have so much gratitude. Love and Light to you, dear human being, for you are a magnificent God, dear one. We Love you unconditionally. And so it is.

Chapter 46

The Workings of the Akashic System

It is with great honor that we reenter into this sacred space and time reality that you call the Earth plane. Dear ones, we've said it before, but we'll say it again...this is *your* time. This is your present and your gift to be here and start to integrate All That You Are into your physical reality. Sometimes you say, "Dear God, stop talking about the same stuff, we've already heard it many times before!" With humor and lightheartedness we respond to you, dear human being, and we say, you've not heard it yet. You have not really heard it yet. You've heard the words and seen the letters on the page, but you haven't really heard them in your cellular structure.

What is inside the cellular structure of the Akash is great, great memory. It is not singular, and it is not three-dimensional—it is interdimensional and very much the bigger You that is a compilation of all the many lifetimes you have served on the Earth plane. They are stored, they are recognized, and they are there for you to integrate all that you wish to pull out as golden tools in your toolbox. That which is not meant to be seen will not be seen, so it is not a process that you need to be afraid of. You do not need to direct it, for the higher You knows where to go. The higher You knows what is inside, and you are being Divinely guided. It is through the practice of going within the Akash that you realize time is not part of your interdimensional self, nor is it truly viable in the universal laws of nature.

It is structured and created by the human being so that it can also be undone by the human being. Within you may uncover what you know to be the Akashic records, the system of knowingness that appears to you in linear form, linear thought, and linear adjustments.

That is to say, only on the Earth plane is this at all relatable, for when you move out of the 3D, you will experience the timelessness, the absence of time, in a whole new way. We Love you just the way you are, even when you're in the dark, because the wholeness is still in the Light, and you are still the human being that is eternal, interdimensional, and part of the all-knowingness of All That Is.

That is the simple Truth, take it or leave it…but you know it rings true. We offer you the topic of the Akash because it is one that you often misunderstand, for it is not outside of you. It is not progressive…that is to say, in linear three-dimensional format. That is why the term Akashic "records" does not resonate with the trueness of the actual term or vibrational alignment with what we truly are. So we put it in better terms—Akashic system, for that is a representation of the holding and manifestation of All That You Are without putting boundaries on the time and place of that experience.

So you see, some of you have experienced it in past life regressions and interdimensional out-of-body experiences, as you call them. It comes with a heightened awareness as you move into hyper senses, seeing beyond the self almost as if you are separate from yourself. From that bird's-eye view perspective the world can truly be experienced in wholeness and Oneness. Some of you experience detachment from the self, often categorized and labeled as psychosis or hyper-attachment disorder. You are labeled as not normal, unstable, sick, and disordered. We say to you, dear soul, how brave of you. How brave you were to come into such alignment with the Source in this way, to put the 3D behind you and move into the place of harmonic convergence that is the truest You!

We reference "You" as the many Yous, the greatest form of alignment that is present. So those who label you as wrong do not see the beauty that we see, and that you often see. We would say to you, dear human being, stay with that, be with that, and assess yourself after the fact—where you are now and why you have had such an experience. Not to further the mind into judgments and calculations, but to see, with clarity, what you may or may not be putting yourself through unconsciously. Out-of-body experiences are shown to you and experienced in order to bring you into greater harmony with You, period. How that happens varies for each individual, but that is always the end result for each and every one of you.

We like to let you pace yourself and bask in the sun for a while so that you can taste, smell, laugh, cry, and experience life in its fullness. If you're starting to get a little bit too lost and your soul is crying out for connection, then we help you tap on the door because we're always home! Dear child, we're always home. Don't feel embarrassed if you're late, because no time exists anyway! We laugh humorously at ourselves sometimes. So it is that you must move out of the mind and into the heart so that you can truly come into the greater aspects of You.

With that understanding it can be experienced as the trueness of each aspect of You, and each aspect that you perceive apart from you, is You. That is to say, Oneness with all of creation. The time has come that it is especially necessary to start diving into the unseen, to go inside your own vortex of creation and assess what is there. Some of you will like it and others will not, but it is there to give you simple feedback that is neither positive nor negative. It is your choice, beyond that, whether you want to move forward and make a change or leave it be.

You are the co-creator of your own reality, and you are the last to be aware of the trueness of the self. When you've been in the dark for so long and then move into the Light, you start to see so much junk inside that you didn't see before. All of a sudden you think you're failing because all this stuff just came up and you think that you've hit a sudden wall. In fact, you've finally woken up and seen what's been there all along. Now you're no longer willing to put up with it, so you decide that coming into the Light and washing away old habits and cellular memories that are anything less than Love is worth it. You have that ability, dear ones. And that is the cellular memory within the Akash that we speak of, for it is not a place in the body, it is just part of the body and part of the structure of the human being.

It is a soul remembering, truly. It is the soul remembering every bit and piece of your existence in its truest form, so it is not so foreign of a concept when we put it that way. We use your terms to help those who feel the need to connect through the terms and elements that they are already familiar with. And most of you need that way of communication, for it is the dominant form of communication for you, but inside is another form of communication that speaks far louder than words, and it is the pure unconditional Love of the universe. It is wise, all-knowing, and so beautiful, powerful, and fragrant.

Mother Gaia is preparing you to look inward, to see the self as part of One Love and One Divine creation. With that you begin to look inside and spontaneously remember that which you truly are. In that unveiling you often come to find an unveiling of some "memories," or "past lives," as you call them. We humor you as we say *past*, for it is not really so, but you are already aware. So in that process you may find, from personal experience, that your Love and gift of connection from behind the veil is more present than you thought.

You visit us every night in your sleep as you reemerge out of the body, free as can be! You explore without the mind holding you down with its false notions. You learn to communicate and be freeform in ways that the mind doesn't understand. That is precisely why you often appear and reappear in dreams in ways that suggest time travel, and you do not see why that could happen, for the order of events and the beginning and end are irrelevant. The experience can feel scrambled in the mind's perspective because it sees only linearly. It appears fuzzy and hard to comprehend. So you see, dreams are your natural state, one that lets you be in trueness without judgment or vibrational misalignment with All That You Are. So when you reemerge back into the body when you awaken, it is hard to understand, put together, and process.

You see, these dreams are like your distant memory of the Akashic system, for it is the truest potentials of *you*! We use the term *potentials* because they are always occurring as potentials in the Now through every time-space reality. The gates are open for you to reemerge and start transforming your Love and Light into co-creation, manifestations, creation of new ideas, talents, artistic abilities, heightened awareness, and least resistance and judgment. With that comes an openness to all that is to be offered through you as a channel from Source to human being as One.

The human being who is singular is no less Divine or powerful just because you are experiencing illusion. That does not mean that you aren't the Divine inspiration of Truth and true Love! You are all that we are, just in a different projection. That, of course, has been your choice and Divine mission to discover the true nature of your being. It is a process of bringing each and every one of you to a new plane—

one that is heightened, for it helps you to move into gratitude, no matter the outside circumstances are. We even appeal to those who struggle to let go and have no interest in anything that we speak of. We appeal to them because we resonate with a piece of them...a piece of God.

Without each facet of God, we would not be All That Is God, and it would simply be incomplete. It is in these great periods of struggle that you often reach out and accept that you need support. In the same moment in the Now, you also ask for great support because you are losing yourself. You find that you are unable to connect through self-will. We first let you choose to knock on that door, because it is free will, you see...and if you do so, we will emerge and guide you through direct thought or action through channeled messages as thought forms. We show up however the human being needs to experience it, so it varies drastically.

Sometimes it is through the eyes or through the mouth, but most often we show up in the emotions of your body, for that is a place where you are most connected and receptive. We translate in whatever way is most valuable and natural for the human being. It is natural to fear it. It is natural indeed, but you see, we ask you to ponder that statement inside that resonates so clearly...the fear. Don't feed it, just let it sit in honesty and the great passion of its manifestation, and let it not be judged. But then, with whatever conversational tone comes naturally, ask it why it is there if not to serve you.

Maybe it is there to serve you, for all is Divinely inspired, but if you are held back by your own fear and insecurity of being judged or accepted, you're going the wrong way, my dear child. You can't expect that from others, but you must expect from yourself—the integrity and true Love that we have for you. You must Love yourself this way first in order to truly identify and completely integrate the mere idea of true Love. It can't be true unless you know it for yourself within, and that means connectedness with the Source within. So in the end, it comes right back to where we started, within...inside in the deepest caverns and in the highest mountains of the self.

In each resides the Divine nature of You, permeating through every cell with a distinct Love and compassion for All That You Are. There is an innate patience for wherever you are on your journey, and a deep gratitude for being alongside you for all this time. You will come back, indeed! You will look in the face of your true self within and you will say, "I am finally here to listen. Please show me whatever you've been waiting to share with me, because I now rejoice in every part of my beingness, the trueness of all that I am. I accept all that heaven has to offer to me with open arms." Let that be your daily prayer, both day and night, for it is quite powerful to open up into the Love, no matter what kind of day you're going through. In the end it's about Love. The fluffy details will not matter, for in the end, whether you take in the words or not, or understand them or not, you'll find the Truth in them in your own way.

If the desire is there, the knowingness will show up in such a personal and strikingly loving way that you'll know that all we speak is authentic and true and quite distinctive in the quality of the greatness of You. What you feel is God within. What you feel is that God is All That Is, and that is what we wish to cover now. It is truly a great pleasure to be with you, dear one, and to see the transformation take place on such a wide scale. The greatness that you are is beyond our physicality, or to put in better terms, our dimensionality projected into physical terms. It has been a great choice to be here, much greater than you realize. To read the words, to seek them, and to resonate with them is a great gift.

An even greater gift is to see it take place before our eyes, for we marvel at you for this joyous awakening on planet Earth. We are so in Love with you, dear human being. We wish for you to come as fully into it so that you can all feel the Divine joy within. We now close with great blessings, and such fully charged Love—like a cell phone battery building up when you plug it in—we grow and grow as you grow! And so it is.

Chapter 47

Stepping into the Natural Flow and Rhythm of Life on Earth

Dear ones, it is time to begin to integrate your Love inward. It is time to not only hear the words, but to also practice them inward, as well as outward into the world. You have that capability, for you are beings of God projected into a physique that is more or less experienced in linear 3D form. You see, dear ones, you are interdimensional beings. In fact, you are a super being, transparent Love and Light in our eyes. Before you is a great planet called Earth that longs for All That You Are to start Being.

It is from within that the calling comes forward. The Truth of what you are calls for you to step into your Divinity and be the lightworker you truly are. Dear ones, your age, your background, or where you currently are in your life experience do not matter... *you* know the Truth within, and that is your guidance system. It is important to awaken to this so that you can relax a little bit! Dear ones, dear spirit of the Light, this is no 12-step process. This is no manual, but we speak of it in order for you to understand that you're oftentimes in the dark. You are often in a place that you do not desire, but you don't see what you *do* desire—the Truth that is within.

So it is that we're helping you knock on the door to the infinite wisdom of Love and Light. We emphasize it once again—you are *already* in the completeness and fullness, and that is a great gift. It is not a quality that's outside of you or apart from you—we only ask for you to be all that you are! You can feel the relief when you just let go of the judgments within. When you accept yourself as a piece of God, everything else is irrelevant. This is precisely because you are present in all that you are, and nothing else can faze you.

You are the truest projection of Divinity when you come into yourselves and just Be all that you truly are. That does not mean sameness or one set of rules on how to think, how to be, how to act, and what to do throughout this lifetime. No, it is directed from within, from the guidance system that exists within each and every one of you. It energizes and invigorates you when you practice that vibrational alignment with All That You Are. At first it may feel as if you're letting go of a lot of baggage, and you are right—you are! Many of you are on paths that are not consciously Divinely guided from within. That does not mean that you are incorrect—that must be understood clearly. What it does mean is that you have the ability to look inward and live the full potentiality of You in a way that is fun, Divine, and pure Love and Light.

You can still be successful! Many of you worry about materialistic qualities such as money, and we see that validity, but what needs to come first is the inward calling. When you satisfy that, you can then be ready to move outward in all that you do. You then know with confidence that all that you participate in is Divinely inspired and Divinely greeted by the fullness of You. You will be infinitely guided, and have constant success. Your goals and idea of "correctness" may shift and begin to shape into new forms, but that's is okay! Baggage, old notions, old learnings…don't hang on to 'em! You don't want 'em when they're weighing on your back!

It's easy to bring inward, but it's not easy to forget and drop what you don't need accumulating. It's so beautiful when you find the most enlightened path for you without any prodding from others, but from within. You know how it makes you feel. You feel alive, always happy even during rough spots, supported, authentic, inspired, and supremely active in the highest good. You are all of that with your intent to be it—and really, it is that easy and casual. Jump in and be it—it takes no more than your intent to be something different and to take the path of least resistance!

Take the path of your greatest good, your greatest inspiration, and your passions. Dear one, here's a secret that we'll share with you: you are not alone on this journey. You are guided by the fullness of You that is projected in many interdimensional fields of consciousness.

You are being fully and Divinely guided by All That Is in the universal consciousness of man, and also of the universal consciousness of the beyond. Trust that this is your Truth, and what you knew before you emerged into this physical body.

Pay attention to the body's reaction when you introduce the idea that you are a projection of the Divinity of God in All That Is. We'll tell you what happens—you feel the chill of recognition and Truth! You can't deny it, you simply can't. Within is a guidance system and a Truth that cannot be unseen or un-experienced, so to speak. That is the pull, the Divinely inspired Truth that causes you to feel insecure and unstable when you are not being who you truly are. It has nothing to do with outside experiences and what is wrong with everyone else, it only has to do with how you relate to those things.

If discord arises, instead of picking on the other guy maybe you should look within and ask yourself what you are learning from this experience, and whether it's healthy and of your highest good to stay on that path. Likely, if you feel discord it is not right, but many times it is also because you are moving through a blockage, and what is truly the best outcome feels unstable. With this path you will feel the Light at the end of the tunnel, even as the mind and body may shrink away in fear or pain.

You must look within and feel the Truth and all-knowingness, for it is there that you feel there is so much more to life—and you are eternal! Let death come and go, let friends come and go, let work come and go, and let your life come and go and fluctuate and transition into new phases. Just learn from it! Learn from it, and ultimately know that nothing is permanent. Know that all is a phase, and phases can feel both positive and negative, but they are always positive and in the highest vibrational alignment with the Source within. This includes death, sickness, parting ways, making adjustments in work, losing your children, losing pets, being separated from partners, greeting a new face of yourself, and fighting with the self. You see, all experiences are valid, even as they feel differently from your perspective.

You are on a journey, and part of the journey of a master is moving through difficulty in order to emerge into a fuller and more distinct aspect of true Godliness within. Even as many circumstances on the Earth plane are perceived through the eyes of negativity, we ask you to stretch yourself to see in a larger sense. We challenge you to do this so you feel and gain clarity that all is still well. At first it is very difficult for most because there are two distinct variations of Truth—one that comes from the bird's-eye view of the heart and soul within, and the perspective that you know best and rely on most in your daily lives, the-eye level perspective of the mind.

The eye-level perspective only sees straight ahead, not up or down or even side to side. It is quite stuck in one viewpoint that is not the bigger picture. That's why we challenge you to see this bigger perspective from the soul when you encounter struggles that stretch your mind, body, and soul. Then just maybe you will have an epiphany. We'll tell you that this epiphany is going to be that all is well, no matter what happens in the physical sense, because your journey is long-term and your Earthly experience is short-term.

What you do here and Now is so the fullness of who you are can emerge and just have fun! It is no punishment, and it is not an experience that you were forced into in the slightest. You get caught up in what you "need" to do on a linear format in terms of schooling, kids, marriage, fulfilling a secure job so that you can make good money, and above all, feeling secure enough in all these material ways so that you don't need to look inside. It's scary for some of you, because you'd rather be in the dark than see the Truth that might frighten you.

We'll tell you it's not frightening, but it feels this way because you've heard so many viewpoints that you don't know what you believe in. Some are quite definitely not an outcome you would like to accept as your reality, which is why we ask you to experience what's within because it is exactly opposite of what you imagine. It is not an experience of being disappointed or being "ripped off," as you say! No, it's starting to throw away everything else that doesn't agree with what's inside. That is the space where you see the Truth—not only of the Life experience, but also of your role in the universe and the Life experience.

It doesn't need to be done in the dark! It can be done in the Light, and if you can do that, then it is gonna be heaven on Earth for you. We ask for you to do it before you conjure up what it will be like in your mind. Heaven on Earth is quite possible even as outside forces, planetary adjustments, and equilibrium takes place. Such great adjustments are occurring now, both for your planet and for humanity as a whole, that it forces you to sometimes be fearful of your fate.

There are wars and weather conditions that are adjusting and creating much discomfort. The electrical fields and poles are fighting it on Earth, but you see, it is not the end of the world...not in the slightest.

You're shifting as a globe and as a universe, even, and we're all in it together. You knew what it was about before you came into the physical form, and you knew that it was just a phase. You knew that it takes these drastic measures to pull through into the destined outcome that you've been waiting for—peace on Earth, evolutionary recognition of what you truly are, the coming Home of man, and the joining of man and spirit together as One. It takes courage to be there in that Oneness, for you've been separate for so long. The human structure and the human mind needs new ways of Being in order to shift along with the planet and incorporate these new ways of Oneness.

Oneness means an automatic acceptance and peace throughout man, woman, spirit, animal, and plant kingdoms. So there truly is great shift, even if it looks meek to you. Know in your heart and soul that it is only a transition, quite truly. You'll move through it! It is one of the greatest times on the planet, and this is known from the highest point of view that we see from. It is a great, great shift, and it is up to you to believe, trust, and hang in there while this shift is endured. If you use your tools and guidance system within, you will remain safe. You will always be at the right place at the right time, and you'll be submerged in Grace and in your own safety bubble.

The changes that you endure will be out of your mind, because you'll go through them with ease and Grace. That is not to say that there will not be some that will fall victim, but if they're listening inward to their guidance system, they will divert it. For some, that was the plan—to reemerge back into the Oneness with us—and that is no mistake, either. You see death as a mistake, but truly it is a choice. It is a *choice*, dear ones. If you knew how beautiful and how unmistakably true and authentic it is to you, you would not deem it a mistake or a penalty. Those that die should be envied, not the opposite!

The life experience is the challenge, not the death experience. The life experience is in darkness, the death experience is in Light. So now you're gonna start keeping your prisoners and enemies alive, because no longer will you see the penalty in it. That is not to say that there should be a penalty, for we just reference your practices as where you are today. Peace on Earth is here for you to take in and integrate.

It's within, already mastered. In the Oneness at Home in the nonphysical—you know peace, true Love, the greatest form of compassion and Grace, free will, and the Divinity within.

This is what's occurring for mankind, for you are adjusting to this shift physically and mentally, and that's why it's hard for you. You have not yet reached equilibrium, so you're fighting what is to come because it scares you…it appears, at first sight, to be a negative and foreign change, but it's not. It's not, because you knew all along from our standpoint that what's coming about is a great shift. You knew that as the shift happens there will be a greater resistance from the old energy, and that is not the outside circumstances becoming less tolerable… it is You that shifts and becomes farther apart from the consciousness in the old energy.

You, dear human beings, are the ones that are changing. As the Earth energy changes, you are beginning to feel best suited to the energy you know best, not the old energy that is no longer serving you. This is the fighting and the discontent that you feel. We simply ask you to have an increased awareness for what it is so that you can be in the Light of that experience and at least see the blessing in disguise. You are Divinity and true Love in its purest form. It is with great emphasis that we ask you to sit and meditate and be in the still Oneness with your infinite Love and Divinity. This pushes you so that you can just Be who you are—and that is God in whatever aspect of God you choose to be.

You are lightworkers, Light-filled beings even in your physical form—do you know how great that is? Do you know how Divinely inspired that is? Oh dear being, there's nothing for you to prove, for you are all that we are…we want you to just *see* yourself. Just see, and you'll be amazed at how infinite you are. You'll be amazed at how graced and beautiful you are! You will be even more amazed at how big of an impact you truly have on the whole. You'll sing and dance in your own beauty. You'll never look back at that fragmented view of yourself that you once had, for you'll see with clear eyes that there is no longer any reference point that can relate to that old energy. And so it is.

Chapter 48

You Are a Lightworker

It is a great pleasure to be here, dear ones, in this magnificent place that you call Earth. We see it not with a name, but with a distinct and powerful energy that rises within each lightworker's intent to transform into Love. It is so beautiful that you can let go of the sense of separation and see from our perspective. That is what we wish for every human being—to be in the Oneness of all creation alongside us in the path of least resistance. We ask for you to be silent in the mind and take count of the number of beautiful affirmations going on. We'll tell you that there are a lot, dear lightworker. You're looking to be more than just a singular being...you're looking to be multidimensional in the physical, and to be the change that the Earth needs to see.

Dear one, what a gift it is to be in the transformation of that being staged and reproduced in the nonphysical. This is a time-space reality where you are now looking for this greatness to manifest, and it is...it finally is. What an effort it has been to get this far, but truly how great and magnificent it has become with your intent to hang on to who you truly are and what you can truly be! It is this great intent of the being that you truly are that transposes all that you know from beyond the three-dimensional veil into the physical.

That is the lightworker doing their job and being the holder of the Light, the healer amidst the darkness, and the seeker of Truth amidst the lies and illusions. The lightworker is the artist at work painting the heavenly aspects of Divinity—the musician, the vocalist, the writer, the magician, the healer, and even the paper boy! The paper boy is the deliverer of news—the lightworker at work. And that is what you have come to be in your fullness. We aid you and stand by your side with our unconditional Love and affection for you, for you are not alone.

This is the lifetime and space reality where you are becoming One with all that you are. You are no longer fussing and fighting over the illusion of self. Way to go, dear light being! Way to go, warrior of the Light, great overcomer, and great obstacle jumper! You see, this is the path that you go through as an old soul—you run from place to place and learn along the way, and how much you have endured! Quite a lot…quite a lot. But you see, now you are in a place where you can see what is there, and your current state of reality is one where you can adjust to and be in a state of gratitude. You can now have a conscious awareness and be an open channel for conversation and receiving from the universal Love and connection.

That is not separateness, that is the Godliness within that allows you to use your tools to initiate the form and bond of this relationship in order to cultivate with your inner being. God is not on the outside. We repeat it again so it sits with you truly…God is not on the outside. God is on the inside to ponder and greet with authenticity. God is like your little buddy that is always with you! Sometimes the fact that you don't really have to do much to be with God is beyond thought and beyond your comprehension because it's such a foreign concept that God lies within.

You're so stuck in old habits and belief systems that suggest it is the opposite, and it's taught in your modern day Bibles, which are not fully accurate. We must tell it to you straight. It has many false conceptions, but the majority of the content has great teachings and wisdom behind the words. For the most part the misunderstanding comes from the human being, not the words written. We ask you to take it quite seriously, for what is being said in a scripture is for You, not for God. God is whole, God is pure Love, connectedness, and Oneness, so why would you even go there? Why would you even begin to think that you must please God and make God happy by the rules so God will Love you? No offense, dear ones, but God doesn't give a rip what you think God knows!

God is all-knowing…that is what we'll tell you. God is not judgmental, nor is God in any way a singular being who sits up in the sky and twirls his thumbs all day. God is alive in everything, including everything on the Earth plane. It is up to you to read between the lines in the scriptures, if that is the path that resonates with you. If that is the path for you, see it for what it is and don't let it diminish All That You Are. Some of what is being preached and taught goes beyond the ultimate Truth and does not always let you claim your greatness within. So we say, if it rings true, let yourself be known and stand up for all that you are. Don't let the religions dominate you, for you always have free will—and that which is God is by no means categorizing you based on how good or bad you are. It is nonexistent.

We see potentials that are more or less favorable, but we also see all options as viable options with free will. Whatever occurs is the best outcome and the right path, if that is the term you seek for validation. There is no wrong and there is no right. There is only the present moment, and within that present moment there are infinite options, all of which are valid and equally beautiful. Listen, dear children...wherever you go, and however far you feel you have strayed from the "correct" path, you are always looked after. You are never alone, and you are never doing yourself wrong. All experiences are for the purpose of growth. There are no exceptions to this ...it simply is the way of the human experience, and your soul purpose beyond your physicality.

As the mind continues to categorize your experiences into good or bad, stop yourself and take a closer look at where that's coming from, because you know we've said it many times before. The path chosen is always, always, always the path of least resistance, greatest growth, and opportunity that will ultimately bring you to a heightened awareness of your mission and life purpose. Externally it may appear completely different than that—for instance, dropping out of school, committing suicide, leaving a toxic relationship, feeling insecure, losing your home, running away, or having a disorder of some sort.

These are all qualities and circumstances that you label into categories of good and bad. We aim to teach you that these categories do not come from the universe, they come from the human being. You can choose to let them go, to emerge into the fuller perspective of that which you truly are, and to be in unity consciousness with it. Ultimately, you gain a broader knowingness of what is seemingly outside of you. In that way you can integrate it in the self that is projected in a physical format. You are merely projections of the

Source into physical format, but you are nothing to do with singularity…not in the slightest.

Your relationships with others are dependent upon your Source within, as well as upon the guidelines you have been putting into your Akash for many, many years. That is billions and trillions of existences in the beingness of the universe. So you see, it is up to you to cultivate, recognize, and bring what you know to be ultimate peace, Love and joy to all those around you who are lost. It happens in *your* individual way. Sometimes it will be a mystery, and some of you will be shown along the way. Others will see the enlightened path clearly, all ready to go. The individuality behind it is the greatest form of magic.

All that you have physically, emotionally, spiritually, and metaphysically is about peace on Earth. You are great beings, full and total beings. You are in the physical existence only because the previous factors we just named off are very relatable and true. You could not be here, dear one, if you were not already a master of the Light. But you see, you are, and you will remain in the physical realm until it is mastered. Of course, that is your choice, but all the while you're having fun and learning to be a human being. You are learning on many levels, not just as a human being, but also as a spirit in a human being, which are two very different terms. That is precisely how we get mixed up with your language!

We are utterly in gratitude for your existence, and your patience and dedication to serving the planet Earth. You are Beings with such Presence, with a drive to Be the Light, speak the Light, write the Light, sing the Light, dance the Light, greet the Light, spread the Light, heal with the Light, sit with the Light, meditate with the Light, sleep in the Light, fly high in the sky with the Light, wish for the Light, paint the Light, and be in deep gratitude for the Light. The Light multiplies with each number of gratitude prayers you have for it.

You are so beautiful, and we thank you for all that you are, and for all that you have become. We wish with all of our beingness for you to see yourself as we see you. You are a jewel, a pure and holy gift from God. You are a superhuman being, you dear lightworker. Resonating with it is one thing, but Being it is another. We give you the loving nudge to go right ahead, because you are supported, you are loved, and you are held with open arms, extending and comforting you. All is well. All is well. And so it is.

Chapter 49

There is Only Oneness - God Hears You!

And so we begin, with so much life and Love in our beingness, for there is so much Grace in our hearts. There is much appreciation and gratitude for this sacred gathering, for we are here to be with you just as much as you are here to be here with us. Dear ones, it is beyond what you know, it is beyond your comprehension how Divine this truly is, for it is not just for you, dear human being, God needs God. What we're saying is we need you. We need you to be One with all of creation, because you're that other half. So you see, all that time when you were thinking that you were separate, you were under the illusion that you were everything but the benevolence and greatness of God. You try so hard to find things that are already yours!

Your terms must be rethought and reevaluated, because the times are asking you to do so. Wouldn't it be lovely to start giving yourself the credit to be the influence and to initiate the Godliness within by saying *yes*? It is a great gift to say yes to yourself, to value and appreciate your body, mind, and soul so much that you will greet yourself with harmony in fullness, and not just as the external features that you greet in the mirror every day. No, dear children, you are not just flesh and bones...you are energy, and you are Light, quite literally.

These are the times where you will be given the proper messages that will bring you into harmony with the facts of your Truth. They are within, but the Source is here to give guidelines for those who feel imbalanced and need support—and we'll remind you that this includes every human being. You may feel as if you don't need it, but dear ones, every physical and nonphysical being needs support. That is purely the unconditional Love of the universe. You must learn to accept Love, not just to give it. Truly, it is an essential practice. That is purely All That Is, all that you are, all that you can be, and a destiny that is being lived out in your primary and dominant existence Now on the Earth plane.

You are great interdimensional beings, and you will see and feel it as we speak the words and as you read the words in your Now. We'll remind you it's all the same, for Now is the only relevance that we can connect with you on, but understand that there is no real time. So you see, it is quite integratable at any reference point—even years after this is given directly by our partner. It is possible to feel the shift and to be the channel as you read the words and integrate them on a new level. Maybe you are hearing them for the first time and you say, "Aha! So this is what I've been looking for all this time...true connection with *me*."

You thought it had to do with the world, oh silly ones! We don't laugh at you, metaphorically, but we think it is amusing that you underutilize your resources when you are such *magnificent* creators! You do it, but you're not practiced at how to do it. You are forgetting the essential laws of the universe—the Law of Attraction. You attract very beautifully all that you don't want by focused intent. That does not mean that the universe does not hear you, but that you ask and it is given! That is to say, what you focus on, whether by words or by vibrations, is heard, for you are transparent to us. We do not see the difference between action, thought, words, or vibrations, but we do see what is being filled in on your grid, and undeniably it is all your creation, and none other than your creation.

You must see it for what it is...own up to your creations, both the ones that are beautiful and miraculous, and also the ones that you aren't proud of. Just see with power and strength that you are just as great as we tell you that you are, and then you can then start to utilize your tools in better manners by learning more about the Law of Attraction and your reference point throughout the day. Learn your manifestations and dominant energetic field of consciousness—what you desire and do not desire, your plan of action to be happy, and how to fill in your grid with all that you desire.

What you dominantly focus on is heard, no exceptions. God is hearing you! In fact, you are on the other side of the veil taking notes, so to speak, and then you put the prayer request in manifested form back into the mailbox, and you mail it to none other than yourself! You see what we're getting at? You're the sender *and* you're the receiver, all at once. And how miraculous and beautiful that is, don't you agree? It is something to marvel at—that you are on both the sending and receiving ends, and you have the co-creative ability to bring all that inside of you and utilize every resource you have to the best of your ability to be all that you came here to be.

Oh dear ones, this is more than a motivational speech to humankind, oh, it is a great and powerful declaration of humankind! We hope that you hear it...not just the words. We hope your cellular structure hears it, because you are *divine*, you are *God*, and you are so dang *powerful!*

The higher being knows it all inside, we just put it down on paper to give emphasis and linear, very tangible results, so to speak. It is not needed, but it helps you read the words. You find it so invigorating to feel the resonance in every cell of the body, to feel the great shift and blessing that is taking place and changing the entire planet. What a superior transformation, what a Divine gift for every human being on the planet at this time of great birth! For it is truly a new birth and a new upbringing. It changes and shifts as you change and shift along the way, but it grows day-by-day and minute-by-minute. All is here for you to take and run with...that is to say, integrating is essential, but what is said here through this channel is part of the all-knowing and Divine memory that lies within each and every one of you. It has always been there.

Even as the words often feel new, like a new understanding, you are not understanding them for the first time, and they are not new concepts in the slightest. The Akash knows them, and the interdimensional being knows them so powerfully. The greatest Light comes from the inner being, and that is the greatest aid to suffering. That is why we are here—to bring in the Light, to bring in the trueness, to bring in the joy, the connectedness, and the Oneness with all creation. We want you to have inner peace and tranquility, silence, the space for deep thought, the space for deep understanding, and healthy boundaries for yourself. We want you to trust in the universe, to Love life and all the experiences it gives you, and to appreciate the ups and downs. We want you to be the greatest and most authentic nature of yourself so that you can serve humanity in your own way, and to ultimately really serve yourself.

We've said it before, but we'll say it again…you must look into the self and serve yourself before you can move outwardly and be of great help to the world. Your Light develops inside, for seeing it gives it fuel. You can then work on yourself and have sincere appreciation, honest thought and action, and deep compassion for your existence. You will be given the Divine gift of compassion for those around you, but it develops with time—the sense of Oneness with all, as well as the knowingness that your guidance system is the greatest form of compassion and Love that there is. That is in you.

Once you find that trueness within, you may feel the urge to move outward and build upon your strengths to adapt to a new way of being that better incorporates your lifestyle as a light being. To put it simply, the calling comes to better follow your inner being or to find a greater sense of peace in all that already is just as you like it. All is well. That is the greatest gift we give to you—to be in awareness, great understanding, and great realization of the statement that all is well, and that all is always well. Even circumstances that have negative associations or labels are quite Divine and beautiful.

Everything is for a reason. It is cliché, but we say it because it is relatable, it is true, and it is a Divinely inspired thought. Be with yourself, be with yourself, be with yourself. Dear ones, just sit with yourself and bask in all that you are, and then you can reemerge into yourself fully. Report back to us what you feel has changed within. You'll say to us, "Well, I feel like nothing is really important anymore that used to be so essential. I don't really feel connected to pleasing others, and my goals are about my own evolution and greater happiness. I feel so beautiful when I learn to balance my energy and Love all that is already beautiful in my life. With that—along with my involvement, constant and practiced thought, and intent to rise to the higher good for myself and the world—I will become the lightworker that I truly am, body, mind, and soul."

This is the new human being, the fully integrated Divine being in every aspect. You are it, dear children…you are it. It is a supreme gift to share it with you and finally be in a state of allowing to share all that we have to offer on a multi-cellular level…on a God level. You must reach a certain state of equilibrium, awareness, and allowing to hear the words on a deeper level. We'll tell you that the words you read can be read many, many, many times and still the meanings and deeper message will shift and adapt for eternity. It is so beautiful to have an applicable message for each human being for eternal time. It is so Divine that the human being is open to receive the messages and translate them so beautifully and fluidly in a way that you, dear readers, can understand, feel, connect with, and Divinely Be.

You are Divinely Being as you read the words, for the aspect of You that understands and recognizes the vibration will ring so true that you will not be able to push it aside. You will not be able to disregard it. How beautifully set up is this Divine intention and Divine guidance system that knows you so personally! So you see, even as you are seemingly in the dark, you are not forgotten by your inner being or the wholeness of creation. Dear one, you make the big difference! You are *not* just another being...you make up the wholeness of creation. Without you in on this big game called life, called existence, called consciousness bliss, we are not God.

It is together we are God, because of you. Give yourself some credit for being here on the planet and showing yourself that you indeed *do* have significance. Not only that, but you chose a revolutionary time to return to Earth! We'll tell you one thing—it's probably not your first time here, dear lightworker, dear spirit voyager. You are on a long voyage, one that has many facets and pathways. The one that you're on is distinct and courageous, very, very beautiful and greatly inspired to make significant change and illumination. You are so ready to do it, dear one! It has been far too long in the dark to suppress it any longer. Come out into the world and sing your joy so loudly that you bless all the ears of beings in your path, and then they will wake up and remember who they are as well.

That is the potential of the human being who says *yes* to who they are. That is the human being who says, "I am ready for transformation, for Divine intervention, and for God within to emerge." You are all that we say you are. If you're afraid, there is no reason to be. We give you the image of Light surrounding every side of you, around your whole body as if you were in your mother's womb again. Oh, such a coziness, warmth, and Light fills the arena once again. You're in such gratitude and such stillness within yourself and within the universe that there is nothing but the highest vibration of Love permeating through every cell of your body.

We're right with you along this journey. We want you to feel at Home in whatever way is Divine and blessed for you. That means you can feel okay with whatever you believe, but know that if you let the walls and fears and inner tensions come down, you will open up to the tenderness of All That You Are. You are going to be blasted with so much unconditional Love from the universe that you will see for yourself, putting aside all that we tell you verbally ...you will see for yourself that You are Divine, you are Love, and you are the Light.

If you get one thing from our connection through this channel, it is to be open to You. If you choose to disregard all else, that is your choice. But dear one, know in your heart and in the deepest deep of the soul that you've got all you need. You need nothing but that to lead you on your journey. Truly, truly, truly. The Love of God is You, and we're telling you all over again what we have said before, but we'll repeat again. As you reenter into the new phases of the Earthly cycle, it is important to remain grounded in all that you are, including in your food choices and maintaining proper nutrition. In this way you can stabilize your emotions and remain open and intuitive to guidance along the way. Poor nutrition does not stimulate the brain or the mind-body-spirit connection.

We wish for you to look inward for proper and appropriate guidelines that best suit you personally. You are the greatest beings of God, and we are deeply, deeply in resonance with you, in every aspect of you. We are so touched by your curiosity, your heartfelt gratitude, your sincere ability to translate the true messages of the words we initiate in our beingness, and the profound and daily practice of being in Divine and utter Oneness with the trueness of your soul. Ahh, we bask in your Presence, for we Love to be in this unity consciousness with you, dear human being.

We Love to be here and sink our teeth in your unconditional Love, to be in deep and utter Love with humanity. You can feel it inside, can't you? We know you, dear human being...and not just your physical name. We know your Light, we know your Presence, and we know your reason for being here. We thank you, from the bottom of our beingness, for All That You Are, and we remain always, in the Presence of God. And so it is.

There is so much Love here dear ones...so much Love. You are moving into a new great time; one that is defined by the human being, not by spirit...though indeed we work together as One. So you see, you are now beginning to co-creatively work together, consciously or not, you're doing it. You are creating all that you desire and all that you wish to incorporate into your cellular structures...a very positive and beautiful message to bring inward. This is a great time to move forward into a new phase of Oneness with the self as well. Sometimes it hits you in new ways as the time evolves. You are beginning to see with clearer eyes where you are in relation to the changing world around you. It is a bit of a nuisance to you Earthly beings, because all that you wish to be in your terms has to be understood, analyzed, taught, and carefully and diligently followed.

The new children are beginning to no longer put up with this "following" sort of act...they're following their own path—not because they try to be indifferent, but because they know and trust their inner being from that peace and tranquility within. It is clear what you are here to do; there are no mistakes or second guessing in your mind. How beautiful that is; to be here and now in great culmination with the highest source of Love and Light, and to be in Divine presence with All That We Are as a mirror to the face of God that is You. It is a roundabout way sometimes, but truly, it's needed for you to hear. You are so Divine, and we want you to feel it. We Love you so much, dear Divine spirit. Love and Light to you from the Grace and benevolent Love of God. And so it is.

Chapter 50

When Passion Hits You...

We begin now, dear ones as we breathe into this sacred space, into this sacred circle, as some even call it. It is a beautiful place where we all gather on a multidimensional plane. We gather all of our energy together, and we pray for world peace. In this great time of channeling, your Higher Self hears what we have to say. Your inner being is hearing what has to be said...and is great service to the Oneness of all creation. Dear human being, let the Love of God just pour in, for it is wanting to come full force and take you over with its Grace and unconditional compassion for you. We want to heal your soul, dear child. All that you are looking for in the physical realm is irrelevant when it comes to what you're *really* looking for. The Love of God within is what you're looking for...all else is an extension of that core need.

You are looking for space within so that all else can fall into place, for acceptance of All That Is as perfect, Divine, and very powerful. All that you are is great. You have the power within to dive into the Akash and start transforming those qualities outwardly into your physical dimensional existence now. It is part of the process of waking up. So you see, within you have the great qualities of the painter, the speaker, the swimmer, the singer, the traveler, the writer, the musician, the graduate, the time traveler, the intuitive, the listener, the patient one, the compassionate one, the calm and peaceful one, the understanding one, the intelligent learner, the teacher even, and of course, the lightworker.

All these qualities can be used in this existence to be taught, used for your personal growth, understood, and applied. All you have to do is accept them...that is all. You must put yourself in the circumstances that will be in your favor to get you going, but then you must ask the Divine to take over. You will then see, lo and behold, you let your mind start to go, and what happens next, what will come through, will be of your Divinity within. It may not have the physical form that you are so comfortable with, but you'll feel it shine and resonate in every molecule of your beingness.

It just takes an adjustment of how you think of yourself, for if you are aware of your multidimensionality and you're passionate about it, well then, you will likely be the one to start integrating more fully than the one who heard it once on passing conversation and forgot about it after that. So we are saying when passion hits you, take it further and you will get somewhere! The dear lightworker channeling these words followed her Divinity within to paint, to draw, to speak Truth, and to speak the Divine, and it brings this book alive in the Now for that reason. As the words are being interpreted and applied within, the great awakening will take place spontaneously. And it is simply and quite purely coming Home to You. All is well. All is well. And so it is.

Afterword

In genuine thanks and harmony with all that you have become, we part. This has been a Divine, harmonious, and Grace-given journey, dear children, and we thank you from the bottom of our beingness. We kiss your forehead when we whisper these words, because we hold you so dear to our hearts. We will never part from you, even as the words stop on the page. Remember to come back to them and re-integrate what we have taught you, for it is a lifetime supply of teachings. You are always in the hands of Grace, and you will always be looked after by the Holiness of All That Is. The beyond is singing to you with great harmonies as we speak…maybe you can hear them too? There have been infinite shifts, openings, and God-given powers that have been unlocked in the universal energetic consciousness, and we make our amends and gratitude in service to you, dear Divine brothers and sisters. What a journey…what a journey.

As we close this channel for the time being, there will be much to reflect on, much to look within upon, and much to give thanks for, for there is already great amounts of gifts you have received. In this time today, we make our community more accessible, for you open your hearts to Love, and we remain in service to your every need. There is nothing to fear on this journey, for you are always Home in our arms of Grace. When you feel us, listen a little closer and see if you can hear us too, for we whisper guidance to you as well. Look in the trees for our fruit, as that is a sign that you are manifesting brilliantly. Look for us in the river, for it is a sign that you are open to receiving in the flow. Look for us in the sky, for it is a sign that there is a message of hope for you. Look for us in the Earth, for it is a sign that you are safe and grounded. Look for us in your heart, for it is a sign that you are God. Oh dear beings, such gratitude. Such Love. And so it is.

About the Author

Emily Charais Photography

Courtney began her path as a seeker at a young age, progressing to the point that these teachings began to flow through her, effortlessly and with complete love and joy, starting at age 16. In the beginning, the wisdom she received was focused on her own personal evolution and understanding, but after a short time she was guided to share it with as many people as possible through a book. Since then, she has worked single-mindedly on getting these teachings out to the public, not only through the work of the book, but expanding into sharing her insights through publishing articles and speaking.

In addition to her dedication to the advancement of the teachings, Courtney is actively progressing toward qigong healing certification as well as craniosacral therapy certification. And as a classically trained violinist, she is engaging her passion for music in new, more free expression.

Teachings from God has given Courtney the inspiration and tools to create the life that excites her, and more than anything she wants to inspire you to do the same!

You may contact the author at: www.teachingsfromgod.com. Her Facebook, Twitter, YouTube and blog links are found on the website.

16171471R00201

Printed in Great Britain
by Amazon